WIND
IN THE REEDS

by Philip Wayre

Collins

ST JAMES'S PLACE, LONDON

First Impression   *1965*
Second Impression   *1968*

© *Philip Wayre, 1965*
Printed in Great Britain
Collins Clear-Type Press
London and Glasgow

Contents

Illustrations

Illustrations

1. In the Beginning

Animals must have fascinated me at an earlier age than I can remember, for I cannot recollect much before the age of six. I had then learnt to read and my favourite book was *Nests and Eggs*, in a series called "Shown to the Children." Although I was not actually encouraged to do so, I was not discouraged from spending most of my spare time looking for something alive to catch and keep—all kinds of creatures, from caterpillars, beetles, newts and lizards to dormice and field voles. I had a passion for making cages; cardboard boxes, jam jars and butter muslin were the first materials, but I soon graduated to old orange boxes and perforated zinc bought from the local ironmonger with my pocket money. Birds appealed to me specially, though I never kept cage birds as such; on the other hand I well remember my older brother having a mixed collection of finches, among them orange cheeked waxbills.

My own earliest venture into keeping animals was when my parents gave me two rabbits one Christmas. I dearly wanted to breed them and could not understand why no babies appeared despite all their antics; but then I didn't know that my parents had been careful to choose two bucks! One of them called Brutus remained a favourite pet for nearly seven years.

There are certain pursuits that require a sense of dedication; doctoring is one, and I think being a full-time naturalist is another. I still prefer the good old-fashioned word naturalist to its modern counterpart coined by certain television ornithologists, natural historian (I wonder how many historians aren't). As a young naturalist my collection grew—to embrace not only mice and lizards, but snakes and rats.

This obsession with animals and birds intensified when I was sent to Sherborne. One has far greater freedom at a public school and at Sherborne I was lucky. Though I cordially detested school life, there were compensations. I have always been poor at games, perhaps partly because I have never been able to see any point at all in running about after a ball; and in the summer term, the few of us for whom no cricket team existed were allowed out on bicycles to draw country churches. I could never draw and, since all churches look roughly the same, used to get mine done in a matter of minutes and then go off in search of birds. There were many in that part of Dorset new to me, cornbuntings singing from the telephone wires alongside the Yeovil road, wood wrens in Honeycombe Wood, reed warblers and sedge warblers along the River Yeo and many more.

The nesting season over, those of us who were budding naturalists turned our attention to rabbits; there were always plenty in the Sandford Valley, especially in one place where there had been an old firing range. In the winter term, especially on Sunday afternoons, we often went that way and set snares, or surreptitiously slipped a ferret into one of the smaller rabbit warrens. In those days the killing instinct was still strong, and our little clique of two or three was forever trying to find ways of catching anything from rabbits to foxes or badgers, both of which lived in the same valley and preyed on the rabbits. We were rarely successful, but the main thing was that we learnt quite a lot about wild creatures and their ways.

After I had been at Sherborne for about a year I came into contact with a young assistant master called George Yeates; he was a fervent bird photographer and during the summer term spent every moment he could photographing birds at the nest. He often took a boy or two either to build a hide in a tree or to help him get his camera and equipment set up. Needless to say there was great competition between us to be chosen to go with him, partly for the chance of seeing some rare birds and partly for the fun of the car ride.

I learnt much from George Yeates both about birds and the art of bird photography; his pictures were first-class and his methods classic. No hide was ever rushed up too quickly, and no severe " gardening " to open up the nest for photography was ever permitted. Any twig or bough in the way had to be carefully tied back temporarily with black thread and replaced after the day's session was over. Sometimes he allowed me to spend a short spell in a hide to try to take some pictures of my own. I had a second-hand Thornton Pickard $\frac{1}{4}$-plate reflex bought on Yeates's advice and this old contraption takes good pictures to this day.

Sherborne days saw the start of my real interest in birds of prey. Another boy with whom I was friendly, Gordon Jolly, was already a keen falconer and I soon became absorbed in this new pastime, and so did several others. Now it was a school rule that no pets of any kind might be kept. We managed to keep a ferret or two on a neighbouring farm, but hawks would need more looking after. We discussed various ways to over-come the difficulty without success. Then one night in the dormitory our house-master turned as he was leaving the room and said, " Oh, by the way, Wayre, no hawks." This made me all the more determined to keep hawks and so, seeing no other way, I sought permission to go before the headmaster Ross Wallace. This was an unusual request from a boy in another house and I did my best to put the case for keeping hawks and starting a falconry club.

There was a disused and tumble-down shed on a piece of waste land adjoining School House. We could soon repair it and fit it out as a mews in which to keep the birds; they could be tethered outside by day on the waste land which we would clear. Ross Wallace sat behind his desk and appeared completely uninterested. When I could think of no more to say he suddenly said, " Provided the birds are properly looked after I see no reason to stop you. You and Jolly can go ahead but remember, you must do the job properly."

We soon had the shed converted into a mews. The rubbish was removed, the earth floor cleaned out and vertical slats nailed across the windows to prevent the hawks damaging their feathers by flying against the glass. Perches were put up and a new door made with a lock which worked; all was ready except that we had no hawks. After reading several books on falconry, including Blaine's classic, we decided to start with two kestrels and eventually we found a nest in a very tall elm tree along the Yeo valley. By watching the parent birds we concluded that there were young in the nest, but the climb was more than Gordon or I could manage. The nest was a good seventy feet up and there were few branches to help; furthermore the bole of the tree was immense and the previous owners of the nest, a pair of carrion crows, had built it right out at the top of one of the highest limbs. A boy called Peter Twiss, who afterwards became the famous test pilot, was mildly interested in our hawking scheme and volunteered to climb the tree and take the young birds. This he did one Sunday afternoon. There were four youngsters, quite large but still covered with white down, rather too young to take; but Gordon and I were afraid to leave them longer in case Peter wouldn't go up again, so we yelled up to him to take two. They were lowered carefully to the ground in a sack and taken triumphantly back to school.

For the next two or three weeks the young kestrels were kept loose in the mews and fed twice a day on pieces of rabbit or shin of beef. This presented another problem since, although we were allowed out in the town, we were not allowed into any food shops; so permission had to be obtained to go into the local butcher's. Gordon, who was in School House and close to the mews, fed the young hawks immediately after breakfast, while the break before lunch found three or four of us cleaning out or feeding them.

At length the last traces of white down disappeared from backs and heads and the youngsters were ready for training. They were fitted with a light leather jess a few inches long on each leg together with a bell. The jesses we made ourselves out of thin supple leather bought from the local saddler: they were secured to a large-size fishing swivel which, with a leather leash about four feet long, completed each bird's furniture. The bells were made of special alloy, they were extremely light; yet their tinkle could be heard over a quarter of a mile away in good conditions. We bought them from an Indian called Chaudri Mohammed Din of Amritsar. It may seem strange that schoolboys should buy bells in India, but I have no doubt that the information was given to us at the time by the secretary of the British Falconers Club. Makers of hawking equipment have always been exceedingly rare and as far as I remember two addresses, one in India and the other in Germany, had been handed down from generation to generation.

The hawks spent the night back in the mews, tethered about three feet apart to a screen perch; this perch was padded and a weighted strip of canvas a yard deep hung from it. If a bird should jump off in the night it could only hang down the length of its jesses—a matter of five inches—and it was easily able to climb back up the canvas to the perch. On fine days each bird was tethered by its leash to a small wooden block outside. A pointed steel rod pushed into the ground held the block secure.

Every day we spent as much time as we could carrying the hawks about on our fists to tame them and get them accustomed to strange sights and sounds. At feeding time they were encouraged to jump a foot or more to the gloved hand holding their food.   After several weeks both birds would fly a few paces to the fist, and it was time to enter them to a lure. This was a small leather pad to which some birds' wings were sewn; attached to it were tapes to tie down the pieces of raw meat. The lure was joined to a length of cord by a swivel, and it was supposed to represent a dead bird. A hawk would be taken out, secured by a long light line called a creance, and placed on a convenient wall or post. Then we would walk away a few paces and swing the lure round and round before letting it drop to the ground. Gradually the birds learnt to associate the lure with food and would fly to it more promptly and over increasing distance.

One Saturday afternoon, Gordon and I were flying our hawks in the gravel yard outside the school squash courts. He was holding my bird at one end of the yard while I swung the lure at the other. At that moment the headmaster arrived showing a couple of parents round the school. We both stopped what we were doing and stood still, but he told us to carry on. I swung the lure again, and to our imense relief the little falcon jumped into the air and came sailing in to land on it. The headmaster beamed with satisfaction and walked on, no doubt impressing the parents with tales of how Sherborne was reviving the ancient sport of falconry.

Our kestrels were soon safe to fly loose, and though we never attempted to catch anything with them, we had great fun watching them fly and making them chase and stoop at the lure which we swung round and round trying to jerk it away at the moment of impact to prevent the hawk catching it and thus make it throw up to stoop again. Sometimes the birds were not keen, having been too well fed. Then they would sit on the Abbey or the roof of one of the school buildings and refuse to come down to the lure however much we tried to tempt them. We were always terrified lest we should have to go in to a lesson or prep. and leave them out, which would have meant a lost hawk. In those days we had not heard of weighing hawks daily to find out their best flying weight and so regulate their food. But with a bird as small as a kestrel, weighing about six ounces, there is very little margin of error. So perhaps it was a good thing we didn't try.

Soon after getting the kestrels we were lucky enough to get three young merlins from a gamekeeper in Yorkshire; no doubt he would have destroyed them otherwise. These tiny falcons were easier to tame and train than the kestrels, being altogether quicker, keener and more co-operative. We soon had them flying loose and at the end of term I took a kestrel and a merlin back home to my parents' seaside house at Bexhill for the summer holidays.

We lived not far from the Pevensey Marshes, and I got permission to fly my hawks there. Transport was a problem, but one of the family, usually my mother, could generally be persuaded to drive us over for an hour or so.

One August day the little merlin whom I had called Imp had her first chance to catch wild quarry. We had left the car by a small inn called The Lamb right in the middle of the marsh, and I was walking along the bank of a dyke with Imp ready for immediate release. She was held on my gloved hand only by her two jesses, the leash and swivel having been removed. There was a fair wind blowing, and she had some difficulty in sitting still on my fist; a sudden gust sometimes blew her wings open, and she would almost lose her balance. She would only remain sitting while facing the wind, and as it was essential that she should see anything which moved in front of us I was obliged to walk into the wind. The country was open with only a few scattered and stunted thorn-bushes. The fields in which bullocks and sheep grazed were divided by dykes, most of them jumpable. Larks were numerous, while carrion crows could usually be seen in twos or threes, flying over the marsh, sometimes diving earthwards, sometimes soaring to float on the wind. Suddenly a lark rose almost at my feet and Imp was after it in a flash. The lark rose into the air and swept off down-wind with the merlin close behind. It was making for the nearest thorn-bush which grew on the bank of a dyke about three hundred yards away, and by the time it got there the hawk was a bare yard from its tail. The lark closed its wings and dived like an arrow into the bush below it; the merlin put in a stoop a fraction of a second too late, grazed the topmost twig, failed in its headlong dive to pull out in time, and landed in the dyke. Running up I breathlessly fished her out and sat her on a gatepost to dry in the wind.

After that Imp had many flights at small birds including larks, meadowpipits and wagtails, but she only caught two or three before the holidays ended. While I was thrilled and excited whenever she caught anything, I think that this was mainly due to a sense of completion and pride in having trained her. The main thing was the fun in watching her fly and in running after her across the sheep-cropped turf.

Later on in the same summer holidays Gordon came to stay, bringing with him from Devon a very small male peregrine or tiercel which he called Midget. Small though this tiercel was, he was still more than three times the weight of the tiny merlin, and by comparison a much more powerful bird with long slender toes tipped with needle-sharp talons. Unlike the kestrels and merlins with their docile tameness the peregrine had to be taught to accept the hood. This is basically a light leather cap which is slipped over a hawk's head in order to blindfold it. Once hooded the bird is unable to see but is otherwise not inconvenienced at all, being able to breathe freely and even to eat whilst remaining with its hood on.

There are two types of hood, Indian and Dutch. The former are lighter and easier to make, but they are also much easier for the hawk to get off since there are no braces at the back by means of which the hood can be tightened once it is on. Dutch hoods are heavier and far more difficult to make, but once on they are not easily dislodged by the hawk. Some

Photographing sparrowhawks was more fun than hoeing sugar-beet

The tufted duck on her nest in a Surrey bog was one of my first subjects

A trained falcon in the early days

Partridges or a pheasant? Venus on point and waiting for the falcon to fly

modern falconers use Indian hoods which have been fitted with braces in the same way as the traditional Dutch hoods. This compromise is perhaps the best of all, and I always use such hoods.

Hooding a hawk is not in any way cruel, but of course the bird has to be taught not to fear the hood and to allow it to be slipped quietly and quickly over its head. The best way to start this training is in a darkened room with just enough light to see by. As the bird gets used to the hood so the light in the room can be increased. The more highly strung the hawk the more useful the hood, since once hooded the bird loses all fear of strange surroundings and will sit quietly while being carried through crowds or riding in a car. There is a knack in hooding, and generally speaking the larger the bird the easier. Some small hawks learn to duck or shift their heads sideways to dodge the hood just as you are going to slip it on, and they move far quicker than the hand that holds the hood.

Our great ambition was to catch a partridge with Midget. A few coveys were to be found scattered about the marsh, but of course we were not supposed to hawk them. Flying partridges or grouse with peregrines is a very difficult manœuvre, requiring considerable skill on the part of the falconer. Peregrines are true falcons or long-winged hawks and they catch their quarry in the open by stooping from a height. In level flight the game birds will easily outfly a peregrine, especially upwind. The principle of game hawking is therefore to teach the peregrine to " wait on "—that is to climb to a height of perhaps two hundred feet or more and then circle round over the falconer watching for the game to be flushed down below. Hurtling down from such a height, the falcon has a fair chance of catching one of the covey provided the timing is perfect. The quarry must be flushed when the hawk is upwind and coming in towards the falconer. The partridges are fully aware of the danger of getting up at such a moment and will do their utmost to upset the operation either by getting up too soon when the hawk is downwind and turning away from them, or by waiting, crouching low, until the falcon has just passed over, then springing and flying like bullets upwind. Either way the hawk has little chance of making a kill, having lost the initiative.

When Gordon brought Midget he was already almost trained. He would accept the hood and flew well to the lure stooping hard at it. The last thing to teach him was to " wait on." To do this we would go daily to the marsh and one of us would unhood the tiercel and throw it off while the other swung the lure fifty yards away. As the bird approached, the lure had to be jerked up, caught and concealed beneath one's jacket all in one movement. The sudden disappearance of the lure made the hawk climb steeply and circle, looking to see where it had gone. It was essential to throw out the lure and allow the hawk to swoop down and feed from it before it had started to lose height, since the object was to reward the tiercel with food on the lure while it was at its highest pitch, and so encourage it to go even higher next time.

To begin with we thought ourselves lucky if Midget made one complete circle twenty feet up; and though we never succeeded in training him to " wait on " properly at any height, we did at least manage to persuade him to hang around at about the height of the telephone wires. This was not high enough to enable him to catch a partridge, even when we were lucky enough to flush a covey while he was still in the air. Nevertheless we got two or three flights this way, and although the quarry always escaped unscathed it gave us a lot of fun and excitement. Above all it taught us how difficult peregrines are to fly properly.

2. Birds in War

Upon leaving school I was faced with the impossible task of deciding what to do for a living. Other than natural history I had no particular interest, and between the wars there were extremely few jobs available in that sphere. Finally it was decided that I should attend the College of Estate Management in Lincoln's Inn Fields. I hated the daily journey to London and used to spend every moment of my free time looking for birds on the Surrey commons, particularly Thursley Common near Godalming. Two rarities which nest there always managed to elude me: the tiny Dartford warbler, the only warbler to brave the English winter, and the hobby, a summer visitor and perhaps the most graceful of small falcons.

The tufted duck was another bird which kept me guessing for some time. During May I made daily counts of them on the trout lakes and gradually the number of ducks declined, showing that they were sitting on eggs. A thorough search of the reeds and sedge bordering the lakes produced several mallard's nests but no tufted. I had no idea where to look next until one evening, as I stood watching from beside the sluice gate, I suddenly noticed two tufted ducks come swinging in over the trees to land beside their drakes out on the water and at once begin to dive for food.

It was clear that they had left their nests some distance away, but I had no idea from which direction they had come. After nearly an hour one of the ducks got up and flew off;

her flight was direct and purposeful. A study of the map revealed no more lakes or pools in that area, but it did show a swamp called Podmore about a mile away. A day or two later I went there. It was heavily overgrown with sedge and reeds intersected by open patches and lanes of water about eighteen inches deep, but fortunately the bottom was fairly firm.

After beating backwards and forwards through the bog I eventually flushed a tufted duck from her nest deep in a clump of sedge. The eggs were nearly hidden in the dark, almost black, down lining the nest. Within thirty yards I found another and this time a run or tunnel led through the vegetation to the back of the nest, showing the route by which the duck came and went. The second nest was in the best position for photography and within a week I had moved up my hide in daily stages to a range of seven feet. Although all this took place nearly twenty-five years ago I clearly remember the excitement of waiting in that hide the first time for the returning duck and watching her squatting bright-eyed beside her eggs before settling down with much wriggling of her body to incubate.

Not far from the tufted's bog, in a more open part of the heath, several pairs of common curlew nested. There is something most attractive about the curlew, his stature and stately walk, his long curved bill and wary eye, but above all his glorious bubbling spring-song. Many other birds were to be found on those Surrey commons. Nightingales could be heard singing in May almost anywhere along the main Portsmouth Road. Tree pipits nested out on the heath near scattered clumps of fir, and once I found a crossbill's nest built right up in the topmost twigs of an old Scotch pine.

During the first winter of the war Gordon and I set off in my car, an ancient two-seater Morris, for Wells-next-the-Sea in

Norfolk to try to shoot a wild goose. In retrospect this may sound rather an odd thing to have done, but that first war winter was a strange one. The war was without battles, petrol though rationed was not particularly short, the calamity of Dunkirk was five months away, and the bombing had not started. We arrived in time to go out for the evening flight with a local fowler of renown called Sam Bone. He took us to Holkham Gap and I remember how horrified we were when we saw half a dozen other cars there. We walked along the beach beside the sand dunes and there seemed to be a waiting gunner every fifty yards. At last Sam told me to wait in the dunes at a place called Towers Low. It was a starlit night with no wind, and the geese, which we could hear talking in the fresh marshes beyond the trees, suddenly went silent. Then with a clamour they were up and flying towards us, nearly two thousand of them.

Most of them passed to the east of my position when suddenly I could hear more coming straight for me. Looking up I could just see a thin wavering line of birds against the sky. I raised my gun, swung far in front of the line, and fired both barrels; the flock split in two and flew clamouring seawards, but one bird remained and appeared to be growing bigger and bigger; then I realised it was falling. A moment later a young white-front crashed into the dunes behind me. Of course it was a fluke, but one which did much to raise our stock locally, for staying in the same hotel were two Cambridge dons who had been out for ten days without getting a single goose.

After a fortnight Gordon had to return to Devon, but I stayed on and went out before dawn one morning with the two dons for the early flight. We left their car at the end of a drift leading down to the salting and walked out across the mud to a shingle bar called the Binks. It was freezing hard so that the mud was covered with a film of ice and was very slippery in rubber boots. We were late and it was beginning to get light; one or two ducks were already flighting, so we loaded our guns. At that time I had a double eight-bore hammer gun, a heavy weapon, and hearing ducks approaching I cocked both hammers. A second later my feet shot from under me, and as I fell I threw the gun aside. It crashed spinning on the ice, mercifully without going off. It spun like a top and every time the barrels pointed at the dons the two of them jumped into the air together as though over an invisible skipping rope. Altogether on that trip we shot four geese and a good many wigeon and mallard. No doubt we were lucky with the weather, which was hard with heavy snow at times. Much as I enjoyed the shooting I kept wondering how to set about wild-fowling with a camera.

At length it occurred to me to dig a conventional hide in the middle of the geese's favourite marsh so that only three feet or so stuck up above ground level, and to camouflage this very carefully with natural vegetation. One evening I waited for the geese to flight out to sea since I did not want to disturb them, and as soon as they had gone I set to work in the failing light. Apart from the fact that the hole, two feet deep, quickly filled with water all went well and by the time it was dark the job was completed and the low hide well concealed.

My plan was to get into position before dawn so as not to disturb the birds and to wait until the sun was strong enough for photography. The following morning the flocks came in from the sea as usual and settled in the right marsh but several hundred yards away. In daylight I was surprised to see how obvious the hide was; even an object barely three feet high looked conspicuous against the flat marsh. The next day the geese had moved to another field farther away and for the rest of my stay they never went back to the original marsh.

These first efforts at wildfowling with a camera, unsuccessful though they were, marked, I believe, the beginning of the end of shooting with a gun so far as I was concerned. I was to shoot a lot more ducks and geese in many different places, but all the time I was dreaming of shooting them with a camera. It was to be seven years before I should be able to try again, for that summer I was caught up in the war.

During the spring of 1940 I volunteered to join the Navy and was sent to Northern Ireland as a seaman in the Royal Naval Patrol Service. There I was drafted to a converted yacht and within a few days we sailed south to take up patrol duties in Strangford Lough. Many things about the lough impressed me: its grandeur and loneliness, the grassy islands uninhabited save for a few sheep and rabbits and the curious atmosphere of a land-locked sea, but above all the bird life.

We made many trips in search of greylag geese and quite often succeeded in getting a bird or two. On one occasion I stalked a small flock of wigeon sitting at the water's edge on Green Island; it was not a difficult stalk as the wind was in my favour and there were some low bushes to give cover. As they rose I fired. One bird fell on to the shingle. It was a drake wigeon, and when I picked it up it appeared to be unscathed although unconscious, so I concluded that a stray shot must have grazed its skull and stunned it. A live wigeon was far more exciting than a dead one; so I took off one of my socks and carefully pulled it over the bird, leaving its head and neck free. After a little while it recovered and looked quite bright. I had visions of clipping one of its wings and keeping it alive with any other wildfowl I might get in the same way.

We spent the rest of the afternoon looking for the greylags without success and, as the sun went down, we returned to Green Island and went ashore. There is a small water-hole near the top of the island; the land then slopes down to the south, ending in a shingle spit running out into the sea. We decided that I should dig a small pit by the water-hole and lie up there in case any geese came in at dusk, while Johnnie (part-owner of one of the ferry-boats) would lie out on the spit. Taking a spade from the dinghy I handed my gun to Johnnie; he had his own gun under one arm and put mine under the other. I laid the wigeon carefully on the short grass and started to dig. A moment later Johnnie shouted and I turned round just in time to see the wigeon flying off, having escaped from the sock. Johnnie stood there, a gun under each arm, roaring with laughter but quite unable to do anything about the bird.

The moon rose as it got dark, and some geese suddenly called quite close to me. Then I saw them, five greylags gliding in on set pinions to land by the water-hole. They looked huge, they were so close. I sat up so hurriedly that I fired the first barrel prematurely by mistake, but I got a gander weighing $9\frac{1}{4}$ lb. with the second. Johnnie got two wigeon when the moon rose, then we heard brent geese in the direction of Salt Island and decided to go after them in the dinghy.

Johnnie rowed very quietly close along the shore while I sat in the bows with gun at the ready. The brent could see us long before we could see them, and kept getting up ahead of us. We turned back towards the motor-boat when three geese suddenly appeared crossing our bows. I dropped one and it immediately dived. We rowed like mad and chased it every time it surfaced; then we saw it in the moonlight swimming just below the surface. As quick as lightning Johnnie thrust his arm into the water and grabbed it. The extreme tip of one wing had been damaged by the shot, but otherwise the goose appeared unharmed. I was even more thrilled with the little black brent goose alive than I had been with the wigeon. We wrapped it up carefully and in due course it was turned out, with one wing clipped, into a disused chicken-run in Strangford with a sunken tub for a pool. The following day it was cropping the short grass of the run as though nothing had happened.

The little brent goose was doing well and getting tame, but

I badly wanted another to put with it, or even a greylag. Several trips up the lough on off-duty days had failed to produce a single wing-tipped bird. Then one day I was given permission to try for a goose on the Hollymount marsh near Downpatrick. The weather was still quite hard and there had been a heavy fall of snow. Quite a number of geese and mallard were flying about looking for open water. Occasional parties of wigeon and teal came by, but most of them had left for the mud flats and the unfrozen waters of the lough. We spied a small group of geese feeding on the marsh fairly close to a reed-filled dyke. The keeper was keen for me to get a shot and suggested that I should creep along the frozen dyke under cover of the reeds until I was opposite the geese; then he would walk out on to the marsh and put them up, hoping that they would fly over my position.

All went according to plan, the geese passing about forty yards to my left. I dropped one and it was obviously only winged, so I ran out and chased it through the snow. When I caught it I was disappointed to see that its right wing had been broken clean by the shot in the vicinity of the main joint corresponding to the elbow in the human arm. Since the bird seemed otherwise untouched, I amputated the wing at the break then and there and put on a tourniquet with a piece of string to prevent bleeding; then I rubbed snow over the wound. It hardly bled at all and that evening I put the bird out in the pen with the brent.

People who breed mallard nearly always seem to have more than they want, and a friend who had heard that I was keen on keeping wildfowl offered to let me have a pair of his birds. He lived farther up the lough on Mahee Island, which was connected to the shore by a low concrete causeway. This was normally outside the limit of our patrol, but I managed to persuade the skipper to take the boat up there so that I could row ashore in the dinghy and pick up the ducks. As we approached the island the boat suddenly ran aground on a mudbank. We tried to push her off without success. The skipper was not pleased and shouted at me, " damn and blast your ruddy ducks." The rising tide eventually floated the boat and we started back but not before I had been ashore and collected a pair of nice fat mallard. These were soon turned out with the geese and we christened them " Damn " and " Blast."

Some time in March we were given a long week-end leave and I decided to fly home from Belfast to Liverpool and thence by train to my parents' wartime home in Lancashire. I had written to tell them to expect two geese and a pair of mallard which were destined for the pond in the garden. We left Belfast in mild weather, but when the door was opened at Speke airport it was many degrees colder and a powdering of snow lay on the ground. The brent goose and the two ducks were soon grazing peacefully on the lawn in our garden; they were to be the beginning of a considerable collection of wild-fowl.

In the autumn of 1941 I was sent as a sub-lieutenant to an M.G.B. stationed in Dover. Our task was to attack German convoys trying to slip through the Straits in the dark and, since we were at sea at night and attempting to snatch a few hours' sleep by day, I had no time for natural history, though two incidents remain clear in my mind. The first was the wonderful clamour of a flock of brent geese flying low over our boat just at the start of a Commando raid on the French coast. Their music momentarily eased the tense silence before the landing. The second was a considerable movement of small birds across the Straits one sunny April day; most migration takes place at night over the sea, so this was something of an exception. An M.G.B. at speed throws up a white plume of water six or seven feet high astern, and during the trip I counted no less than twelve small birds who met their doom by attempting to settle on this arc of water only to be instantly engulfed.

One morning in April, 1944, I woke to find the sun streaming in through the window of my room—cabin we used to call it—in the Royal Temple Yacht Club which was our mess at Ramsgate. As I came to, I realised that a bird was singing on the chimney stack outside my window. His song was quite loud and I had never heard it before. It consisted of three simple phrases constantly repeated, with a curious noise like someone rattling a handful of small pebbles towards the end. I went to the window and could see the songster quite plainly, a dark almost black bird with a whitish patch on the wing and the stance of a large robin. It took me some time to grasp that here was a very rare visitor, a cock black redstart. Up to that time only a few scattered pairs of these birds had bred in this country although the species was a regular, if rather uncommon, winter visitor.

Black redstarts prefer to nest in ruined buildings or amongst rocks, and are found breeding over much of Europe as far north as Denmark. That they were not found as a regular breeding species in this country before the war was presumably because of lack of suitable habitat. German bombs provided an abundance of ruins, particularly in the south-eastern corner of England, and from that time on the birds started to colonise this country.

Bird song has always intrigued me although I have no ear for music as such. This black redstart provided a wonderful chance for a detailed study and I spent many hours listening to this particular bird, stop-watch in hand, timing every phrase and complete song. There was plenty of opportunity since he sang from the 13th April to 26th June, occasionally in July, and sometimes as late as mid-September. His full song lasted about three and a fifth seconds (average of fifty complete songs timed) and consisted of three distinct phrases: the first a short warbling sound, the second a harsh rattling note like a handful of small pebbles being shaken together, and the third a short chirring trill always ending in a double high note. The shortest complete song timed lasted two and a fifth seconds, the longest nine seconds. The variation in duration was largely accounted for by the differing interval between phrases one and two, while there was rarely any appreciable interval between phrases two and three. This bird sang on sunny days and even when it was raining, especially if the light was bright.

In addition to the cock's song, both male and female black redstarts had their own vocabulary. The cock uttered a quiet and mellow " swit swit " nearly all the time when in the vicinity of the nest; this became louder and harsher whenever an intruder ventured near. He also had a loud and harsh scolding note " tuc-tuc-tuc " which he would sound with his beak full of insects. This scolding note was given only under conditions of extreme alarm, as when a cat strayed into his territory. When his hen was within the nest feeding the young the cock would sometimes sit outside uttering a low churring note as if of impatience.

The hen had the same quiet and mellow " swit swit " as the cock when near the nest, and she also had a low scolding note " tic-tic-tic " uttered quietly and in quick succession. Sometimes she would include a high-pitched " seep " in between the " tic-tic " thus: " tic-tic-seep-tic-seep-tic-tic." Once she sat a few feet away and through a closed bill made the tiniest bat-like " swee swee swee " so shrill as to be scarcely audible.

Towards the end of May we found the first black redstart's nest in the bombed ruin of the Granville Hotel on the east cliff. It was built about twelve feet up below the wrecked balcony and was hidden behind paint and plaster peeling off the ceiling. We could hear the young calling, a harsh churring cry whenever they were being fed, so we assumed that they were at least a week old.

While it was obvious from the start that we could not photograph the birds actually at the nest, I hoped somehow to get some pictures. So a day or two later we returned with a borrowed pair of step-ladders and started to construct a hide of green material over the top of the steps. There was another minor snag: the nest was just inside the perimeter of a six-inch coastal defence battery. We approached the battery commander and explained the position, emphasising the rarity of the bird. He agreed at once to let us try to get some pictures. About a week later I fixed up my camera inside the hide at the top of the steps, and focused on the top strand of the coiled barbed wire entanglement surrounding the battery. This wire was immediately beneath the nest and I had noticed that both birds sometimes perched on it before flying up to feed the young.

That first day I spent two hours inside the hide during which the adults fed the young fifteen times. But not once did they sit on the coil of barbed wire. I had to think of a new plan and so a day or two later I went to the town refuse tip, and after much searching managed to collect some maggots. I set the camera up again and tied the maggots to the strand of wire with black cotton. During a spell of one hour and forty minutes the young were fed eleven times, and three times the hen bird perched for a second or two on the strand of wire near the maggots, giving me the chance to get a picture. I was excited with the result because as far as I knew black red-starts had not been photographed before in England.

In the years after the war the numbers of breeding pairs declined as the stricken areas were cleared and buildings repaired.

In the spring of 1945, I took up my last appointment in the Navy at a shore base in Poole harbour. My job there was to supervise the laying up of M.T.B.s and M.G.B.s on a mud-bank in a little-used part of the harbour. When they arrived the boats had been stripped of almost everything, including guns, engines and stores. The lifeless hulls were then lined up to be disposed of when the war was over. I had seen many of these boats at the height of their active service, and could remember those who fought in them. Now their fighting days were over and they lay there silent and deserted, a roosting place for sea birds.

A few months later the war in Europe was over and I was invalided out of the Navy.

3. The Ducks that flew to Russia

Once again I was faced with the difficult task of deciding what to do for a living. I could not bear the thought of life in an office, and so it was agreed that I should become a farm pupil with the ultimate aim of running my own farm. After a year on a small mixed holding in Oxfordshire I became a pupil on a typical large Norfolk arable farm. This was much more fun because I had plenty of spare time and could get away to the coastal marshes wild-fowling or photographing birds.

Sparrow-hawks were still relatively common and I found a nest with eggs in a fir tree in the middle of a wood bordering a large field of sugar beet which I was supposed to be hoeing. Within a week I had built a hide in a nearby tree and spent several afternoons photographing the birds instead of hoeing beet.

About that time a very unusual bird, a pectoral sandpiper, turned up on the marsh at Salthouse; it frequented a rather wet place amongst the sea-aster not far from the coast road. Surprisingly, it was quite tame and we discovered that, if I set the camera up by the side of a shallow pool and remained motionless behind it, the bird could be gently driven or walked right past me and with a long focus lens it was possible to get some pictures. I believe that these are the first, perhaps the only, shots of this species to be obtained in the wild in Europe, for this sandpiper is a rare visitor from America.

Eventually my parents set me up on a farm of my own of 387 acres at Mileham in mid-Norfolk. A pond had been made in a corner of the home meadow and into it went the surface water from the yards. One of the first things I did was to have this pond and about an acre of land surrounded by a stout fence of wire netting seven feet high.

That winter I went to Ireland for a holiday and the original inmates of this enclosure were a pair of Greenland white-fronted geese which I brought back from Wexford slob. They had been wing-tipped by shooters on the slob and I first saw them grazing peacefully in a farmer's orchard. When I told him I would dearly like some geese like his, should he ever get any more, he promptly gave me his pair. They were in perfect condition and are both alive and well to-day, fifteen years later.

One of the pair had a ring on its leg inscribed Zoolog. Museum Copenhagen Denmark 270814. Later on I learned from the Danish authorities that it had been ringed as a youngster by members of a Danish expedition to West Greenland the previous summer. This was quite exciting since the Greenland white-fronted goose was then a new sub-species which had only recently been described and my pair was therefore one of the first to be kept in this country.

The north slob was a wonderful place for wildfowl, and I spent many days that January watching the geese. The slob itself consists of about two thousand four hundred acres of reclaimed marshland, and the birds, though shot by the sporting tenants, have been protected since the beginning of the century. Up to 1930 the geese wintering on the slob were mainly greylag with a few barnacles. Then the white-fronts started to arrive and their numbers steadily increased over the

Next stop Russia?   I release a mallard after ringing it at Mileham

Above: left, white-winged black tern photographed with my Heinkel lens; right, the greater black-backed gulls fight while the hooded crow stands by. Below: left, American pectoral sandpiper, a rare visitor; right, hen black redstart, 1944

years until at times there are over four thousand on the two
slobs, north and south. Having heard that there were two
snow geese amongst the white-fronts, I spent several days
searching for them. Local opinion was that the white goose
had been wintering there for several years.

On the slob the geese, though apparently in huge flocks,
were found on closer inspection to be in family parties. This
collection of family parties within the main flock is common
to all wintering geese, but is not always apparent, particularly
just after the flock has pitched. As the birds feed undisturbed
and spread out, so the families become more obvious—a pair
of old birds and their three or four goslings of the previous
summer, with here and there barren pairs, newly betrothed
couples, two or three years old, and of course odd birds. The
family bond is very strong in geese and each little group grazes
on its own within, as it were, an invisible movable territory.
The moment another family or odd bird enters this area the
old birds rush at it cackling and hissing with their necks
stretched out parallel to the ground.

One afternoon I felt sure I had at last found the snow goose,
sitting by itself close to a group of white-fronts. By slipping
through a barbed-wire fence and along a shallow ditch I got
close enough to have a good look through glasses. Suddenly
the white goose shot up a long white neck topped by a long
bill and there stood not a goose but a spoonbill. Seeing me
the geese got up and the spoonbill flew off by itself in fast
erratic flight, its short pointed tail and long spatulate bill being
most conspicuous. I watched it disappear as it glided down and
landed out of sight in the middle of the slob. By crawling
along the ditches I eventually came to a small creek which
gave good cover; this creek suddenly ran into a large channel
or lagoon of golden sand with water lapping between the
miniature sand-bars. I was glad of my careful approach
because more than a thousand wigeon sat sleeping in the
lagoon with several small flocks of teal, mallard, curlew,

lapwing and golden plover. The afternoon sun shone on this galaxy of wildfowl, while the blue sky with its white cumulus clouds was reflected in the still water of the channel. Not fifty yards away the spoonbill stood asleep at the edge of the water with its bill turned back and hidden in its scapulars. Its snow-white body and duller wings reflected the sun and I knew by the black tips to its wings that it was a young bird. After I had been watching for some minutes a party of teal saw me and jumped in alarm. Once again the spoonbill's long neck shot up and it too flew off in the same fast, curving and flapping flight, while the air was full of whispering pinions and the whistling of hundreds of drake wigeon.

As the sun started to sink low over the hills inland I noticed a white blob amongst a hundred or more feeding white-fronts. Stalking closer I could see through my glasses a smaller white blob which appeared to be the head and neck of a goose. I got close enough to watch them and could see the snow goose and its companion the blue snow goose, owner of the white head and neck. The two birds appeared to be mated as they kept close together and wherever the snow goose went the blue snow followed. Both birds were noticeably larger than the white-fronts. These snow geese are of course colour phases of the same species—the lesser snow goose, which breeds in Arctic Siberia, Alaska and as far east as Baffin Island, from where no doubt these two birds had wandered east-ward and become caught up in the flocks of white-fronts migrating south from Greenland. At this time the lesser snow goose was not on the British list since it was thought that existing records were of birds which had escaped from cap-tivity. But there is no reason to believe that the two snow geese on the slob were other than truly wild birds.

There is a pool at Mileham in the middle of a large arable field, well away from any road. It is roughly half an acre in extent and oval in shape, the northern end being deep and the southern end shallow. This end dries out in summer and grass grows which, when flooded in winter, attracts ducks. There is no cover round the pool, but during successive cleaning out operations the spoil has been left round the edges and now forms quite a high bank sheltering the water. I first noticed three or four mallard dropping in at dusk one October evening and so I started to feed the pond each afternoon, tipping about one and a half pails of barley into the shallows. I had no idea of shooting the birds, but I used to enjoy hiding nearby and counting the duck in against the last of the sunset. With regular feeding the number coming in each evening rapidly increased until by the end of November well over a hundred birds would arrive in the last half-hour of gloaming to feed on the barley. Standing in the shadow of a hedge a hundred yards down wind, one could listen to the quacking and murmuring of the ducks as they splashed and dibbled in the shallows.

Quite a number of teal used the pool and as I wanted some for my waterfowl collection I decided to build a trap in the shallow end. This was done by driving four ash poles into the bottom of the pond forming a rectangle eight feet square and six feet high which was completely covered with small mesh wire netting. A door in one side and a funnel-shaped tunnel of netting in each of the other three sides completed the trap.

The way the funnels were set was important. They were nearly three feet wide at the entrance where they were joined to the side of the cage and the top was about eighteen inches above water. Each funnel was about three feet long and tapered so that the innermost end was only eight inches across and about four inches above the water at the top. The sides of the funnels like those of the cage itself were pegged down to the bottom of the pool. To bait the trap, corn was scattered in the shallows round about and a trail led right through each pipe into the cage. While I had seen something like it else-where, I had no idea whether this particular trap would work in practice. After baiting it for the first time I went up the next morning with Gordon who was staying with us. We had seen over a hundred duck go into the pool the night before and, as we crept up to the edge and peeped over the high bank, a party of mallard rose from the far end.

The sight of the trap astonished us, for it appeared almost bursting with ducks and indeed it was. It held nineteen mal-lard and four teal. We rushed back for a landing net and soon had the teal safely in the bag for the short journey to join the collection by the house. The mallard we released. Two things had become clear; first, that we must have another elongated and narrow addition to the main cage into which captive ducks could be driven and easily caught up; and secondly that all the birds we trapped should be ringed before release.

For the next four years I worked the trap during the winter months whenever I could and caught nearly six hundred ducks. Most of them were ringed and released, but many were birds which had previously been caught and ringed. The record catch of thirty mallard and teal was made on a night in January with a full moon and the pond partly frozen.

Wildfowl using this pool spent the day resting on largish lakes, the nearest of which was four miles away, but some of them also came from the coast twenty miles distant as the duck flies. Odd parties of wigeon came in, particularly in hard weather; but although we could hear their whistling calls at dusk, none was ever caught.

Of the 284 ducks I ringed at Mileham, forty-five were recovered; that is to say, they were shot by somebody who sent particulars of the ring number back to the British Museum. Ducks are great travellers, and thirteen recoveries were from abroad. Perhaps the strangest were two mallard which were caught on the same night in February and ringed and released the next morning. Both ducks were shot within three days of each other the following April, one near Leningrad and the other on the Volga.

While I have rather mixed feelings about ringing wild birds, I must confess that I enjoyed learning to what distant places ducks which I had once held in my hands had subsequently journeyed. Nobody can deny the wealth of scientific knowledge which man has acquired through large-scale ringing of birds. Migration routes have become clear, hitherto unknown breeding grounds or wintering grounds of certain populations have been discovered; mortality, life span, and a host of other facts have been learned. Without some means of marking individual birds it would have been impossible to accumulate such knowledge.

It was at Mileham that the seed of our game hawking sown twelve years earlier at Sherborne finally bore fruit. For the first time we had both land and a fair amount of game. Gordon Jolly was the chief organiser and for a couple of seasons we tried each September to catch a few partridges with trained falcons. That we achieved any success at all in those days was entirely due to another friend, Jack Mavrogordato, who had many years' experience of hawking both in this country and in the Sudan. Despite the fact that we had no dogs Jack caught several birds with falcons which he had brought home with him. One of his most successful hawks was a tiny lanneret who weighed scarcely as much as a partridge. It soon became obvious that it was impossible to do much without a good pointer or setter. Once again Gordon took the initiative and we became joint owners of a pointer bitch called Lorfred Venus.

Game hawking is to my mind the most exacting of all field sports and under modern conditions it is without doubt the most difficult. Perhaps this is one of its attractions. If the number of birds killed is any criterion, game hawking can hardly be classed as a field sport. The killing of a single partridge or grouse with a trained falcon requires patience, experience and skill plus a large percentage of luck coupled with highly specialised conditions.

Perhaps I should describe the sort of flight at which one aims but which is so rarely achieved. For this purpose we will assume that we have a fully trained and experienced falcon and an equally experienced pointer though months of hard work and skill will have gone into the production of each.

Really open country is essential because all falcons are inclined to wander off unless the quarry can be flushed straight away and this is often impossible. Peregrines are powerful fliers and will soon be lost to view in any but the most open countryside. Having arrived at a large stubble field, the pointer is taken to the down-wind end so that, as she gallops criss-crossing the field, she is always working into the wind. With any luck she will suddenly whip round and stop dead in her tracks, crouching low with nose well forward and parallel with the ground, one front paw raised and tail out-stretched, a picture of statuesque immobility. When on point these dogs have a peculiar glazed expression in their eyes as though they are almost entranced by the scent of game; and well they may be when one considers that under favourable conditions a pointer can scent a covey of partridges sitting unconcerned in the stubble twenty or thirty yards away.

The dog on point being in a reasonable position for a flight its handler has to decide whether she really is pointing par-tridges and not a hare, or even a lark, for sometimes the best of dogs can false point. Having decided that the dog is speaking the truth, the handler tells the falconer who then removes the hood from his bird and holds her up. The falcon often appears in no hurry as she sits looking round; she may even mute, that is defecate, and then rouse or shake her plumage. Suddenly she jumps into the air and flies round in circles gaining height, her bells jingling with each thrust of her powerful wings. During this time she cannot see the partridges; but an experienced falcon knows that the dog and the men down below will probably flush birds for her. Her circles may be as much as a quarter of a mile in diameter and, as she gains height, she commands an enormous area of countryside and with her incredible eyesight can see a pigeon flying two or three miles away. Any bird moving in the vicinity is a temptation to her to stray.

When the falconer knows that she is up as high as she is likely to go he signals to the dog handler who flushes the partridges when the falcon is upwind and coming in towards him. As the covey rockets away into the wind there is a moment's pause while the falcon assesses the situation. Then she flicks over and with a few quick wing beats she drives downwards in a vertical death-dealing stoop. If her aim is true and she means business, one of the fleeing partridges is killed.

There are minor variations in the procedure of game hawking, and I have merely described a system which, we found from experience, worked. Old writers often described, and their artists depicted, kills in which the falcon comes down from a great height in a vertical stoop, striking the quarry a tremendous blow from above so that it falls dead to the ground leaving a puff of feathers floating earthwards. This does sometimes happen, and I have seen it on several occasions; it is the classic game-hawking flight and is quite breath-taking, especially if the falcon starts her stoop from a height of several hundred feet. You can then hear the rushing of wind in her feathers as she plunges down. But in my experience it is rather difficult for the falcon to score a direct hit of this kind, and many successful game hawks stoop behind their quarry and then pull out of their dive, relying on their impetus to carry them up so that they grab the bird from behind while they are swinging skywards. Besides being easier to seize the partridge, this method is advantageous to the falcon since, if she bungles it, she is gaining height and so can stoop again. Much has been written about the speed of a peregrine's flight, but it is quite impossible for a trained falcon to catch a winter partridge or grouse in level pursuit unless she has the advantage gained from the stoop. Many find this fact hard to believe.

We found that keeping a pointer for hawking was rather like keeping a pony for one's children to ride. It soon turns out that one is useless because it cannot do all the work, so a second is acquired, and thus the rot and the expense starts, and before long you find you have got three or four. As the dogs lived with me at Mileham my contribution to our combined game-hawking each September was to work them for the others while they flew their hawks. To improve our chances of success, Gordon and I hired between us the sporting rights of some twelve hundred acres of land which included what had been a wartime aerodrome, but was then being farmed.

Handling the dogs was a wonderful relaxation. I love pointers and never tire of watching them work; and I could also watch the hawks in action without the awful anxiety of flying them. Then I knew that the success of the flight depended ultimately upon my flushing the partridges at exactly the right moment; this gave me exceptional opportunity to watch a good many peregrines actually catching quarry, in some cases only a few feet above my head. What struck me most was that every falcon adopted the same method: during the stoop both feet are tucked up and invisible and just before striking or grabbing the quarry one foot only is lowered ready for action, the other being held up and not used unless required. Often the speed at which the hawk is travelling causes the quarry, and the foot grasping it, to trail out behind. The second foot is then available for the falcon to land.

The flight I have just described is the kind one tries to achieve, but only a very few are so successful. The rest are spoilt for one or other of many reasons. The dog may be pointing a hare, or the birds may have recently left that particular spot though their scent lingers; the covey may be too close to the sanctuary of a hedge or a copse; the falcon may not try very hard or she may rake away after a wood-pigeon; the partridges, who are fully aware of the danger a falcon presents and who are watching her every move, may get up when she is wide and down-wind; or, if they are Frenchmen, they may refuse to fly and simply run in front of the dog. All these and many other circumstances too can ruin the chances of a successful flight, and each falcon can only be put up two or three times a day.

In case anyone imagines that many birds can be killed with a trained hawk, let me put on record the result of one of our best seasons. In September, 1955, after three weeks of daily endeavour, we caught ten partridges, most if not all with a young falcon flown by another friend, Bill Ruttledge, who is a very fine falconer. Somebody worked out that, taking into account our combined expenditure, each partridge killed cost us nearer one hundred pounds than fifty! I realise of course that on really well-stocked partridge manors or grouse moors larger bags have been made. But of all sports game-hawking is one where the size of the bag matters least. Its attraction lies in its difficulties and frustrations and the sight of that noble bird, the peregrine, on the wing. Bill's falcon once killed a brace of partridges in one day, and we afterwards had them for dinner. There can be very few people alive to-day who can claim to have eaten game in this country taken by a falcon.

4. Wildfowling with a Camera

Most bird photographers concentrate on their subject during the nesting season with the result that there is a sameness about their work. The angle is nearly always looking slightly down on the bird at its nest. Nowadays such pictures are often technically perfect, classics in their sphere, but rather dull when you have seen several hundred of them.

I would go so far as to say that the most interesting scenes that I have witnessed in the bird world have been away from the nest and often outside the breeding season. It was this kind of thing that I was set on photographing, and wildfowl were an obvious choice. Of all birds wild geese seemed to me the most rewarding for the pictures I envisaged.

Shortly before the war Peter Scott had shown me some fine photographs taken by American photographers of flocks of geese wintering in Louisiana and California, but at the time no comparable pictures existed of wild geese taken in Europe.

The American photographers enjoyed many advantages, not least of which was plenty of sunshine. In addition their goose grounds were well organised with permanent hides or "blinds" from which to observe and photograph.

In the early winter of 1946 I heard that large numbers of white-fronted geese often fed fairly close to the sea-wall on a salt marsh in Gloucestershire known as the "Dumbles." Peter Scott had already rented the land behind the sea-wall where he intended to build up a collection of waterfowl to replace his pre-war flock which no longer existed. He had

42

already started work on the construction of permanent observation huts or hides built into the sea-wall itself, from which it was possible to watch the wild geese in comfort. Thus it was that I arrived at Slimbridge at about the time that the large flocks of white-fronts were also arriving, and spent several days watching and photographing them. It never occurred to me at the time, and perhaps not to Peter either, that he would make such a huge success of the now famous Wildfowl Trust at that very place.

I remember well how the geese came in one morning. Little parties kept arriving over the marsh high up in the mist. They came in all day in lots of seven or eight, and sometimes eighty or a hundred in one skein. These newcomers were easy to distinguish as they arrived, for no resident birds ever flew more than a hundred feet above the ground when moving from one part of the marsh to another, whereas the strangers always came in at a great height. They would appear over the hills, thin wavering lines in the mist, come round on the wind, and then begin to lose height over the marsh, descending on stiff pinions with their paddles down, and finally dropping with vigorous wing-flapping amongst the ever-growing flocks.

We noticed that these new geese always pitched right amongst birds already on the ground, and never just outside a flock. Those feeding took no notice whatever of the fresh arrivals, not even looking up at them. Now and then a small flock would come planing in on set wings; then suddenly the birds would twist and tumble, diving to within a few feet of the ground, and righting themselves only in time to land—a delightful evolution known as whiffling. Once safely down, the birds always had a quick preen before starting to feed. I wondered where they had last preened and fed, and by what route they had come from their breeding grounds in far Siberia. How many stops had they made on the way? Perhaps one day, when observers all over Europe have pooled their notes, we may be able to answer some of these questions.

Soon there must have been 3,000 white-fronted geese using the marsh, and when a passing aeroplane caused the whole lot to take flight out to the river, the roar of their wings was like the noise of distant surf, and their concerted clamour was beyond description—the most thrilling of all bird noises.

After being at Mileham for six years I more or less gave up farming and moved to Great Witchingham to concentrate on birds. The property we bought was a small farm on the main Norwich-Fakenham road, and though I did not realise it at the time it was an ideal situation for the type of place it was destined to become. The fifty acres of land is undulating and attractive, but unfortunately there was no spring or stream for our collection of waterfowl. So our first task was to sink a deep bore to provide a constant supply of water for the half-dozen small ponds which we excavated. These ponds were dug on a rough meadow by the house and then the whole paddock was surrounded by a fox-proof fence of wire-netting. During the first winter we planted groups of flowering shrubs and quick growing trees, and within a surprisingly short time the ducks and geese, numbering about twenty-five different species, began to look at home. We also had to do a fair amount of work on the house, and since there was no garden to speak of we had to make one, laying out borders and sowing lawns.

About this time a friend asked me if I would be interested in a huge long-focus lens said to have come out of a war-time Heinkel which the Germans had used for high-altitude reconnaissance. It seemed just the thing for photographing wildfowl and waders on the shore, so I jumped at the idea. The only snag was fitting it to a camera, or perhaps I should say fitting a camera on to the lens. To enable this to be done I designed what amounted to a long box complete with its own bellows-extension operated by a rack and pinion. The lens, 7¼ inches in diameter and weighing forty pounds, was screwed into one end of the box, while the camera, the front of which had to be modified, was attached to the other end. Not being a telephoto lens, but having a focal length of thirty inches meant that the whole outfit when assembled was over four feet long and weighed nearly one hundred pounds. It was the most unwieldy piece of photographic equipment imaginable and its size and weight meant that in addition to a stout tripod at the point of balance a bipod at the rear end was also necessary.

That summer a rare visitor in the form of a white-winged black tern arrived on Cley Marsh and spent a few days hawking flies over the Round Pool in company with some black terns. Various people attempted to photograph this rarity with little success since it kept well out over the water and spent the entire time on the wing. One afternoon I took the camera and big lens to have a go. Billy Bishop, the warden, helped me to carry it out across the marsh where we set it up on the bank. I shall always remember the look of amazement on the faces of the other bird-watchers and photographers using more conventional equipment. Seeing my cumbersome apparatus stuck up like a field-gun, one man came over and explained to me that I should never get a picture of the white-winged black tern with that set-up. It would be quite impossible since the bird had to be picked out amongst the more common black terns and then followed in flight—something which was plainly impossible, with my equipment.

For a time I thought that he was probably right, then I noticed that the vagrant had quite a definite beat over the pool which it seemed to follow as often as not. Taking a stick I waded out and set it up so that the top stuck out of the water roughly on the terns' line of flight about twenty yards in front of the camera. Sitting on a stool I trained the lens so that I could just see the tip of the stick in the bottom of the reflex view-finder, and whenever the bird appeared to be flying towards the stick I watched in the view-finder. The trouble was that I never had sufficient warning to be able to focus and shoot in the split second available. There was a young army officer amongst the bird-watchers, and he offered to act as spotter for me by counting the bird down whenever it flew towards the stick. This was a tremendous help as it meant that I could remain watching the view-finder ready to focus and fire the shutter almost at once. By this method we took over thirty pictures in a couple of hours and some of them were reasonably sharp considering the speed of the bird and the range.

With the arrival of winter brent geese invade the Norfolk coast although in a good many years Christmas is over before any large flocks appear. Brent are the most erratic of all wild-fowl and they have always fascinated me, perhaps on account of their extreme wariness, and perhaps because of the mystery which still surrounds them. Our knowledge of other breeds of goose, particularly the pink-foot, has increased enormously during the last few years as a result of large-scale ringing on their breeding grounds and also of flocks having been caught by rocket-netting in their winter quarters. So far very few brent have been ringed at all, and nearly all of those on their Spitzbergen breeding grounds.

During the spell of hard weather in March, 1955, over 3,000 brent congregated in Blakeney harbour and I decided to build a hide amongst the clumps of spartina at the salting edge in the hope of photographing them. At full tide the sea covered the whole marsh and only the top of the hide could be seen above the water. The geese only feed near the salting during the first of the ebb when the rest of the mud is still submerged. They always seem highly suspicious of the cover formed by the spartina grass, and my hide, though carefully concealed, looked rather like the Eiffel Tower in the vast expanse of mud-flat.

Owing to the poor winter light, photography could only

be attempted when high water was between ten o'clock and noon, so that only four days were suitable in every fortnight. Fortunately the day chosen dawned clear and frosty with a light, northerly breeze. High water was just after ten o'clock, so that by 11.30 conditions should have been perfect, with the mud near the hide beginning to show. By the time I arrived the wind had backed and increased and it soon became apparent that this was going to hold the tide up longer than we had expected. It was well past noon before the ebb gained momentum and we were able to set the decoys out.

We had brought the equipment from Morston in Kitch Bean's boat and now we struggled with the big lens and camera, heaving it over the side of the motor boat into a small dinghy for the short row to the edge of the mud. From there we struggled and splashed to the soaking wet hide in which we set up the camera with the legs of the tripod standing in six inches of water. Our decoys were in position on a slightly higher ridge of mud twenty paces away. They were home-made and consisted of two pieces of hardboard cut to the shape of a goose's body and hinged along the top, i.e. at the centre of the goose's back. A separate head and neck made it possible to vary the birds' attitude between feeding and resting.

Parties of geese were by now flying up and down the estuary looking for the first of the zostera beds to be uncovered. A bunch of about a hundred came in from the sea and pitched on the mud at the tide edge. In the brilliant sunlight they appeared surprisingly light in colour; suddenly I realised that they were all light-bellied brent. The juvenile birds had broad white tips to their secondaries and wing coverts and this gave them a strikingly barred appearance. A smaller bunch of fifteen geese swung in towards my decoys and dropped down just beyond them. They at once recognised that something was wrong with my hardboard geese and started to walk away, feeding as they went, plunging their bills deep into the ooze almost up to their eyes to get at the

47

zostera roots—a method of feeding which seemed hardly in keeping with their generally dainty demeanour. Suddenly all heads shot up, and a moment later the mud was emptied as every goose flew clamouring out to sea. A pair of great black-backed gulls, which had apparently been the cause of this headlong flight, continued their quarrel over a dead wader in front of my hide.

The dark-bellied brent has always been by far the most numerous form on this part of the coast and a pale-bellied bird something of a rarity. Yet a careful watch for several days that winter revealed that of the large number of brent in the estuary quite 75 per cent, or over 2,000 birds, were pale-bellied. This goose has now been given complete protection by the Danish Government on its Greenland breeding grounds. But its dark-bellied cousin is less fortunate, for it is now said to nest at all abundantly only on certain parts of the Taimyr coast. Here moreover it is still, according to the latest Russian literature, slaughtered in large numbers during the moult for food for humans and dogs.

Having discovered a technique for photographing ducks and geese with a long focus lens during the winter, I decided to try the same principle with waders on the tide edge of the north Norfolk coast the following autumn. This wait and see photography has its charms for you just never know what will turn up. Often no birds come within range all day, but a hide at the tide edge is a fascinating place in which to sit for there is never a dull moment, and it is indeed a bad day if dunlin, redshank or turnstone fail to materialise. Turnstones are one of my favourites, they are always so tame and busy probing and pushing the green slimy enteromorpha up into little balls with their bills and making lightning stabs at any small creature they uncover.

Since the days of the Kearton brothers at the turn of the century until shortly after the last war, the bird photographer had two main markets for his pictures, apart from illustrating lectures. These were to illustrate articles in the Press and to illustrate books. With the coming of television on an almost world-wide scale the situation rapidly changed. Natural history programmes became popular with the public and a demand appeared for nature films; in addition audiences at lectures were beginning to expect moving pictures. In the summer of 1955 I finally succumbed to the lure of the movie camera and bought a 16 mm. Paillard Bolex.

My first efforts were with waders along the tide edge where the ever present dunlins provided easy chances from a hide. Soon, having mastered the initial steps of film making, I was on the look-out for a bigger assignment. On looking back I realise now how very few, if any, of the initial steps I had really mastered. The following March Kitch Bean and I set off for the Outer Hebrides to film the barnacle geese wintering in the isle of South Uist.

All the equipment, including the still camera with the thirty-inch lens, was loaded into a van, upon the roof of which we lashed a small boat which could if necessary be turned into a floating hide. I think the atmosphere of such a trip can be felt best if I quote direct from my diary which I wrote at the time. Two things emerge very clearly: first how little I should have achieved without Kitch's co-operation, and secondly how lucky we were with the weather.

Friday 16th March

Bright diffused light until 1 p.m., then becoming overcast and dull. Wind SE. but not so strong.

In the hide on the machair behind Grogarry Lodge and ready for action by 11.30 a.m. We approached from the south and saw four or five hundred barnacles feeding beyond the hide along the west shore of Loch a'Mhachair. They stayed there while I got ready with the Bolex and twelve-inch lens. Kitch gave them half an hour and then went round in the van past Grogarry and carefully put them up. They nearly all pitched again to seaward of the hide except for one small party of twenty or so, which landed about seventy yards away. Kitch manœuvred the big flock again a little later on and they all pitched in my field, planing down to land on all sides of the hide with a glorious clamour of yelping cries. They remained feeding all round from about noon until nearly three o'clock when two crofters came with a tractor carting muck on to the machair, and put them out towards Geirinish. I noticed that several of the geese were ringed with ordinary aluminium rings, and at least one bird had a bright orange ring on its left leg[1] and an aluminium one on its right. When feeding the barnacles split up into small family parties and there were the usual quarrels when two such groups got in each other's way. Sometimes a young bird would stray into another group and get chased away.

Monday 19th March

Mainly sunny and bright. Strong SE wind.

In the hide at the end of the cattle-fold by 11 a.m. The geese were out on the stubble on the other side of the road and to seaward of me. At twelve o'clock Kitch, having moved them twice, got the whole lot down in front of my hide but about 250 yards away. I filmed them as they came in, and then they kept walking and flying in twos and threes towards

[1] When the film had been processed we noticed that not one but several geese in the flock had been ringed with orange-coloured rings on their left legs. From subsequent inquiries I learned that these rings had been put on by members of a British expedition to north-east Greenland the previous summer. This was the first definite evidence that the barnacles wintering in the Outer Hebrides nested in Greenland and not, as some had supposed, in Spitzbergen.

me until they were only about eighty yards away at 12.45 p.m., when a crofter drove his cattle down past the hide and put them all up. By 2.30 p.m. Kitch had manœuvred the geese just south of the fold, when a man came across the machair leading a heifer to the bull. Shortly after a shooter arrived and immediately started a lengthy detour, and began to stalk my decoys! Just as he got under cover of the fold I got out of the hide and stood up on top of the bank. He stopped in his tracks as though he had seen a ghost, then slunk off rather sheepishly.

Friday 23rd March

Some cloud, but bright sunny patches. Light E. wind.

In the new hide by 10.30 a.m. Kitch moved the geese over from the direction of the loch almost at once but they pitched half a mile to the north, towards the farm. They soon became restless and started to "roll-over," that is to say those at the back of the flock would get up and pitch again in front of their companions; by this means they drew within range. Then they all got up and came straight in towards the hide, dropping on arched pinions with their paddles down less than a hundred yards away. A wonderful landing shot and my camera ran out of film just at that very moment! The whole army of geese—at least seven hundred birds—walked past within forty yards of the hide while I filmed them.

In the afternoon we took down all the hides and cleaned up generally, and after saying our good-byes we sailed for Mallaig on the midnight boat.

5. Quest for the Gyr Falcon

Once the property of the King of Denmark, gyr falcons were presented as royal gifts to the courts of Europe during the Middle Ages when numbers of them were brought annually from Iceland. Great value was attached to these birds and it seemed strange that those imported and trained for falconry in more recent times had not come up to the high standards expected of them. There must be good reason, and the best way to find out was to go and study gyrs on their Arctic breeding grounds.

Iceland was an obvious choice since it is comparatively easy to reach by sea and we had heard of several eyries which had been occupied within the last two or three years. With local knowledge we hoped to find more pairs. For some years I had imported duck eggs for hatching from a collector near Myvatn, by name Willie Palsson. He was a farmer living in a valley several miles west of the lake and every June he would visit Myvatn to collect the eggs of tufted duck, scaup, gadwall, wigeon, Barrow's golden-eye and harlequin, which he sent to waterfowl breeders all over the world. I had corresponded so much with him that he seemed like an old friend. A few scattered pairs of gyrs were also believed to nest in this region. These falcons depend largely on ptarmigan for their main food supply, although some pairs breeding on high coastal cliffs, especially in the north west, prey on the seabird colonies. Like many arctic species the gyr has a good breeding year when its chief quarry also reaches a peak. We were lucky because in 1956 ptarmigan were very plentiful. Their cycle of abundance follows a five to seven year pattern, and in years when they are scarce, few if any of the gyrs breed in the interior.

On 4th June we boarded the Icelandic ship *Gullfoss* in Leith harbour. All the gear for the expedition was safely stowed in our Land-Rover which was sheeted and lashed to the fore-deck. Most of the other passengers were Icelanders going home; they included a male choir which had been touring the United States and Canada. As darkness fell and the ship left the quay, the choir lined the rails and sang a national song to those left ashore; and very stirring it sounded as the *Gullfoss* moved slowly out of the basin and into the dark waters of the Firth. The following day was calm with a light south-west wind. Herring gulls followed the ship through the Pentland Firth and in the afternoon fulmars put in a casual appearance, and one shearwater passed to seaward. Once out into the North Atlantic, the weather deteriorated and by next morning there was a fairly high beam sea running; the ship was rolling so that most passengers remained in their cabins. Like many northern races whose lives are tough and to a large extent dependent on the weather, the Icelandic people are rather religious, crucifixes and bibles being much in evidence. A copy was in every cabin printed in both English and Icelandic.

Fulmars were with us in force sweeping and gliding amongst the white-capped breakers with swift ease and scarcely a wing movement. They were quick to feed on any garbage thrown overboard but in a quiet and dignified manner and not like the quarrelsome raucous gulls. As we approached the West-mann Islands kittiwakes and a great skua joined the procession astern. I spent some time filming the fulmars by wedging myself against the after guard-rail so that I could lean over the stern and follow the birds better. After some time I could tell from experience which birds were likely to be worth photographing, since they all used the slip-stream of the ship in much the same way, and whether they would pass close or not depended on their angle of approach. The sea set an exposure problem. One moment the bird would be flying against the sparkling white foam on top of a huge roller, and the next minute it would sweep down into the dark bottle-green trough of the wave. This, combined with the rolling of the ship and the fact that I had to hand hold the camera—with a cord round my neck for safety—resulted in rather poor pictures.

We docked in Reyjkavik at nine o'clock in the morning and Gordon met us on the quay, having flown out the day before. After much delay we eventually got the Land-Rover ashore and through the Customs; then we all went off to lunch at Gunnar Sigurrdsson's house. Gunnar could speak English and he was a great help in getting our expedition organised. All his family seemed to be there and they gave us a magnificent meal including a huge boiled salmon and lots of rich cakes. Gunnar's younger brother Olaf very kindly acted as our guide and interpreter that afternoon in Reykjavik. We had to go to the government offices to see about the permit for filming the gyrs; this took a long time. Then we had to send some crates on to Akureyri by road as there was no room in the Land-Rover, for we hoped to take some live ducks back for the collection and had brought the specially designed crates with us. Finally there was paraffin to be got for the Primus and this caused no end of trouble because the Icelanders call paraffin " petroleum." They were taken aback when I insisted that I must have paraffin and not petroleum, and I nearly ended up with 25 litres of the medicinal variety!

The thing which surprised me most about Reykjavik was the sight of two pairs of whooper swans and a colony of arctic terns nesting in the gardens in the centre of the town.

Late in the afternoon we left on the drive north and covered about a hundred miles before camping beside a river. It was a fine clear evening but rather cool. On the hill behind our camp redwings were singing amongst the dwarf birch scrub, rather a monotonous little song starting with a tri-syllabic twitter, followed by a noise like several starlings chattering together—during this part of the song the bird sits quite still with its beak open but hardly moving. Just before we turned in a pair of greylag flew up the river calling and passed low over our tents. Next morning we struck camp at 8.45 and set off for Akureyri. The first part of the journey was mostly dull hill-farming country. Iceland's agriculture is chiefly confined to the coastal strip and river valleys. No crops are grown other than hay, and sheep are the predominant live-stock, with a few cows. After Blunduos the road runs through fine mountainous country with snow-covered peaks and rivers hurtling down through gorges of volcanic rock and scree. We reached Akureyri at 6.30 p.m. in torrential rain. It was so wet and cold that we decided to spend the night in the Kea Hotel. We had covered 283 miles from Reykjavik in about ten hours' driving time. This may sound slow, but the road was not surfaced and was single track for most of the distance besides winding and twisting amongst the hills and along the valleys. I kept a note of the birds we saw on the journey—a total of twenty-three species—raven, eider, great black-backed gull, ptarmigan, ringed plover, redwing, grey-lag, whimbrel, snipe, whooper, meadow pipit, redshank, arctic tern, red-breasted merganser, scaup, wigeon, red-throated diver, red-necked phalarope, teal, wheatear, snow bunting, black-tailed godwit and lapwing.

The following day I managed to contact Willie Palsson by telephone and arranged to meet him in Akureyri at three o'clock that afternoon. We spent the morning driving up the fjord in the rain. In the marshes at the head of the fjord we saw many wigeon, pintail and mallard while on the river itself we found our first pair of harlequin. It would be hard to imagine a more gorgeous bird than the drake with his dark blue plumage, russet flanks and white streaks especially when seen against the wild background of his native torrent. In the river below one of the bridges we saw a grilse of seven to eight pounds. Willie Palsson turned up about five o'clock in a taxi laden with duck eggs to be sent off by air to England, Holland and Belgium. There were 300 for us in the consignment. In the early evening we set off for the Myvatn area and some miles short of the lake Willie told me to turn down a very rough track across moorland country towards the deserted farm of Brettingsstadir on the Laxa River. This was about three miles from the road and, leaving the Land-Rover, we crossed the river by a foot-bridge and made our way towards a gorge in the hillside where a gyr falcon's nest had been reported. A pair of Barrow's golden-eye jumped out of the river as we approached the bridge and on a small green pool at the foot of the cliff was a pair of long-tailed ducks. On the way to this place we kept putting up ptarmigan every few yards, sometimes six or seven cocks at once, and we counted six ptarmigan kills from the Land-Rover, all the work of gyrs. This raised our hopes and we searched eagerly for the birds.

After scanning the cliff face and scree above the gorge we found the eyrie fairly low down in a well-sheltered position just above the small pool. It was obviously that year's site, but the eggs had been taken which accounted for the absence of the birds. We were to find this a common occurrence wherever gyrs nested in reasonably accessible places. Despite their being strictly protected, farmers would take their eggs and, having found some means of smuggling them out of the country, sell them to collectors abroad. We reached the village about 10.15 a.m. to meet a farmer who knew the whereabouts of another gyr eyrie in the Odadahraun desert to the north-east of Myvatn. He was out having a Turkish bath in a new bathing house he was building on the fringe of the desert over a steaming hot spring. We ate a meal amid the lava outcrop by the lake while awaiting his return. Finally we set off in two Land-Rovers about midnight, and after visiting the new bath-house and a stop at the sulphur springs in the desert we drove for about an hour. Then we left the Land-Rovers and walked to the south-east into the forbidding lava desert. The going was fairly good, mainly dry ling, dwarf birch and willow but with many lava gorges and crevasses to negotiate.

About 2 a.m. we were approaching a rocky hill when a gyr falcon flew out to meet us. It was the tiercel, and a moment later the falcon joined him and the pair flew round mobbing us with harsh cries of "kwek-kwek-kwek." We were thrilled at the sight of them and everyone increased pace up the hill. At the top we rounded the cliff face and came out along a wide ledge about sixty feet above the desert floor. Gordon climbed the cliff to a likely-looking shelf, but it was empty. All the time the two birds stooped at us screaming—a sure sign that we were very close to their eyrie. Then I noticed what from our position looked like the nest. At the same moment Gordon, who was by now on the cliff face, shouted that he could see two young on the ledge below him. Fortunately for us an outcrop of rock at the edge of the cliff was only twenty feet from the nest and gave a fairly good view into it. Here we decided to build our hide during the days that followed. We set off on the four-mile walk across the desert back to the Land-Rovers in high spirits, and by 4.15 a.m. we were back by the lakeside a mile or two south of Reykjahlid where we made camp. Three hours later we had unloaded all the gear, pitched the two tents and were ready to turn in for a few hours' sleep. We got up again at 10 a.m. and although we had had less than three hours' sleep we felt quite fresh. There is something about the Arctic air and the perpetual daylight which gives one a reserve of energy entirely lacking in more southern climates.

After collecting Willie we set off once more for the eyrie in the desert at the cliff called Burfellshraun. This time Willie said he thought he knew an easier way to reach it by driving farther along the track and then across the desert itself for about a mile. We left the Land-Rover at the edge of a steep gorge and set off to the west towards the eyrie. After covering five miles it became apparent that none of us could tell which range of cliffs amongst so many was the one where the gyrs were breeding. We decided to go back to the car and drive back to the old spot and start again from there. Having wasted all this time and walked an extra ten miles we eventually approached the breeding cliff and saw both adults leave from the vicinity of the eyrie. For three-quarters of an hour we all worked at the hide. Gordon was the mason while the rest of us collected slabs of lava and clumps of dwarf birch for him to use. The effect was a remarkably well-camouflaged structure on the extreme edge of the outcrop with a sheer drop of seventy feet beneath it. When the walls of the hide were half up we left it for the birds to become accustomed to it, though I doubt whether they even noticed it since it appeared to be part of the cliff. We had brought with us several of the usual portable hides of green canvas four feet square with duralumin uprights; but we decided not to use one of these because the position was exposed and likely to be windswept, and the green canvas would not blend with the grey lava; furthermore we could not drive the uprights into the rock. On the way back across the desert we found a golden plover's nest, our third that day.

In the evening I sat outside our tent writing up my diary and the account of the day's events ended thus:

I write this back at base camp, the wind has dropped, the flies are out and a pleasant smell of cooking fills the air. The midnight sun is casting long shadows and there is peace across the tranquil waters of the lake. Redwings sing in the birch scrub behind our camp and now and again a cock ptarmigan rises into the air with his distinctive croaking note and sails down like a white handkerchief against the grey rock. Our tents are in an almost perfect position sheltered by the outcrops of lava which jut out in a jumbled chaos interspersed with close-cropped greensward. The lake edge is but ten yards away, and there the springs entering the water from the lava are warm enough to wash in comfort. Ducks are everywhere. A wigeon sits on eight eggs under a slab of rock not twenty yards away while scaup, tufted, Barrow's golden-eye and merganser dot the surface of the lake a few yards from the shore. The nearest Barrow's nest is fifty yards away across a tiny bay.

The next morning Gordon, Willie and I completed the hide in pouring rain. The finished product looked like dry-stone walling from the fells of Westmorland. We used the dura-lumin uprights from one of the portable hides to support the roof; across them we threw the green canvas hide and covered it with thin slates of lava and clumps of heather. The adult gyrs mobbed us for some minutes, then cleared off and left us to work in peace. In the afternoon we went to Vidafell gorge west of Masvatn to look for gyr falcons.

After quite a long walk past a ruined farm we entered the gorge and strolled along the banks of a tiny stream which flowed down the centre of the valley. Cliffs of grey jagged rock towered up on each side of us. We saw a gyr fly out from beneath a huge slab of rock high up on the east face and a few moments later a second bird appeared and the two of them soared high above the valley, passing over us without mob-bing. They soon cleared off and though we searched the cliff and found an old eyrie on a ledge beneath the slab of rock, we could find no evidence of an occupied nest. In the next valley we found two ravens' nests which had been raided by farmers; the young had been left lying dead on the ground below. Gyrs too are not popular with the farmers because they prey on the ptarmigan, so it seemed probable that the same farmers had destroyed or taken the gyr falcons' eggs.

Having left the gyrs of Burfellshraun for forty-eight hours to become accustomed to our hide, we set off at 6.30 in the morning for the first of many days spent watching and filming the birds. We had some difficulty that first morning in setting up the camera—we had built the hide so close to the edge of the cliff that one leg of the tripod hung over the side with nothing to support it. Fortunately the tripod was fitted with a central column and by removing the leg, we used this column as the third support, thereby getting the camera as close as possible to the edge of the cliff with a good angle of view down into the nest.

Shortly after 7.30 a.m. my two companions left me and started on the four-mile walk back to the Land-Rover. It was agreed that they would return at 1.30 p.m.

Once they had reached the vehicle and set off for our camp, there would be no living soul within fifteen miles of the hide. I felt very much alone in my tiny cell as I looked out to the east through a chink in the wall. There a hundred feet below me was the view the sitting falcon must have gazed at day after day as she sat incubating her eggs. It was utterly silent, no birds called. I could see across mile upon mile of the endless wastes of the Odadahraun desert. Rock formations like Roman amphitheatres were broken by crevasses, lava of all colours from jet black to purple and red broke up the land-scape in a jumbled chaos of gorges, hills and ravines. Snow still lay in all the hollows but there was no other water. Save for the ptarmigan and a few scattered pairs of snowbuntings, this silent and godless country belonged only to the gyrs. The whole of Iceland is of volcanic origin and, as I sat there straining my ears listening to the emptiness, I could sometimes hear faint belly rumblings from deep down in the earth where molten lava still simmered.

After half an hour, the falcon appeared and sat on top of the highest crag behind the hide. Forty minutes later she landed on the nest ledge without food. Both eyasses sat up and screamed to be fed but she merely looked at them, her head on one side. She was a magnificent bird, very light beneath her wings and on her breast and having a beautiful pale blue-grey back streaked with silver, the colour of reindeer moss. The larger of the two youngsters reached up and pecked at her beak. A couple of minutes later, as if satisfied that all was well with her family, she turned and flew off. Nothing further happened for two hours and there was no sign of either of the adult gyrs. As time passed the two youngsters became more active and indulged in periodic bouts of wing flapping. To do this the eyass would stand up and face out over the ledge and flap its wings, and with each flap would pitch forward on to its beak. After one bout the largest eyass picked for a while at an old piece of bone, then turned carefully and muted out over the edge of the eyrie—hence the tell-tale white splash marks below occupied nests. As they became hungry, the eyasses would both scream every few minutes; this screaming rose to a crescendo whenever they saw one of the adults approaching. Without warning the falcon suddenly arrived on the nest ledge carrying a headless cock ptarmigan in her left foot. Plucking it carefully and deliberately she fed the youngsters, breaking off morsels of meat and passing it to them in her bill. They screamed all the time and the larger eyass seemed to get most of the food. After a quarter of an hour the falcon turned round and flew off taking the remains of the ptarmigan with her. The well-fed young settled down to sleep.

Soon after midday a heavy shadow fell across the nest ledge as the sun disappeared behind the hill so that further filming became impossible. We had to confine our activities to the mornings. Our routine varied little for the next few days. We were up soon after 5 a.m. and I was in the hide by seven o'clock, remaining there until relieved by the others five and a half hours later. After a meal back in camp we would spend the afternoons exploring the district and searching for other nesting gyrs. On two days Gordon took over on relieving me and remained in the hide watching and making notes until I went back for him in the evening so that we gained a fair idea of a complete day in the gyrs' life at this stage. Upon our arrival each morning the falcon, sometimes, though by no means always, accompanied by the tiercel, would fly out and mob us. Then, as the others walked away, she would sit on the highest crag near the nest and watch them go.

On most days she arrived on the nest ledge without food sometime before eleven o'clock and after looking at the eyasses for about a minute and a half she would fly off. Of six feeding visits watched from the hide, three were by the tiercel and three by the falcon, although she only fed the eyasses twice. The third time she arrived with the tiercel, each carrying a ptarmigan and left at once, the tiercel remaining to do the feeding.

In addition to this visit by the pair, one more visit by both birds was observed and filmed. This time they both arrived on the ledge together with much wing-flapping and screaming, though only the tiercel had any food. The falcon left almost at once and sat on her favourite crag while the tiercel fed the eyasses. He was gentler with them than she was and took far more trouble in tearing up the food and seeing that both chicks got a fair helping. They were always fed midst much screaming and the larger, probably a young female, got the lion's share and was always fed first. Both adults took away the remains of a carcass after feeding. It seems that at this stage, with the young about a month old, the tiercel does most of the hunting for the family, often handing over his quarry to the falcon to do the actual feeding, although the tiercel does sometimes feed the eyasses himself.

While the falcon spent most of her time in the vicinity of the nest sitting on one or other of her favourite crags, she also went hunting on occasions and brought her kill to the eyrie. There were two high pinnacles of rock north and south of the nest and from either the watching gyr must have been able to command an extensive view of the surrounding desert. When satisfied that no one was in the area, she invariably flew down to her favourite rock almost opposite and only eighty yards from the nest. Here she would sit by the hour, occasionally preening or picking her toes. We were sure that the chicks had been fed once in the early hours before we reached the hide each morning for there were fresh fragments of food on the ledge and the eyasses themselves were sleepy as they always were after a meal. Every day when we kept watch they were fed again between 11 a.m. and 1 p.m. and once more after 5 p.m., so that there were three feeding visits daily. Every time we watched the youngsters being fed a whole cock ptarmigan was brought to them except on one occasion when only part of the bird was brought. Once the smaller of the two eyasses, probably a male, was seen to try to tear at the quarry himself.

During our stay in the Myvatn area we located seven gyr eyries and of these four were definitely occupied and another almost certainly so. All of them were in an area covering 440 square kilometres and the nearest occupied eyries were eight kilometres (five miles) apart. They were as follows:

1. Holkotsgil on the Laxa River already described and the first nest we visited. We were told it contained eggs which had been robbed. The nest itself was an untidy heap of twigs quite possibly originally built by a pair of ravens. It contained some fresh down from the falcon and some newly shed gyr feathers. This eyrie faced south and had little white stain below it. Ptarmigan were extremely plentiful in the area.

2. Burfellshraun (Skogarholt), the eyrie which we filmed in the desert, containing the two eyasses about three weeks old. The nest was merely a hollow on a turf ledge about sixty feet up the cliff, and like every nest we saw this one was protected from above by an overhanging

slab of rock. It faced ESE and there was a considerable white stain below it. Strangely enough although ptarmigan were plentiful there were few kills in the vicinity, so the adults had been hunting farther afield.

3. Prihyrningar (Dalfjall) unoccupied. We were told that gyrs last bred there in 1954 (two years before our visit). The nest itself was once more a pile of twigs, perhaps again originally the work of ravens. It was in a cleft in the rock jutting out from the steep scree of the gorge facing SE. As usual it was overhung by a slab of rock. There was no white stain beneath it.

4. Hrfanabjorg (North of Myvatn). This nest was merely a hollow on a small turf ledge on the east side of a steep gorge facing west and about sixty feet up. It contained four eyasses which, judging by their size, were two falcons and two tiercels. They were at least six weeks old and were well feathered but with a good deal of down still about them. One youngster was all alone on a small ledge about a dozen feet below the eyrie. There was considerable white staining below the nest ledge and a litter of castings, bones and ptarmigan wings and feet. The remains of several kills in the vicinity were all of ptarmigan or duck, in one case a scoter. At this nest the adults were much in evidence, both flying round screaming at us and diving repeatedly to pass only a few feet away. It took us an hour to walk to this eyrie from the place where we left the car. The going was good, a sheep track most of the way and no lava, we walked along the floor of the gorge which was rather like a Scottish glen with ling, coarse grass and patches of dwarf birch in the bottom. The hills on either side were a tender green from young birch leaves, changing to the grey of moss and lichen above the limit of the trees.

5. Vidafell (Austurgil). Already described. Here again we were told locally that the eggs had been robbed. The

Uist.   The barnacles came swinging in on to the machair in front of my sea-weed covered hide

Brent geese forty yards from my hide, photographed with the Heinkel lens

Iceland. *Gordon surveys the Odadahraun desert; there is a sheer drop of eighty feet below the hide*

The falcon of Burfellshraun at her eyrie

adults were still present in the gorge. No white staining beneath the eyrie.

6. Vindbelgjarfjall (NW of Myvatn). We were told that this was a regular eyrie but were unable to visit it. Believed to be unoccupied in 1956.

7. Kringlugerdi (Laxa River). The eyrie was on a ledge about fifty feet up the cliff facing west. Though we could not see into it, the considerable and fresh staining below it was a certain sign that it was occupied.

All these eyries were situated in areas where ptarmigan or duck were plentiful and every nest was under an overhanging slab of rock. This was probably necessary to give shade to the young as much as for protection in rough weather. At the eyrie we filmed, I noticed how quickly the eyasses began to pant and appear distressed when the sun shone on a calm day. Then they invariably retreated into the shade of the overhang.

I had always imagined that gyrs would choose the highest and most inaccessible precipices upon which to breed, but all the eyries we saw were either in gorges with steep sides, or in comparatively low cliffs, and all of them were well sheltered. No doubt the severity of the weather conditions, especially early in the spring when the gyrs lay their eggs, was a sound enough reason for their shunning the towering thousand-foot cliffs and seeking shelter lower down. It will be noticed that all the eyries described face the southern half of the compass. Although eyries are often in the same area year after year, there are usually one or more alternative sites. Judging from the ages of the youngsters in the nests we saw, the gyrs in Iceland lay their eggs during the first half of April. This is exceptionally early so far north, where wintry conditions are still apt to last until well into May. It is so much earlier than other birds in the area that the young gyrs have to be fed entirely on adult ptarmigan or duck since these birds are still laying or incubating their eggs while the gyrs' eyasses are being reared. There are no young ducks or ptarmigan available for the adult gyrs to feed to their young. This is quite different from the situation with other birds of prey like peregrines, merlins and sparrowhawks, for with all these the rearing season of their young synchronises closely with the fledgeling period of the birds which yield their main food supply. These fledgelings provide a large proportion of the young hawks' food.

The early nesting of the gyr is an interesting adaptation, for it ensures that when the young gyrs leave their eyrie and start to hunt for themselves, they are able to begin by catching newly-fledged ptarmigan or flapper ducks. The young hawks would almost certainly find an old ptarmigan or duck too fast for them to begin with, thus the early breeding season enables the eyasses to start hunting easier quarry. It must also be helpful to the parents in feeding their young since there is little vegetation at this time of the year and therefore the ptarmigan are conspicuous.

The behaviour of the adult gyrs varies when their eyries are visited. At the nest we filmed both old birds mobbed hard the whole time anyone was near. The falcon was most persistent in her attacks and they would both fly round screaming their harsh " kwek-kwek-kwek " cries of rage. When we stayed to start building the hide, they eventually gave up mobbing. The tiercel cleared off while the falcon sat and watched from the highest crag in the range of cliffs 400 yards away. If one of us attempted to climb down to the eyrie, she would come screaming off her pinnacle and start mobbing again. At the eyrie in Hrafnabjorg both adults flew round and called angrily while we were in the gorge. When we started to descend by rope to the nest their attacks increased in ferocity and, screaming with rage, first one then the other would come over a couple of hundred feet above us and turning would dive straight down with half-closed wings, flashing past with the hum of an arrow leaving the bow string. Throwing up at the bottom of each stoop, the birds would sail skywards looking very pale against the grey cliff opposite, sweeping round to renew their attack. Although they passed several feet away, there was something unnerving about those stoops, their speed and the deadly hum which accompanied them.

The adults whose nest was in the Vidafell gorge only flew round once without calling, then disappeared and did not return. But their eggs had been robbed which no doubt accounted for their lack of interest. I suspect that gyrs with eggs in the nest may slip away quietly when disturbed and that the sham attacks and screams of rage only occur when there are young in the eyrie.

During the whole time we were in daily contact with the gyrs we saw surprisingly little of them hunting. Had their normal method been to " wait on " like peregrines soaring several feet up and then hurtling down on to an unsuspecting victim, we should doubtless have seen much more of them. The terrain, flat lava desert intersected by crevasses and gorges, is not suitable for this method of hunting, which in order to achieve surprise, the cardinal point in any attack by a raptor, requires mountainous country with valleys or steep cliffs and not one in which there are nooks and crannies every few yards into which the quarry can dive to safety. The gyr is a specialist in pursuing and catching ptarmigan. Its method is to fly low and fast across country following the contours closely, thus suddenly surprising and grabbing its quarry, often a cock ptarmigan sitting on a slab of rock in the bottom of a gorge. In any prolonged chase the ptarmigan would soon disappear in one of the numerous holes or cracks in the lava. We were to learn much more about gyrs and their hunting in later years when both Gordon and I had the chance to train and fly several birds from Norway.

The remains of gyr kills, especially when the victim was a ptarmigan, usually took the same form. While in some cases plucking appeared to have been thorough and complete down to the primaries, in the majority of cases the wings had been broken off at the carpal joint and left lying with the primaries intact. Many such wings were found beneath occupied eyries and, although the adults we filmed always took away the remains of the quarry after feeding their young, it is possible that they ceased doing so when the eyasses were old enough to tear up their own food. Some of the old wings beneath this nest were probably the remains of kills brought to the falcon by her mate while she was incubating. We were able to identify the remains of four species of birds amongst them, ptarmigan, redwing and two duck, scoter and scaup. The strength of the gyr's bill is enormous and we frequently saw remains of ptarmigan in which the thigh bone had been snapped, while in others triangular pieces the shape of the gyr's bill had been cut out of the keel or breast bone.

A good deal has been written in bird books about the colour of Icelandic gyr falcons, and there is no doubt that these birds vary a lot. But I am quite sure that age has nothing to do with it, except that all first year birds I have seen have been the same shade. Their basic colour is pale buff, heavily streaked with dark brown, especially on the breast, while the feathers of wings and back are brown edged with pale buff. This plumage is moulted when the bird is about a year old and when completed, which may take several months, the bird acquires adult dress. At the Burfellshraun eyrie the falcon was a beautiful silver grey with darker markings, while her mate was very dark; and of the pair at Hrafnabjorg the falcon was dark and the tiercel very pale grey, at times appearing almost white. Both the Vidafell birds were a typical grey. White birds are probably very scarce and are more likely to be wanderers from Greenland, especially during the winter when birds from the north-east of Greenland migrate southwards and regularly visit Iceland. It is not beyond the bounds of possibility that occasionally Greenland birds have remained to breed in north-west Iceland.

The position in Iceland is not complicated as it is in Norway by the existence of voles and lemmings, since neither occur, nor by competition with other raptors. It is a straightforward case of dependence on one main food species, the ptarmigan. This bird in turn probably depends upon the availability of those plants upon which it feeds. It is thought that in many arctic plants the quantity of buds or seeds varies to a marked degree according to the state of flowering, and thus the amount of vegetable food available for the ptarmigan varies considerably from year to year. From our observations I am sure that, given the two essentials, plenty of ptarmigan and low cliffs in which to breed, the gyr falcon may be a commoner bird than many imagine, though certain factors will affect the breeding population of these hawks: first the ptarmigan cycle already discussed, and secondly the hostility of the Icelandic farmers some of whom rob the eggs and shoot gyrs in the autumn. Although the falcons are supposed to be strictly protected in Iceland, the farmers in the north freely admitted that they disliked them because they took ptarmigan and that they shot them whenever they could in the autumn. They had no reason to tell me this unless it were true. If this practice should increase the gyr will soon be a very rare bird in Iceland. In fairness, however, I must say that with the exception of the one eyrie mentioned above, where we were told that the eggs had been stolen, none of the others was molested in any way during the breeding season. This would not have been difficult had the local farmers been so minded.

After we returned from Iceland, Gordon and I obtained two young gyr falcons from Norway and were able to train them and fly them at partridges. This had long been one of our ambitions and now for the first time we would be in a position to compare the flight and hunting methods of these powerful arctic falcons with our own peregrines. The latter is a serious-minded bird, efficient at his job and, once trained and fit, can be relied upon to try his best day in, day out. But not so the gyr. His is a more fickle nature, shot with humour which makes him always unpredictable. One day the tiercel would mount three hundred feet above my head and there remain floating at ease against the autumn sky; looking up one could see his head craned down and moving from side to side as he watched every movement of the dog. The next day he would be just as likely to chase a flock of passing lapwings, playing with them in the air and making clumsy stoops which they avoided without effort. Tiring of this he would come back over me and keep diving at me in fun—on such days serious hawking was out of the question.

Though the peregrine does of course watch the falconer and the dogs, it never does it so obviously as a gyr who will often turn his head and look down over his own back as he climbs skywards. Of the two birds I am sure that the gyr is the more intelligent, and much faster, for no peregrine can catch a winter partridge in level flight. Once when one of the dogs had a perfect point in the middle of a hundred acre field the gyr, having climbed to a great height, decided to go off and " beat-up " the local rookery. Passing high above the trees, he suddenly stooped, driving downwards through the whirling mass of cawing birds, and caught one of them. While we watched through field-glasses he started to fly back to us still carrying the rook. When a few hundred yards away he suddenly let it go and came sailing down to the lure while the rook made off. Presumably he had decided that he had had his fun, and that in any case a rook was no good to eat.

Most young hawks are apt, through inexperience, to mis-judge their stoops during their first season. But I have never seen a peregrine which was as bad a judge of speed and angle of attack as the gyr tiercel who seldom hit his quarry at the first stoop, and if he did usually failed to bind to it. Once he had knocked his bird down, it was another story, and on the ground he was far more nimble than any peregrine. This poor marksmanship and playful inattention to the sport convinced me that to hunt by flying high and then stooping at quarry was not a part of the gyr's normal procedure, a fact which I had first realised when watching the wild gyrs in Iceland.

At the start of his second season the tiercel showed even less inclination to wait on steadily and on some days persisted in diving down and sweeping low over the ground behind me—" daisy cutting " as a friend so aptly described it. Late in the autumn, when the leaves were off the trees, the hedges thin and bare and most of the land ploughed, when the countryside was as open and bleak as it would ever be, I decided to change tactics and fly him off the fist at pheasants and partridges. The change in his demeanour was remarkable. This was clearly the way he considered the sport should be conducted. He flew with hitherto unseen determination and speed; gone were all signs of frivolity. His first slip was at a covey of partridges flying across eighty yards away. Removing the hood I almost threw him into the air. He made straight for them, cutting across the arc as they swung to the left. After two hundred yards he was obviously gaining fast while the covey made for a distant hedge and, as the last bird plummeted into the safety of the blackthorn, he grabbed it. His powers of endurance and speed were perhaps best demonstrated one November afternoon when a friend was working his dogs for me in a small field of sugar beet. A cock pheasant suddenly burst from the roots behind us and flew straight and fast over the trees and out across the river valley making for the wood on the other side. I was so surprised that I hesitated for a moment before throwing off the hawk, but despite the pheasant's lead he at once started in pursuit. It seemed a hopeless chase, the pheasant was by this time high over the river and the hawk some way behind and far below. Suddenly we saw through our field-glasses that the gyr was rapidly closing the gap, and the next instant he swept up to the pheasant from behind and sent it spinning down behind the trees. Scattered feathers drifting in the wind marked the spot.

Having seen gyrs fly both waiting on and from the fist, I am certain that it is the latter method which caused d'Arcussia, falconer to Henry IV of France, to write that once he had seen them fly he was " disgusted with all the other hawks." Used thus they are indeed the most magnificent and deadly of all falcons.

6. Geese on the Tide

The film of the gyrs at the nest was successful in so far as it was probably the first detailed record in colour of the family life of these magnificent falcons, but I was well aware of its many shortcomings. These only served to increase my determination to produce better wildlife films.

Having spent more than twenty years taking "still" photographs, I regarded motion pictures as the ultimate medium for reproducing the thrill of watching nature at close quarters. A good still photograph, especially in colour, is very satisfying to the photographer; like a fine painting it is something which one can look at and enjoy time and again, and with little or no trouble. Nevertheless it remains a still photograph, essentially a "one dimension" product. To this dimension the motion picture adds two more, movement and sound; these together mean atmosphere and it is this atmosphere which enables one to become completely absorbed in a good natural history film. So far my filming efforts had been without sound but now I was ready to incorporate the natural noises and so produce more realistic films.

There are two ways of recording sound for a film. The more sophisticated is to make the recording at the same time as shooting the picture and to use some method of ensuring that both are accurately synchronised. This is fairly complicated and the equipment is costly. The other and far simpler method is to shoot the picture and record the sound quite separately, afterwards fitting the recording as near as possible to the picture to gain the desired effect. This is known as dubbing and when skilfully carried out by a good editor the result is often excellent. But it has serious limitations. First, it is not possible to synchronise human speech with the movement of the lips in close-up and the same applies to such things as bird song. Secondly, it is rarely possible to record all the correct noises for a given sequence either before or after the picture has been shot, so that the result when dubbed will never be quite perfect to a practised ear.

At this time I was still using a Bolex reflex camera and separate E.M.I. recording equipment, including a small battery-driven portable tape-recorder and a microphone which could be used in conjunction with a parabolic reflector. This is a small dome-shaped steel reflector which, if aimed accurately at the source of the noise, concentrates the sound waves which are then picked up by the microphone placed in the centre of the reflector. The reflector enables recordings to be made with the microphone a considerable distance from the source of the sound and is a most useful piece of equipment for recording wildlife.

Just as wildfowl had presented a challenge to my still camera, so they now beckoned again and, after initial success with the barnacle geese in Uist, I was determined to film the flocks of brent geese wintering on the Norfolk coast. It is true that I had already managed to take still pictures of these geese feeding far out on the mud-flats—pictures which so far as I know may still be unique—but I felt sure that luck had been with me on that occasion and this time I knew that only patience and considerable organisation would achieve results.

Unlike still photography, film making is a continuous process, so that many more shots have to be taken in order to produce a coherent picture. This entails a far more prolonged effort. In order to make sense the sequence envisaged would have to show distant flocks of brent geese flying about the estuary, small numbers in flight in close-up, flocks coming in to land, preferably towards the camera, and then many shots of the geese feeding as close to the camera as possible. To all this would have to be added shots of the other birds and wild-life of the estuary, together with the natural sound-effects. So it is that days and often months of work occupy the screen for a final result taking a very few minutes.

I knew from experience that stalking the brent even with a powerful telephoto lens, was out of the question. Somehow or other the geese must become accustomed to a hide. Not only would this have to be harmless-looking to the birds, but it would also have to stand winter conditions on the exposed mud-flats. Then I suddenly remembered watching some brent on an Irish lough at low tide feeding happily within a few yards of a navigational buoy lying on the mud at the tide edge. Here was the clue, and Kitch once again provided the answer, for he was a qualified boat builder. Together we planned a floating hide with the idea of leaving it moored out in the estuary on what might appear at the time to be the brents' favourite feeding ground.

The craft which finally emerged from Kitch's shed some weeks later was basically a short but wide punt ten feet long, with a beam of four feet; both ends were boxed in to make water-tight compartments so that it was almost unsinkable. The rest of the boat consisted of an open cockpit six feet long and four feet across with a bracket at each corner to hold an upright steel rod two and a half feet high. These four rods formed supports for a light rectangular frame and over the structure thus formed we fitted a green and brown canvas cover.

I knew that it would be hopeless to try to film from this hide once it was afloat as it would be too unsteady. But my idea was to try to moor it on a low mud-bank. Then, hav ng set up the camera inside at low water, I intended to sit and wait for the geese to come up on the tide and to continue filming until my hide floated, when Kitch would pick me up in his motor boat. Over the next two years I was to spend many hours hidden in this and another larger floating hide which Kitch made out of an old war-time pontoon. It was an altogether heavier affair and, being four feet deep, needed only the minimum of canvas to make a roof and narrow sides for the lens. It was therefore far tougher and better able to withstand the winter gales. Yet despite the size, the geese soon accepted it as a normal part of the seascape.

There is a strange fascination about an estuary in winter time, especially if there are geese or ducks about. For here beyond the dunes with their waving marram grass the rolling sand gives way to endless mud-flats where the sky meets the sea—a place at once beautiful yet forbidding, where all life is governed by one thing: the tide.

At low water the wildfowl are scattered over a tremendous area of sand and mud; some may be feeding but many are resting in flocks either along the tide edge or out on the sands. Filming under these conditions is impossible. But as the tide starts to flow so the estuary comes to life. Waiting in a hide at the channel edge, one is warned of increasing activity by gulls flooded off the seaward sand-bars passing inland in silent flight. In ones and twos they come, then in small parties in chevron formation and finally in flocks. Soon after the water in the channel is halted in its seaward flow; gradually it starts to creep across the sand, the channel grows broader as the flood tide, imperceptibly at first, creeps on silently, slowly. Little trickles of water eddy and swirl in the tiny gullies between the sand ripples and, if you listen and the wind is not making too much noise, you will become aware of the sinister rustle of the oncoming tide. A piping from seaward and a moment later a party of oyster-catchers flies along the water's edge to land on their favourite mussel-bed, their black and white plumage and carmine bills brilliant in the sun. Curlews and godwit, redshank and knot all come in from the sea, and at any moment one may expect to hear the distant clamour of geese as they too rise from a flooded sandbar and flight in to join the oyster-catchers feeding on the mussel-bed. Here there is a good growth of zostera and enteromorpha, both plants upon which the brent feed. All too soon the hide is afloat and filming is over for several hours.

At high water the geese either remain swimming in the estuary or, if disturbed, return to the open sea, while the waders congregate on the higher saltings. Shelduck usually remain sitting about near the water while wigeon prefer to follow the geese back to the safety of the sea. As soon as the tide starts to drop, uncovering their feeding grounds again, the birds return. But filming prospects are not so good because the feeding flocks soon start to scatter over the rapidly increasing areas of mud and sand. Although I have spent hundreds of hours filming and watching the life of the estuary, I never tire of it, whether in bright sunlight, in the grey light of dawn, or in the gloaming when the wigeon flight in to feed in earnest; shadowy shapes dropping down to feed against a red sunset, their whistled " whee-oos " sounding on all sides across the mud-flats.

While bright sunlight is vital for filming in colour, I soon discovered that the hours of daylight are not the best in which to record the noises of the shore. The ever-present wind sees to that except on a very rare still day. Other noises also increase as the day wears on, particularly and most annoying of all, the sound of aircraft. Most of my recordings of waders and geese have been made soon after dawn or at night by the light of the moon. When all goes well these recording trips are just as exciting as filming and make a welcome change. One is no longer confined to a hide, for only the microphone need be near the birds, while the operator can be hidden a couple of hundred yards away or more. There are few more fascinating experiences than to lie quietly at the salting edge on a calm night with a full moon listening over head-phones to the calls and conversations of wildfowl feeding along the tide edge. There is always the chance of the unexpected, a flock of brent dropping in right beside the microphone with a tremendous chorus of goose music, or at any time in the new year a curlew suddenly pouring forth his full bubbling spring song for no apparent reason other than the joy of being alive. I have even had my ear drums almost shattered by an inquisitive wader giving the microphone a hearty peck to see if it was edible.

One of the chief attractions of filming wildlife is the number of visits one has to make in order to study one's quarry before attempting to start filming.

On one such visit I had sat in our unsinkable hide for four hours in bright sunshine without exposing a single foot of film. The geese and all the other wildfowl, for that matter, simply refused to come anywhere near me. It is true that a single goose did eventually fly past, turn and drop down right amongst my hardboard decoys. There it stood with head erect gazing fixedly at its companions until, deciding that their statuesque immobility was a little odd, it walked slowly away from them glancing back anxiously over its shoulder. It is most noticeable that single birds and small parties of geese are much more easily lured in by decoys than larger flocks. Often the process is cumulative. First an odd goose arrives in the vicinity of the decoys, followed by two or three more; and then perhaps a larger flock sees the decoys and several live geese and comes in to join them and so on, until eventually several hundred birds are down in the vicinity.

January and February 1963 were, I suppose, the coldest months in living memory and the prolonged ice and snow wrought fearful havoc amongst all forms of bird life. The marshes around Blakeney harbour were ice-bound to such an extent that no boat could enter or leave Morston creek, the mud-flats froze hard the moment the tide left them exposed, great ice-floes formed along the shore and pans six inches thick and as big as billiard tables jostled and groaned at the harbour mouth. When the roads were once again passable, I renewed filming operations and on the 5th February set off with Kitch to the large pontoon hide moored out on the frozen marsh. Although the sun shone it was bitterly cold, the saltings were still snow-covered and frozen solid, while all along the tide mark the frost had formed delicate ice-flowers.

Fortunately the brent had not left during the severe spell and were still about the harbour, but they were no longer in one large flock. Instead little parties could be seen all over the place, some in the channel, others feeding on the saltings, while most of them seemed to be congregated amongst the spartina on the north side. There they were joined by hundreds of wigeon, mallard, teal and waders. Half a dozen goldeneye were diving for food in the channel and as soon as the hide started to flow a pair of wigeon landed at the water's edge within thirty yards and stayed there for some time preening and dibbling in the shallows. The geese were constantly on the move, many of them flying from the channel up on to the higher marsh to feed amongst the clumps of spartina while others came back to drink and wash in the tide. At one time a flotilla of forty brent swam past within twenty feet of my camera, their white sterns in brilliant contrast with their black plumage, just as the dark tidal flats contrasted with the snow-white marshes in a strange and beautiful black and white world.

Towards dusk we landed on the point and walked to the beach. Drifts of snow filled the hollows between the dunes and the whole area was criss-crossed with rabbit tracks. As the sun went down a party of brent pitched at the mouth of the creek where the boats land in summer. I quickly set up my camera under cover of the sueda bushes and was ready to film the next bunch. At last they came swinging in, silhouetted against the snow-covered marsh. Dropping their paddles they swept down on curved pinions to land on the shimmering water touched with gold by the setting sun.

Soon after I started filming wildfowl, I had an idea that it would be fun to look at them from the air and perhaps at the same time learn to fly an aeroplane. I have to admit that I have no head for heights and am genuinely afraid of aeroplanes, so perhaps this was not a very good idea. Nevertheless I persevered and was lucky enough to be taught by Elwyn McAully who ran the Fakenham flying group. Mac was a brilliant pilot and a most patient and understanding instructor. He owned a Proctor with dual controls and, although I cannot say I ever learned to fly properly, I could at least get it off the ground and land it, provided that he was sitting beside me ready to correct my mistakes. It was soon obvious that one could learn far more about the coastal marshes from the air than any other way, for they lay below one spread out like a great coloured map. At first I found it surprisingly difficult to pick out landmarks which I knew well enough from the ground; everything looks so different from the air. But it is a case of becoming accustomed to a new dimension and gradually learning the countryside all over again. Different objects are seen more clearly from above so that a new set of landmarks replaces those familiar from the ground. Mac and I tried counting geese and ducks from various heights. A thousand feet was rather too high, while at a hundred feet one was over a flock of birds too quickly to count them and in any case they scattered in panic before a low-flying aircraft. In the end we found 300-400 feet the best height. Although geese and waders invariably got up as we approached, they only flew round enabling us to count them. Surface-feeding ducks, mallard and wigeon, would also rise and fly round, while diving ducks, eider and scaup, often simply dived as the plane passed over.

A trained Norwegian gyr tiercel

Le Gran Duc (*eagle owl*) *used in France as a decoy for shooting birds of prey which come to mob it. I used Bubo, but only to shoot film*

Once off Stiffkey we found a dozen seals lying on an exposed sand-bar at low tide. I was keen to try to film them and so Mac dived at them out of the sun sweeping over them only forty feet above the sand. They let us make three such runs before flopping into the sea. I found that by running the camera at sixty-four frames per second, thus creating a slow-motion effect when projected at the normal speed of twenty-four frames per second, one could get quite a steady picture, even from a plane flying at about ninety miles per hour. Mac used to fly me down the coast from Cley to Hunstanton and out into the Wash, returning home along the beach in about one and a half hours; and in that time we were able to get a very good idea of the wildfowl population of the area. Sometimes we would fly back along the tide edge at under a hundred feet and I always found this most exhilarating, especially on a sunny day when everything looked its best, the varying shades of sand and mud, the blue sea and the grey-green saltings. Every detail was visible down to the ripples on the sand. It was rather like floating along in a comfortable arm-chair with nothing to do but gaze down at the fascinating pattern of marsh and shore.

These were happy and exhilarating days and it came as a terrible shock when Mac was tragically killed in a flying accident a little time later.

7. Bubo the Eagle Owl

Man has always regarded owls with a mixture of superstition and awe; even in this civilised land they have been surrounded by tales of witchcraft and ghosts until comparatively recent times. Primitive races still fear them on account of their eerie cries and nocturnal habits. For centuries owls have been symbols of wisdom, long before the verse appeared in a Victorian *Punch*:

Here was an old owl lived in an oak
The more he heard the less he spoke;
The less he spoke, the more he heard
Oh, if men were all like that wise bird!

There is something scholarly about the serious unblinking gaze of an owl which is no doubt partly attributable to its round face with both eyes looking to the front. Another human characteristic not shared by other birds is the owl's method of blinking by lowering the top lid across the eye and not by raising the lower lid as in most species. The owl's ability to blink one eye deliberately while still staring with the other adds to the quizzical effect. Even its feet are different. Whereas most birds have three toes pointing forwards and one pointing back, the toes on an owl's foot are more in the pattern of a star and the fourth, or outer, toe is extremely flexible; perhaps double-jointed would be a better way of describing it. The bird can bring this toe forward or move it back so that it is able to sit on a bough with two toes in front and two behind. As the result of this arrangement the owl's foot can be turned at will into a perfectly balanced grab in which the front pair of talons or prongs are more or less equally matched for size as are the rear ones; only the latter are rather smaller. Here again owls differ from eagles, hawks and falcons, for in all these it is the one fixed hind toe which carries the longest and deadliest curved talon. As in other raptors, the owl uses its talons for grasping and killing its quarry, relying on its beak merely to tear the food into portions suitable for swallowing whole.

All owls have loose soft plumage which results in their flight being silent. Most of them have large ears and remarkably acute hearing. Vision varies a good deal between species but is usually somewhat restricted. This is counter-balanced by a longish and very mobile neck which is hidden in the feathers so that the bird appears dumpy. The neck enables the owl to move its head in all directions without moving its body. It can even turn it completely round and look backwards between its own shoulder-blades. Many owls hunt by sitting in a tree or on some other vantage point and remaining quite still for long periods watching the ground below for signs of their quarry. Their barred or mottled plumage affords them perfect camouflage and it must be a tremendous advantage to them to be able to move their heads through one hundred and eighty degrees, thus keeping a watch all round the compass without moving or rustling their bodies.

Good hearing is important both to those owls which hunt by sitting still and to those which hunt by flying low, quartering their territory on the look-out for small rodents. Making no noise in flight they are able to locate their prey by listening for minute squeaks and rustlings in the grass, so that hearing becomes almost as important as seeing. That owls are blind in bright sunlight is a popular fallacy although their ability to see under such conditions varies between species. Of the dozen forms officially on the British list the largest and to my mind the most fascinating is the huge European eagle owl. This was one bird which I had always wanted to keep and if possible to tame.

In the wild eagle owls are creatures of the silent pine forests, preferring those which happen to have rocky cliffs, especially when undisturbed by man. They are occasionally to be seen in this country as vagrants. They make a nest scrape on a ledge or even at the bottom of a cliff and sometimes amongst rocks on a steep slope. Eagle owls are found over most of Europe, breeding wherever there are sufficiently wild and undisturbed forests, from the Mediterranean in the south to the edge of the tundra in the north. In some parts of southern Europe these birds are found in vast areas of desolate uninhabited scrub country. Two or three eggs are usually laid and the young reared on a great variety of food including rodents and birds.

Six weeks after I had returned to England from the International Ornithological Congress at Helsinki in 1958 I received a letter from Finland telling me that a pair of eagle owls were on their way. This was tremendously exciting news and I anxiously awaited them. At last the telephone rang and British Railways informed me that a box of birds was waiting at Norwich station.

I rushed off in the car and soon had the large crate safely stowed in the back. It was a two compartment box covered with hessian to keep the occupants in the dark. Back at home I carried it into a large wooden hut and shut the door. I wondered vaguely what sort of welcome the owls would give me when I prised open the lid. As a precaution I wore a large leather hawking glove on my left hand and worked the hammer and pliers with my right. As soon as the lid was off both owls jumped out and bounded across the floor to the back of the hut where they glared at me with wings spread. When I tried to approach them they snapped their beaks in a most menacing way. Removing the crate I left them to their own devices while I went to fetch two dead rats. I always keep a breeding stock of both rats and mice for owls and other predators, including various small mammals. They took no notice of the rats when I threw them down, but next morning they were gone.

My plan was to tame both the birds and then try to train them to fly loose and return to me for food. I had no particular desire to catch anything with them, so long as I could watch them fly. After giving them a few days to settle down, I decided to start operations. A friend, who was a keen falconer and very good at making hoods and other equipment, was staying with us at the time and volunteered to make two pairs of leather jesses. Bearing in mind the strength of the eagle owls' beaks we bought some extra stout leather from our local saddler. The next problem was to put them on the owls' legs. Knowing just how savage some owls can be, I decided to wear a fencing mask when catching them. With this and a stout glove I felt fairly safe and soon had the male, the smaller of the two, securely trussed up while Roger quickly slipped the jesses on and joined them to a large swivel to which the leash was attached. The first owl was equipped and ready for training.

I took him outside and set him on my gloved fist; he snapped his beak and jumped off. I replaced him and he did the same thing. After a time he remained sitting unsteadily while I carried him to a block in the shade of an apple tree on the lawn. I set him on it and tied the end of the leash to the ring. He promptly flew off but was brought up short by the leash. Finding he could not escape he eventually sat down on the grass like a broody hen. The same procedure was followed with the female. I noticed a difference in their characters straight away, for she was less nervous and far more inclined to attack. When I took her outside and set her on my fist she bated twice then decided to sit still. The power of her grip was terrific and unlike a hawk she seemed to be able to keep up the crushing pressure indefinitely. Her talons bruised my hand even through two thicknesses of buckskin, while the grip was such that it restricted the blood supply to my fingers. I carried her to another block on the lawn and set her down beneath the trees not far from the male.

During the next few days we spent a good deal of time carrying both owls about and gently stroking them. They settled down more quickly than hawks and soon learnt to sit fairly peacefully even in strange surroundings. When trying to train any bird of prey, feeding is important for much can be done by regulating their food supply. While the bird must be reasonably hungry it must not be allowed to lose too much weight, and to avoid this daily weighing is necessary until one has learned by experience how much food will keep it in the right condition. The female eagle owl turned the scales at 5 lb. 2 oz. and the male at 4 lb. 10 oz., but both were on the fat side and I reckoned that they could lose about a quarter of a pound apiece before they would be really keen for their food.

The first big step in taming a bird of prey is to get it accustomed to eating while sitting on one's fist. This is much more difficult to achieve with any of the owls than with hawks or falcons. In the first place it is often difficult to tell whether an owl is hungry or not and on top of this they are exceptionally temperamental. I soon discovered that it was useless to pick up the owl and carry it around with a nice rat or mouse held in one's fist. It took no notice of the offering at all. Plainly different tactics would have to be employed and so I hit upon the idea of a block in the drawing-room upon which to place the bird every evening until it learned to eat in my presence. The room is long and narrow, one end being used as a dining-room, and there is an area of polished boards in the centre between the two carpets. We drilled a hole an inch across in the centre of the boards to take the iron point of the block which passed straight through into the ground beneath. There was the added advantage that the owl sitting on the block could not make a mess of the carpet.

The female, whom we had christened Bubo, which also happened to be her Latin name, spent every evening in the drawing-room. The third night she suddenly flew down on to the floor and seized the dead rat in her talons; she then brooded over it like an old hen for nearly an hour without moving. I hardly dared breathe for fear of upsetting her. Suddenly she got up and gazed down at the rat before picking it up in her beak. Again she remained motionless then equally suddenly took the rat in one foot while she crunched its skull with her powerful beak. This done, she tossed it back whole like some gigantic pill, getting it down in a series of gargantuan gulps until only the tail remained sticking out of her mouth and that too finally slipped down out of sight. I felt that we were over the first hurdle.

Every night I moved my chair closer until she was sitting on her block right beside my arm and eating her rat at my feet. After several more days I sat her on my fist which I rested on the arm of the chair and offered her the usual rat. After half an hour she took it the same way as before and swallowed it while sitting on my gloved hand.

She was getting tamer all the time and I discovered she quite liked me to part the soft feathers on the back of her neck and blow with my mouth close to her skin. She rarely snapped her beak at me now but resorted to hissing if she wished to register disapproval. It seemed the beak-snapping was part of a composite threat display involving arching the wings and spreading them, while raising all the body feathers so that the bird appeared twice as huge as it really was. The beak-snapping is achieved by placing the tip of the lower mandible exactly opposite the curved hook of the upper; then under pressure it slips back into place with a loud clack.

When training hawks or falcons one of the first things they have to learn is to jump a few feet to their owner's fist for food. I was going to train my owls the same way, but little did I realise the difficulties. Hawks can take a long time to make up their minds to jump, but owls seem to have a different conception of time altogether and Mrs. Eagle Owl was prepared to sit for an hour gazing at the rat in my hand in a detached way which reminded me of a cat.

Over a period of time I had reduced her weight from 5 lb. 2 oz. down to 4 lb. 10 oz. at which she showed a slightly more lively interest in her surroundings. For weeks I sat each night with a dead rat in my gloved hand resting on the arm of the chair. The owl, three feet away on her block, sat and stared at nothing in particular. Sometimes she would look at the rat then promptly turn her back as if in complete disgust. After waiting perhaps half an hour she would suddenly appear to notice the rat as if for the first time. Leaning forward she would gaze intently at it, bobbing her head up and down, then she would start rocking from side to side with her wings partly open and after doing all this for some minutes, she would equally suddenly change her mind and lapse once more into her private trance. Usually she would take the plunge and swallow the rat after sitting holding it for a mere ten minutes or so. When I felt she had progressed about as far as she was likely to go I decided to fly her in the room to a dead rat attached loosely to the lure. Once more we had to start from scratch. For the first week she would merely hop down from her block on to the lure on the floor, but gradually I increased the distance until she was flying ten feet. This was about as far as I could go indoors. From then on training would have to be done outside.

Hawks can be flown anywhere once they are trained, but I soon found this was not so with Bubo. She is the most conservative creature I have ever met and unless I took her to exactly the same spot each day and flew her in exactly the same direction she would not fly at all. As I hoped to film her in flight coming towards the camera, I chose a place where the sun would be roughly behind me at midday; this meant that she would be flying directly into it and I wondered what her reaction would be. As it happened she did not mind in the least, but she hated wind and would not fly at all in rough weather. After three months of almost daily effort she would fly a hundred and fifty yards from an old tree stump to a dead rat, when she felt so inclined.

I could never tell whether she was keen or not and nothing I could do seemed to make much difference. Of course if I fed her too much she would refuse to fly at all the next day, but if I cut her food down she was just as likely to go into one of her trances and sit showing no interest in anything. Although I started flying her on a light line for safety I gave it up as soon as possible and flew her loose. Lines are an awful nuisance and liable to get caught up on thistles or stones and drag the bird down. She flew off several times when in one of her moods, but usually settled in a tree with every small bird in the neighbourhood mobbing her. If there were any rooks about they would wheel round in a cawing mass over her tree, so if I had lost sight of her I soon knew exactly where she was. She always flopped down on to the lure even if she kept me waiting an hour or more.

When I first put the eagle owls on their blocks on the lawn during the day our resident garden birds used to make an awful fuss mobbing and scolding, especially blackbirds and blue tits, while the rooks would come over the house and mill round and round cawing. Within a week they accepted the owls and took no further interest in them so long as they remained in the garden. The same thing happened when I started flying Bubo loose. At first the hedgerow birds mobbed her as she sat on the tree stump, but after a few days they took no notice. But when she flew off into a tree it was another matter; this was a breach of the establishment and they joined forces to admonish her. The owl's reaction to mobbing was to sit quite still, but if she was caught in the open she appeared to be rather upset by it. Once a pair of kestrels came over and started stooping at her with harsh cries of anger. As each hawk passed low over her head, she ducked to avoid the attack.

Despite my daily contact with Bubo for the past five years I have never been able to decide whether she is quite intelligent or completely dim. She remains where she was when we started—an enigma. Of one thing I am sure; she is far more sensitive to surroundings and even to my mood than any hawk has ever been. It is simply no use taking her out if one is in a hurry or angry about something. She senses it at once and will remain aloof and unapproachable. If at times she appears stupid at others she shows flashes of brilliance. On many occasions after waiting thirty or forty minutes for her to fly to the lure I have walked over to pick it up having given up hope, only to sense her approach and look up just in time to avoid her talons as she seized the rat. She obviously knew I was about to put it away and was going to get it first. The curious thing is that although this happened many times I could never fool her by pretence.

Over the months I tried several dodges to encourage her to fly, with mixed success. One, which sometimes worked, was to throw the lure out with the rat plainly visible and then walk off out of sight; another was to jerk the lure line to make it move; and the third, and perhaps the most effective, was to drag the lure out of sight behind a tussock of grass. While this did not necessarily induce her to fly it always seemed to excite her. Perhaps she realised that once her unsuspecting quarry had moved out of sight she could approach it silently and unseen to make her kill.

On the wing she always reminds me of a gigantic brown moth and I have never quite got over my initial surprise that such a big bird could fly without making a sound. It took me eight months to train Bubo to fly loose to the lure. By trial and error I had discovered that she flew best at around 4 lb. 8 oz. and that she would keep at this weight on one adult rat every other day, which in turn meant that I flew her on alternate days. But just when I was ready to start filming her she decided she would give up flying for the time being and I could do nothing to make her change her mind. I tried all the old dodges, reducing her weight and increasing it, trying her over much shorter distances, offering different kinds of food and so on; but it was no use. There was only one thing to do and that was fly the male eagle owl instead.

He was already tame and jumping to my fist for food so that, by following the same routine, I was able to fly him loose in about seven weeks. He was much more timid than Bubo, and if anything even more sensitive, but he was far more alert and much easier to handle. Weighing 4 lb. 10 oz. when fat, he flew best at 4 lb. and a rat on alternate days kept him at this weight. Unlike Bubo, he would fly in strange surroundings when he was keen, but only over distances up to fifty yards. For longer flights he had to be flown in a familiar place. It was twelve months almost to the day from the time I started taming the owls to our first effort at filming the male in flight.

Of all owls eagle owls are the most talkative in captivity and my male—he never seems to have been given a name— excels himself in this respect. He is always ready to greet those whom he recognises with a succession of " hoo-boo's," each call being uttered with the owl leaning forward and cocking his tail in the air while the feathers on his throat stand out making a white patch. Every spring, usually in March, he gets very excited and whenever I go near him he tries hard to encourage me to set up house with him.

All our tame birds of prey are brought in at night and put on their blocks in large open-fronted sheds which were once used for breeding turkeys. Last thing every evening I go and see them and during the breeding season the male eagle owl jumps off his block as soon as he sees me and walks to the side of his shed where he makes a scrape in the sanded floor with his talons. Bending down and pecking at the earth, he turns round and round with his head almost touching the ground and keeping up a continual bubbling call quite unlike anything he or Bubo make at other times. It is a strange noise, rather throaty and lasting for a minute or more at a stretch. Both he and Bubo also have another call which they frequently use and which is really just a loud squawk. They sometimes make it at each other and quite often at people. In addition both of them are capable of a minute high-pitched querulous little squeak which they utter if one tries to stroke their heads or play with them while they are feeding.

In parts of central Europe gamekeepers use a live eagle owl to decoy hawks and members of the *corvidae* within range of their guns. These great owls sometimes kill crows, jays and magpies which they catch in the darkness while they are roosting. Perhaps the crow family are fully aware of this and therefore never fail to mob their arch-enemy when they find him abroad in daylight. It is said that eagle owls wreak terrible destruction amongst other smaller birds of prey living within their territory. I was anxious to test these things for myself and so I had a padded perch fitted to the top of a telescopic aluminium pole. The other end was pointed and provision made for four guy lines to hold the pole steady. The idea was to put Bubo on the perch and push up the extension so that sitting twelve feet up she would be plainly visible from a distance. Following the example of European gamekeepers I chose a clearing in a large wood which held a fair-sized population of jays. Early one spring morning I put up the perch, sat Bubo on top and hid nearby to watch what happened. The result was most disappointing. Every jay that saw her let out a harsh shriek of alarm and flew off as hard as it could go; there was no question of staying to mob her.

I tried the same procedure in a variety of places both in and just outside woods and in open country, and all jays behaved in this way. Carrion crows took slightly more interest and a pair foraging early in the morning would croak to each other and wing their way over the owl perhaps even circling once or twice before flying on. Flocks of rooks were always ready to mob her provided they had not seen her in the same place more than once or twice before. Then they would spiral round in the air above the owl cawing loudly.

The only hawks I was able to test with Bubo were kestrels and they nearly always reacted violently, stooping at her continually with harsh " kik-kik-kik-" cries of rage. Often they would go on swooping over her for five minutes or more, then fly off only to return a few moments later and start all over again. When they first saw her they would press home their attack, stooping to within a few inches of her head so that Bubo ducked each time they passed over. Small birds varied in their reactions, but perhaps the bravest were a pair of yellow wagtails who were feeding fledged young nearby. They scolded her incessantly for twenty minutes, sometimes flying very close to her head so that I feared Bubo might make a grab at one of them. I happened to be flying her loose at the time and she eventually got fed up with the fussy wagtails and flew silently away to hide in the middle of a large silver birch whose canopy of leaves shielded her. As she went the brave little wagtails flew after her still scolding like a couple of fighters " buzzing " a ponderous freight plane.

The mobbing of a predator such as an eagle owl has a positive survival value not only to the birds doing the scolding—and they rarely run any risk—but also to many other species within earshot. For even if they cannot see the owl, they are made fully aware of its position by the noise of the other birds' alarm calls and so are safer than they would otherwise be. While the jays recognised the eagle owl as an object to be feared, they failed to mob it, which may indicate that this behaviour is not innate but has to be learned by birds familiar with the predator concerned. Our resident jays would hardly have had prior experience of such a rare vagrant as an eagle owl. All the trials with Bubo were conducted in winter and early spring and it is just conceivable that some of the rooks, crows and kestrels were winter visitors to our shores who had had experience of eagle owls abroad. But this would not account for similar behaviour on the part of the rooks throughout the summer which I had noticed when flying Bubo loose.

With the passing of the years both Bubo and the male eagle owl have become steadily tamer. Of the two Bubo is still the more placid and for this reason she has travelled many thousands of miles with me to film shows and lectures, riding quite happily in the back of the Land-Rover or car and sitting on a padded perch. At first I was surprised how quickly she learnt to adjust her balance to the motion of the vehicle. She leans against the force of gravity when cornering and uses her tail to steady herself when I brake or accelerate. Although Bubo will live contentedly for days at a time in a car, she has one weakness—she suffers from car-sickness.

Of course all owls throw up the undigested parts of their food, fur or feather, bones and so on in the form of a pellet; but this is quite different. If Bubo is fed a few hours before a journey, she invariably brings back the whole meal in the form of a stinking semi-digested mass. The eroding effect of the digestive juices in an owl's stomach has to be seen to be believed and a rat thrown up after half an hour is already decomposed and hardly recognisable. It is as if the creature had started to melt inside the owl. The action of the juices in a heron's stomach may be even swifter; I remember watching one of these birds swallow an eel which it regurgitated less than ten minutes later. In that short time the eel had already started to break down.

A strange feature in owls is the absence of the typical crop found in other birds of prey. When a hawk has had a meal the crop is plainly visible, a distinct bulge at the base of the neck. Falconers make use of this in order to judge the amount of food a hawk has eaten. Owls swallow their quarry whole whenever possible, though they usually crush the skull of a rodent first. A few moments later the bulge of the meal can be felt in the owl's stomach by placing one's fingers between the bird's legs from the front.

There is a curiously cat-like quality about Bubo, the softness of her plumage, her round face and eyes, her mottled brown colour and her habit of sitting still, immersed in her own private thoughts. All these things she shares with the fireside tabby cat. But there is one thing she does not share with the cat and that is her liking for water. All our birds of prey are given the opportunity to have a bath at least once a week. Their bathing pool is a small cement pond on the lawn and on bath days the bird is placed beside it on its block. When it feels so inclined, it can fly down and enter the water. Some like having a bath more than others and the weather has quite a lot to do with it. In hot sun most of them bathe regularly, but in the winter few are brave enough. Bubo bathes frequently, especially in the summer, and if she has been away with me to a lecture or television show, one of the first things she does on returning home is to have a bath. Her routine is always the same. She jumps down from her block and wades slowly into the pool, then she pauses and looks down at the water before putting her beak in and swishing it from side to side. That done she ducks her head under, crouching so that the water flows over her back. Finally she flails the water with her wings. When she is thoroughly drenched she shakes her head and flies heavily back to her block. A soaking wet owl is a sorry sight, its body feathers hang in awkward clusters, its scraggy neck is long and thin supporting a huge spherical head. The rounded and dignified form of the owl is transformed into a dripping gargoyle.

When living amongst animals it is best to avoid becoming sentimental about them and to concentrate instead on trying to understand them. Nevertheless I have to admit that I am very fond of Bubo and her undemanding ways.

8. A Golden Eagle trained to kill

On a narrow mountain ledge in a remote part of Finland a young golden eagle flapped his wings vigorously and surveyed the scene below. The precipice fell sheer from the ledge with its bulky nest of twigs and sticks for a hundred feet until it met the scree which sloped steeply to the valley floor. The eaglet looked out over a vast area of spruce forest, broken by the irregular form of a dozen lakes whose blue waters shimmered in the sunlight. Down below a cow elk with her young calf tottering at her heels moved out of the trees and browsed on the tender shoots of arctic birch growing in a clearing. The eaglet bobbed his head as he caught sight of a hazel hen feeding quietly amongst the salix and lichens on a nearby slope. He was hungry; for close on three months his parents had kept him supplied with food, but lately their visits had become more and more irregular. He walked clumsily along the edge away from the nest and leaning outward flapped again. A gust of wind caught his outstretched wings and lifted him. For a moment he hung unsteadily in the air and then, after two or three flaps he sailed out away from the cliff face. His first flight took him nearly a quarter of a mile from the nest and he landed on a rocky outcrop two hundred feet below.

It was there, as he sat preening his feathers, that the forester first spotted him. The man had finished work and was walking home along the foot of the cliff. He had known of the eagles' eyrie since the birds first started to repair the huge bulk of their old nest early that spring, but it was inaccessible without a rope and so he had left them alone. Eagles were unpopular with the foresters because they preyed upon game and took the occasional lamb. His first thought on seeing the young eaglet sitting on the ground was to kill it, but then he remembered that it would probably make more money if he could catch it alive and send it to the zoo in Helsinki.

He got within a few feet before the eaglet flapped away, scarcely rising three feet in the air and landing again two hundred yards farther on. He chased it and after another short flight came up with the exhausted bird and threw his jacket over it. The eaglet fought at first and tore one of the sleeves but soon gave up and lay quiet while the forester carried it home. Almost a week later that same young eagle was sitting in a roomy and well-made plywood travelling box while a friend of mine made the last minute arrangements to send it by air to England.

I had often seen eagles before, both wild in Scotland and captive specimens, but I must confess that on opening the crate I expected to see a much larger bird. Bokhara, as he was christened, was full-grown, but even so he was quite a small male weighing seven and half pounds. Best of all he was feather perfect and with a beautiful bloom to his rich brown plumage. Even his long tail was undamaged, so that the feathers appeared snow white with a wide band of greyish brown across their tips. It is this white on the tail of a young golden eagle which causes the inexperienced to confuse it with a white-tailed eagle. The young eagle's feet were most impressive, for the toes were long and slender in proportion to the size of the bird and each was tipped with a large curved talon, black and polished. The talons on the two hind toes were really massive and each foot had an enormous spread. I was soon to discover the power that lay within those yellow feet.

I left Bokhara alone for several days so that he could recover from the shock of capture and the journey. During that time I made sure that he was eating well. His shed was semi-darkened so that he would settle down and not try to fly with the attendant risk of damaging feathers. During this time I cut a pair of jesses out of really stout leather. They looked enormous, but I wondered how long they would last should the eagle really set to work on them with his great hooked beak.

When I felt I could no longer delay the business of catching up Bokhara, I went into his shed wearing a thick coat and a fencing mask. He was sitting quietly on his perch and as I approached he leant back raising his crest, half dropping his wings and puffing out his chest. His fierce eye glared at me and he hissed in disgust. But that was as far as he went and without any trouble I grabbed him by the legs, tucked him under my arm like a turkey and carried him outside. His only reaction was to utter a pathetic little squealing noise quite unbecoming to the king of birds. Once his jesses were safely on we measured his head and drew an outline of it for the hood which would have to be specially made. Thereafter the process of taming and training him went on in the same way that it did for the eagle owls.

Bokhara's temperament was of course quite different, more like a slow and rather lazy hawk. He was quite highly strung and afraid of strange objects, so that I used to spend at least an hour each day carrying him about on my fist. At first I found his seven and a half pounds balancing somewhat unsteadily on my fist rather tiring, but gradually the muscles in my wrist and arm accustomed themselves to the load and now I can carry him for several hours without undue fatigue. When anything disturbed him his immediate reaction was to grip my fist for all he was worth. This was painful even through a thick leather gauntlet, especially when one of the huge hind talons found a tender place. Nevertheless the most uncomfortable part of training was having to wear a fencing mask which becomes unbearably hot and stuffy after a while. At that time I had no idea whether he would strike at my face or not and I was taking no chances.

Every day I fed Bokhara on my fist; usually he had a large piece of hare or rabbit. Not only did this keep him occupied but it taught him to expect me to give him his food which would help when I started to train him to jump to my fist from his block out in the garden. He was rather slow to learn to fly to my outstretched hand holding the raw meat, but perhaps he lacked confidence, having hardly flown at all before capture. When the new hood arrived I started to get him accustomed to it. Curiously enough birds of prey do not mind being hooded in the least, once they have overcome their fear of the hood being pushed over their heads. If you take a freshly caught wild hawk and set it on your fist it will flap and bate and distress itself and will not begin to look at food. Hood it, and the same bird will settle down and start to feed within a few minutes. It seems to be a case of out of sight out of mind. Eagles are not as a rule difficult to hood as their reactions are slower than a hawk's and they never become so adept at dodging their heads this way and that just as you think you can slip it on. The snag with Bokhara was that one had to remember to hold his jesses very short since he soon developed a habit of striking with his talons at the hand that held the hood. After he had gouged the back of my hand several times I remembered to shorten my grip on his jesses first.

Before Bokhara's arrival I had often wondered how to keep our dogs and cat out of his way when he was sitting on the lawn. It was therefore interesting to see how they all kept clear of him by instinct. Though I am quite sure he would not attack a dog unless provoked, a cat might well be too much of a temptation. Since there was no need to rush his training I decided to give him a very thorough grounding before attempting to fly him at wild rabbits or hares. After six weeks of regular daily carrying and hooding he had become quite tame and would fly twenty or thirty yards to my fist when hungry. He seemed keen if he weighed around 7 lb., which meant giving him the equivalent of a smallish rat each day. When he would come over a hundred yards to my fist and had learned to dispense with any form of line I started to fly him to the lure. For this purpose I had made a much larger affair to which chunks of raw hare were tied. He soon flew at it with a certain amount of drive, but he was always lazy. Never have I seen a bird so determined to fly as low as possible, often his wing tips brushed the ground as he flew and nothing on earth would make him rise even six feet in the air.

Rabbits and hares do not wait to be caught, so Bokhara had to be taught to catch a moving lure. For a start my wife Pat unhooded him and I swung the lure two hundred yards away; when he was approaching I dropped it and ran as fast as I could swerving from side to side and pulling the lure behind me. He soon learned to chase and grab it. About this time he developed a new trick. Normally falcons wait quietly on the lure even after they have finished all the food and either step up on to the falconer's fist or fly a short distance to it. Bokhara took to flying hard at me the moment he had eaten all the meat on the lure and sometimes even before. If I " made in " to him while he was still eating he often left his food and flew straight at me. I soon learned to have my gloved hand ready, for this was distinctly more aggressive than the normal way of flying to the fist. To this day it is unsafe for strangers to approach him when he is on the lure as he will leave it and chase them off when they are still twenty yards away. He has evolved an even more curious ritual when I go to pick him up; as I approach he starts to run, grasping the lure firmly in one foot and bounding along with a sort of " dot and carry-one " action, his wings dropped down to hide his feet. I have to run alongside and it is surprising how fast he can move in this ungainly fashion. I hold my gloved hand in front of him as we run and suddenly he will drop the lure without warning and grab my fist instead. It must appear a very strange performance to the uninitiated.

It was time to see if Bokhara could really turn on the steam and catch a fast-moving quarry. My idea was to tow a dead hare behind the Land-Rover, the end of the tow line being held in somebody's hand so that it could be dropped the moment the eagle grabbed the hare and thus prevent it being dragged along. A large field was necessary so that the Land-Rover could reach forty miles an hour as it passed the assistant holding the eagle ready. Fortunately Gordon happened to be staying with us that week-end and volunteered to slip the eagle at what he judged to be the right moment. We decided to have a trial run. A dead hare was securely tied by the back legs to thirty yards of nylon cord. I sat on the floor holding the other end of the line with the back door of the Land-Rover fixed open. At a signal from me the driver was to reach forty miles an hour as fast as possible and to stop at the other end of the field. All was ready, so I gave the signal and was immediately shot out as if in an ejector seat, to land on my back on the grass—I had not realised how fast even a Land-Rover can accelerate.

Next time I wedged my feet either side of the open door and we roared past Gordon with the hare bouncing along behind. He slipped off the hood and held Bokhara up just as we shot by. The eagle saw the hare almost at once and started in pursuit, so that I had a magnificent view as he chased after us coming up astern and easily overtaking the hare. As he put out his talons to seize it, I let go of the line, but even so the impetus carried him along for a few yards.

While I was training Bokhara I often discussed the chances of catching a hare with various friends who were also falconers. Those who had seen him fly to the lure were sure he would be too slow to overhaul a fast-running hare, while a rabbit would probably turn too quickly for him. I was not sure that they were right and now that I knew Bokhara could easily exceed forty miles an hour I was ready to fly him at a wild rabbit. He was always weighed before being flown and for his first chance at wild quarry I brought him down to a few ounces under seven pounds. It is essential to give a trained bird of prey a comparatively easy chance the first time it is flown at quarry since if it fails to kill it may become disheartened.

Rabbits are scarce in these parts but there were a few left on a disused airfield where I had permission to fly Bokhara. We took him there one January afternoon. Removing his swivel and leash, I held him by the jesses with the braces of his hood half undone so that it could be pulled off in an instant. We started at one end of the main runway, walking with the gentle breeze in our backs. Along either side of the concrete strip was an area of coarse grass, thistles and the odd small thornbush and it was in this cover that I hoped to find a rabbit. Pat took the right-hand side with our old pointer Whisper while I took the left-hand side.

Half-way across the airfield the dog disturbed a rabbit which crossed the runway some fifty yards ahead. I whipped off Bokhara's hood and held him aloft. He saw the rabbit and bobbed his head; then he turned round and jumped off my fist into the wind. I thought he had left it far too late for the rabbit was by now over a hundred and fifty yards away, its white scut bouncing across the open plough as it made for the cover of a thick thorn hedge on the perimeter. Slowly it seemed Bokhara came round and started to fly after it. Within a few seconds he was close behind and the rabbit swerved first one way then the other but the eagle followed each move and then swept in to the attack. The rabbit jinked and, turning on a sixpence, tried to double back past him, but a huge foot shot out and grabbed it.

By the time I arrived breathless the rabbit was quite dead

and Bokhara crouched on it, his wings embracing his first kill and his crest raised, a picture of aquiline ferocity. Since that day I have flown Bokhara at rabbits a good many times and, provided that the country is open enough, he nearly always catches his quarry without appearing to exert himself.

Hares are quite a different matter and although he has had many opportunities he has only caught one and that was more or less by accident. A friend who was staying with us expressed a wish to see Bokhara fly, and so one afternoon we went out to some open country. I stood on high ground swinging the lure while our guest unhooded Bokhara and slipped him. When he was roughly half-way between us a hare jumped up unexpectedly from a tussock of grass near my feet and ran away left-handed. Bokhara saw it at once and swung off in pursuit. Unluckily for the hare there was a low fence of wire netting put up to keep rabbits out of a young plantation bordering the hedge towards which it ran. As it turned on reaching the netting, Bokhara swept in and seized it. After a brief struggle he managed to hold it down and I ran towards him to make sure the hare was dead. When I was still half a dozen yards away Bokhara looked up and without warning left the hare and flew to my fist. The astonished animal seemed none the worse for its adventure and immediately ran off as fast as it could go.

Why he let it go I cannot explain, but I never feel he tries very hard to catch a hare. Perhaps they are a little too big for him and struggle too violently when caught. One thing is certain: a golden eagle flies much faster than it would appear to. Whether he catches it or not, Bokhara can always easily overhaul a hare even if it has a hundred yards' start on him.

Bokhara had been flying quarry for some time before I realised that his training would make a good subject for a short film. In theory we put the clock back to the time when he was first jessed and put out in the garden on his block. We then filmed every stage in his training, Pat did much of the camera work when I had to be in the picture so that between us we covered the whole film with the exception of two shots where we appeared together. Several sequences of the eagle flying to the lure were taken at half speed, so one is able to watch the movement of every feather as the great bird sails in towards the camera. Of course we had to repeat the performance of towing the dead hare behind the Land-Rover, only this time it was even harder to judge when to slip Bokhara. It obviously had to be a crossing shot and it was essential that he caught up with the hare and grabbed it opposite the camera.

Although catching a wild rabbit was difficult enough without having to film it, I felt we ought to try in order to show that Bokhara was indeed " an eagle trained to kill." We spent a good many days on that one sequence and would not have succeeded even then but for a neighbour's kindness in allowing us to fly him over an exceptionally favourable piece of country. It was very open grassland with rough patches of thistle and nettle and two marl pits about a hundred yards apart. There were thorn bushes in both pits as well as rabbit burrows. Usually one could find several outlying rabbits in the rough grass and it was here that our pointer Whisper helped us. She would point a rabbit in its form without disturbing it, and if we were very quiet and careful we could then get the two cameras into place. The first was mounted on a lorry which was driven up and placed so that the sun was behind it; the second was at " square leg " to follow the flight should it go that way.

When all was ready our team of six or seven helpers would spread out with Pat in the middle carrying Bokhara. Meanwhile I was behind No. 1 camera with somebody else behind No. 2. The object of having so many people was to try to force the rabbit to run in the right direction—across the lorry and towards the second camera. You may think that the

Bubo would often sit in a tree for hours

Bokhara reveals his six-foot wing sp

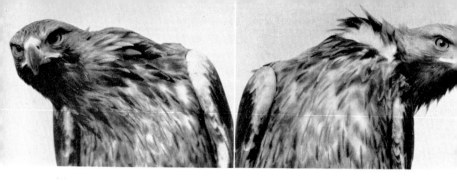

Bokhara sizes it up

Wings spread and talons poised to kill: Bokhara coming to the lure

rabbit had little chance against a dog, an eagle and seven people, but you would be wrong. The cameras and the people hindered Bokhara and helped the rabbits, for most of them ran in and out amongst our helpers while several merely ran straight for the lorry and squatted underneath in perfect safety. I cannot remember how many unsuccessful flights there were, but I know we tried for a good many days before Bokhara at last took a rabbit in front of the camera, even if it was rather a long way off. Not all unsuccessful flights were complete failures photographically, as quite often we would get some nice shots of Bokhara in action or a rabbit running. In the skilled hands of our editor Raoul Sobel all those odd shots were finally built up into an exciting sequence full of action and suspense.

But happy as I was with the results of this film, I began to work on one which was much more ambitious. It set out to illustrate what became of the wild life of the Norfolk Broads during the four seasons of the year: I called it *Wind in the Reeds*.

9. *Wind in the Reeds*

Speak to anyone outside Norfolk and you will nearly always find they imagine the whole county centres on the Broads. People who come to stay with us often say they would like to visit them and are a bit incredulous when we explain that it is rather difficult to see much of the Broads without exploring them in a boat.

The truth is that comparatively few roads actually skirt these land-locked waterways. The slow-moving rivers wind their tortuous way for the most part through low-lying grazing marshes, and the Broads themselves are often surrounded by dense reed-beds or swampy woods. Where there is hard ground and a road adjacent to river or Broad, there you will nearly always find houses, boat-yards and, in the summer time, crowds of holiday-makers, all of which are apt to give a misleading picture. Yet despite the holiday crowds, the cruisers, the sailing boats and the transistor radios, there still exist a good many miles of quiet waterway, secluded marshes and great reed-beds where wildlife is little disturbed. Such places are, however, subject to ever increasing pressure from commercial interests and the few that remain are largely due to private landowners and to the Norfolk Naturalists Trust which controls several large areas, including the famous Hickling Broad.

The increasing popularity of the Broads as a holiday resort has brought its own special problems, all of which conflict with the requirements of nature. Thousands of cabin cruisers pour their effluent daily into the sluggish water, not only sewage but detergents which have a disastrous effect on aquatic plants and fish and ultimately on wild bird and mammal life. The wash from speed-boats undermines the banks and swamps the floating nests of great crested grebes. Add to all this an increase in irresponsible shooting and you will have some idea of what the wild creatures are up against. It was perhaps this conflict between the recreational needs of people and the continued existence of many unique forms of wildlife within our own county which prompted me to devote my first full-length film to the natural history of the Broads.

It takes several years to make a film of this kind, especially when shooting in colour and therefore dependent upon the sun. So it was that for the next three years I was to spend a great deal of my time in and around the Broads. Perhaps the most important part of any film is the " idea " or story-line; it is necessary to have a definite plan before shooting any film at all. Natural history films of this kind cannot be shot to a script, since the unexpected so often happens and it is these sequences which frequently turn out the best.

My idea was to attempt to show the wildlife of the Broads through the eyes of a local reed-cutter, a man whose work takes him out into the waterways and reed-beds at all times of the year. I was extremely lucky in knowing just the man for the job. His name is Russel and, apart from being a reed-cutter, he is a first-class naturalist who takes a tremendous interest in the wildlife around him. Perhaps his interest and powers of observation have been sharpened by his surroundings, for he lives with the Ellis family at Wheatfen on the edge of Surlingham Broad. Ted Ellis is without doubt one of the finest naturalists East Anglia has ever produced and his work in the fields of botany and mycology has gained international repute. In spite of this, Ted is no highbrow scientist, but a sound all-rounder with a wide knowledge of every form of our native wildlife. With his long experience of the Broads, he helped me draw up a list of the subjects which we felt ought to be included in the film, from plants and insects to birds and mammals. Sometimes I had a pretty clear idea of the actual scenes I wanted to portray. In the case of the coypu, for example, I was anxious to show the mother suckling her young while floating in the water; but for the most part I should have to shoot all I could of each subject and hope that in the end it would be possible to build up an interesting sequence.

No film is ever the product of one man but the result of team work. Already three of us were involved and before the finished film reached the screen many more would play their part, including that most important individual, the editor, not to mention dozens of technicians employed in the various processes on the way. Soon after starting the film I acquired another camera in addition to the reflex Bolex. It was a Cameflex 16/35 mm. complete with blimp and linked to a Perfectone recorder for shooting in synch. as already described. A blimp is a most necessary piece of equipment, its object being to deaden the noise of the camera motor. In effect the blimp, though complicated, is only a sound-proof box with a glass front in which the camera is fitted; but in order to deaden the noise it has to have a good deal of special packing and the camera must have no direct connection with the exterior which would transmit the sound. In addition the controls for focusing the lens, altering the stop and so on, must all work from outside the blimp, again without transmitting noise. The result is a large, heavy and cumbersome piece of equipment which again requires an extra-heavy tripod to support it. My blimp with the camera weighs nearly a hundredweight.

Few people see the Broads in winter when the boats are laid up. Trees stand bare and gaunt by the water's edge and wild-

fowl from the coast seek shelter from the northerly gales.
Yet I often think that this is when the Broads really come into
their own, especially when snow covers the marsh and all
save the most open water is ice-bound.

During one such spell Ted told me of a heron which, weak
through hunger, had taken up residence in the garden of a
house near the Broad. In the garden was a large pool. Like
every other piece of water for miles it was frozen, but the
owner of the house used to throw sprats on to the ice every
day and the heron would soon arrive to pick them up. A
hasty phone call and I was given permission to try to film it.
For once the next day was bright and sunny, but it was also
appreciably warmer and I began to wonder how long the ice
would remain. We arrived after breakfast to find the whole
pond in deep shadow from the large house which stood almost
on its bank. There was no sign of the heron. I reckoned that
it would take two hours for the sun to clear the house and,
while there was not a cloud in the sky, this condition could
change in two minutes let alone two hours. Anxiously we
waited, then suddenly the heron was there, sitting hunched
up, a grey sentinel on the far bank; neither of us saw him
arrive.

The day grew warmer and little pools of water began to
form on top of the melting ice while slowly the patch of sunlight spread across the dark surface of the pond. At last there
was a big enough area in the sun to start filming. We set the
camera up and the owner of the house came out with a bowl
of sprats. Calling the heron in his usual manner, he threw two
or three fish well out on to the ice. They skated to a stop right
in the middle and the heron's grey neck suddenly shot up
from between his hunched shoulders as he saw them. He made
no other movement but stood watching as still as a statue,
then equally suddenly he jumped into the air and flapped across
to land slithering, with wings flapping on the ice. With
cautious steps he walked towards the nearest fish and each

time he put his foot down it slid forward so that he appeared to waltz more like a creature from a Disney cartoon. He had just swallowed a fish head first when the ice gave way beneath him, quite slowly at first so that he sank gracefully.

This was too much for the poor bird and he struggled into the air and flew back to the bank. His appetite whetted, he was soon back again, landing with a slide; again the cautious waltzing steps to seize another fish. That done he started towards the next and as he went the ice began to give. He quickened his steps but it was no use: just as he lunged at the fish with his long bill, the ice broke and he flopped down into the water. After sitting for a moment looking rather surprised, he flapped into the air and returned to the bank to digest his meal, standing silent and still beneath the towering beech tree.

When the frost returned I set off with Russel to film duck flighting in to feed on a marsh where there were still some open places. It was a clear day with a blue sky, the reeds were white with frost and ice-encrusted twigs of alder and willow glittered like jewels in the sun. The punt moved silently through the still water where the channel wound its way between alder thicket and reed-bed. Several hundred ducks were already down in the marsh when we arrived. While I set the camera up behind a low bush, Russel went off in the boat to land on the farthest end of the marsh with the idea of putting up any birds feeding there. The plan worked well and after circling high in the blue sky they started to drop in to join their companions in front of the camera. Filming over, we walked through a nearby alder carr to get warm; the thin layer of ice covering the ground crackled under our feet. Suddenly we saw a stoat disturbed by our noise leap from an old alder stump and disappear in a red-brown flash beneath the over-hanging fronds of a large tussock sedge. We tried to find it again without success, then I examined the alder stump. The main stem was hollow and had broken off about four feet up. Something was wedged a foot down inside the hollow, so I put my arm in and pulled out a freshly killed moorhen still warm and undamaged save for the teeth wounds inflicted by the stoat in the back of its head. This hiding of food in a larder is quite a common habit amongst carnivora of all sizes from weasels to lions. The light was beginning to fail as Russel pushed the punt towards the home creek. Seven whooper swans flew south over the Broad and a party of field-fares came flocking in to roost in some osiers; a squawk from one and we were in time to see it fling itself into cover and safety, just avoiding the stoop of a merlin. A few minutes later a protracted despairing scream indicated that the next victim had been less fortunate.

The reed harvest takes place during the winter after the summer growth has stopped. Then the men mow the reeds with scythes and afterwards tie them into bundles which they stack near the water's edge. These stacks often remain for several months before being carted away. Then one day in spring on a high tide the men arrive with a large flat-bottomed barge, the bundles of reeds are loaded and taken to the nearest quay where they are picked up by the merchant. Norfolk reed is in much demand for thatch, being most durable and of good length—often exceeding eight feet. Russel usually works alone or with one other companion, and it was while I was filming him loading reeds one day that he disturbed a weasel from its nest cleverly hidden in the stack. This tiny hunter of harvest mice and voles was away in a flash, pausing on top of a pile of reeds just long enough to take stock of the situation before disappearing at lightning speed down a mole run. A moment later an inquisitive little head with beady eyes popped up again as if to make sure we were still there. Harvest mice are still found fairly frequently in the great reed-beds for this is their traditional home and has been since time immemorial, long before there were any cornfields. Weighing less than a farthing, these diminutive creatures climb nimbly about the swaying stems and make their nests from the slender leaves, lining them with the feathered tops of the reeds.

A gentle " plop " beneath the willows overhanging some quiet backwater is a familiar sound to any angler, for water voles are common all over the Broads. Ever since the time of Kenneth Grahame—and before for all I know—these unfortunate creatures have been misnamed water-rats. This vole is an attractive, inoffensive little animal, not much like a rat when you see one close to—its short tail, about half an inch long, and little round face with prominent whiskers and nose a-quiver are all quite unrat-like. The first water vole I filmed had been flooded out of its burrow in the river bank by the spate which followed a sudden thaw after weeks of frost and snow. I watched several voles that day, all busy moving to drier ground. The thing which struck me most was the amount of time spent grooming their coats. As soon as a vole left the water it would lick and nibble its fur, combing it dry with lightning quick strokes of its forepaws. After wiping its face on its paws, it would start on the back of its head, pulling its front legs over from behind its ears—the same sort of action that both rabbits and coypu have when grooming and which always looks so attractive. This done, it would start on its back reaching round towards its tail, nibbling the fur and combing it out with its front paws, first one side then the other. Every movement was performed at lightning .speed, almost too fast for the eye to follow. The grooming over, a quick shake, a dart and the vole had disappeared

A moment later it emerged from a clump of meadow-sweet and started to dig a new burrow in the face of the bank. Again there was the lightning speed of the forepaws scrabbling at the earth, small roots were quickly bitten through and in less than ten minutes the animal's head and shoulders had disappeared inside the hole. The tiny grains of soil were pushed back under its body and kicked clear with the hind legs so that soon a little pile of loose earth threatened to block the hole. A pause for a rest and the vole whipped round and literally bull-dozed the soil away with its blunt nose; the earth trickled down the bank and into the river, making a noise like grains of rice being dropped into a bowl of water. And if you wonder how I know what that sounds like, the answer is that I used it to reproduce the noise to accompany the film, as there was far too much background noise and wind to record the actual sound at the time.

Water voles are usually reddish-brown in colour but one day Russel caught a most unusual specimen which was dark brown, almost black. He told me he had seen several like it round Surlingham. Even more excitement was caused when, a few months later, he caught a curious rat in a trap set out on the marsh. Although plainly an ordinary rat, it was an extraordinary colour, being bright russet red instead of the usual brown, and having very pale almost white underparts coming right up under its chin. I kept this animal for some weeks, so had plenty of opportunity to study it.

Owls frequently hunt the reed beds and marshes in search of voles and mice, and both barn and little owls quite often start hunting in daylight, while the commoner tawny rarely comes out before dusk; all of them, and in winter the short-eared owl as well, take their toll of water voles. One's attention is often called to a marauding little owl, long before it can be seen, by the scolding of hedgerow birds. Tits and chaffinches, sparrows and blackbirds follow the owl with a chorus of alarm calls. They know perfectly well when they are safe and I have seen blue tits perch within two feet to scold a little owl I was filming, while the owl just kept on bobbing up and down as though embarrassed by all the row.

With the arrival of April, spring is really here. The scent

from countless thousands of pussy willows, now a mass of yellow flowers, fills the air, while tortoiseshell and peacock butterflies feed on the nectar. Bumble bees are busy filling sacs on their legs with pollen to store in their underground nests. New bird song swells the chorus each day and at the water's edge the striking water iris bursts into a blaze of yellow flowers.

Soon the first mallard ducklings will follow their mother through the reeds to the open water. Mallard quite often nest in trees where both the eggs and the sitting duck are quite safe from floods as well as from foxes and rats. The flat crowns of pollard willows make excellent nesting places although the nest we filmed was in the hollow where a large bough had broken off some fifteen feet above the ground.

When the ducklings are dry, about twenty-four hours after hatching, the duck flies down from the nest and calls to them from the ground to follow her; and follow her they do without hesitation. Sometimes singly, sometimes two together, they run to the edge, peer over and fling themselves into space. Down they fall, head first, spinning with tiny wing-stumps held out, to bounce on the ground and lie still as if winded by the drop. Quite suddenly they jump to their feet and run " peeping " loudly to join the duck who waddles up and down calling a low " quark " to tell the rest to come on down. The ducklings never seem to get hurt by their fall and if you pick one up and replace it in the nest, as we did to film them, it immediately runs to the edge and hurls itself down again. For each ball of down the most urgent thing in life at that moment is to jump from the nest and rush to join its mother. Once at the water's edge the old duck waits to collect any stragglers from her brood and, while she may start with a dozen or more ducklings, she will be lucky to have half that number in a fortnight's time, for pike swallow most young ducks hatched on the Broads each year. Stragglers are particularly vulnerable and a duckling swimming alone is apt to disappear without warning, only a ripple remaining to mark for a few seconds the spot where the pike seized its victim.

Foxes, despite their liking for reed-beds, are uncommon around the Broads, but most years a few are seen and as quickly persecuted. I was once lucky enough to watch a fine dog fox making a meal of the remains of a large pike lying at the water's edge not many yards from my hide.

Three birds are virtually confined in the breeding season to the Broads and east coast marshes, the bittern, bearded tit and marsh harrier. While I have filmed all three, I have only done the first two at the nest. The bittern strikes me as a strange, shy, reptilian bird with an uncanny skill for camouflaging itself among the reeds by remaining motionless with neck upstretched and bill pointing skywards; it relies on its mottled plumage and the play of light to conceal it. The bittern's boom is one of the most arresting sounds of the great reed-beds in the spring. The males boom most in the early morning and again in the evening, but also at odd intervals during the day. It sounds like a foghorn at sea or somebody blowing into an empty beer bottle. As the summer advances the birds boom less and, instead of producing five or even six " booms " each time, the number gets down to one or two at the most. Young bitterns are curious little creatures as they crouch on their reed platform nest, all long olive-green legs and bills and gawky bodies covered with brick-red down. They are fed pre-digested food and, as soon as the parent arrives at the nest, they set up a querulous piping call and first one then another reaches up to seize the adult's bill and drag it down. All this results in the parent bittern finally throwing up a nice juicy meal of eels or frogs which the young greedily swallow.

Most small birds at the nest are rather uninteresting, but there is something special about the bearded tit. Perhaps it is the beautiful colouring of the male, with his lavender blue head, black moustache, bright yellow bill and chestnut body as he clings swaying to the top of a reed, his bill crammed with flies for the chicks. The nest is nearly always built above the water and resembles a calash woven out of the dry leaves of reed mace, semi-domed and lined with fine grass and the flowering fronds of reeds. The adults approach the nest in a series of short flights from reed to reed, uttering their high-pitched single note "ping-ping." While the cock frequently perches at the top of a swaying reed, the hen usually keeps to a lower level. Both parents make their final approach to the nest from mid-way down the reeds and quickly slither down to feed the young. Luminous spots inside the babies' beaks show the adults precisely where to place the food, even in the gloomy depths of the reed-bed. Bearded tits often cling to a single reed, but they are equally at home gripping two reeds, their legs splayed wide apart and turned outwards to grip the stems. The adults feed the chicks every few minutes on flies and other insects. Quite often both birds arrive at the nest together and, when this happened at the nest I filmed, the cock always fed the young first while the hen waited for him. Each parent appeared to feed only one chick each visit, quickly dropping the food into the open mouth and flying off at once to search for more. The youngsters deposited their droppings on the rim of the nest by turning their backs on the outside world and raising themselves with their legs and wings. The next parent to arrive at the nest would carefully pick up the fæcal sac and swallow it there and then as soon as it had fed the chicks.

Recording the calls of the bearded tits caused us some trouble since their single "ping-ping" notes have very little carrying power and are often drowned by the rustling of the birds as a small party of them moves through the reeds calling to keep in touch with one another. As usual the solution seemed to lie in a very early start on a calm morning when the reed-beds would be as still and quiet as possible. The population of bearded tits fluctuates from year to year and reaches its lowest ebb after a succession of severe winters when many of the birds die of starvation. That year, 1960, was a good one at Hickling and the warden, Ted Piggin, had found several nests. We arranged to make a really early start, and so a few days later, when the weather seemed settled, we left Whiteslea Lodge well before five o'clock. It was a perfect June morning, dead still, and with the water like glass; a heavy mist shrouded the reed-beds and lay in swirling patches above the grazing marshes. The noise of human activity was non-existent, save for the gentle thud and swish of Ted's pole as he pushed the punt through the narrow channels, and once the drone of a distant motor-cycle. The marsh was alive with bird song at that hour, the fluting calls of redshank, and the continual churring of grasshopper warblers mingled with the chorus of reed and sedge warblers on all sides. A bittern boomed quite close to us, while from seaward we could hear the monotonous " woomph " of the foghorn on the South Haisboro' light-ship, twelve miles to seaward, telling us that the mist was not confined to the land.

After half an hour we reached a large reed-bed and Ted anchored the punt firmly against the bank by thrusting the pole deep into the mud, wedging it against the boat. Twenty yards away in the middle of the reeds was a bearded tits' nest with half-grown young, built in the usual position, about a foot above the water, which was only a few inches deep. Leaving the recorder in the punt we laid out the cable and hid the microphone close to the nest on a dry platform of reeds. All was set and we waited in the boat for the parents to return. It soon became apparent that, not having any idea when one of the adults was on the way to the nest, we should waste an awful lot of battery power, since we should have to run the recorder all the time. It was Ted who suggested that I should remain in the punt, listening over the ear-phones, while he stood hidden in the reeds not far from the nest. As soon as he heard or saw a bird approaching, he would warn me to switch on by holding his hand high above the reeds.

The plan worked well and we made good recordings of the parents approaching the nest and feeding the young, as well as the call notes of parties of already fledged young as they moved through the reeds. Listening over the head-phones I could hear the background noise of bird song, a snipe drumming and the distant moan of the Haisboro' foghorn. Suddenly up shot Ted's hand and almost at once I could hear the parents arriving at the nest and the calls of the young being fed followed by an exclamation in broadest Norfolk from Ted which nearly broke my eardrums, " Blast, there's three b . . . . s ! " Later he explained that three birds had arrived at the nest together all carrying food—there appeared to be a cock and two hens, but we both thought the third bird was more likely to be a youngster from a previous brood since it was well into June and the parents may have had one or even two earlier broods. We poled slowly home to breakfast. The warmth from the sun increased dispersing the mist while a gentle breeze rustled the reeds. As the punt slipped noiselessly round a corner there was a splash and a swirl in the middle of a small bay. At first I thought we had surprised an otter, but Ted stopped poling and in silence we watched two large bream performing their courtship gyrations. Sometimes a dorsal fin would slice through the surface of the water sending ripples shimmering outwards. Their bodies flashed gold and silver in the sunlight as the two fish twisted and turned in the ecstasy of their mating.

During May parties of black terns or blue darrs, as they were once called in Norfolk, pass through the Broads on their migration. At one time they used to stay to breed, building their floating nests on rafts of vegetation, but now they are only travellers calling in on their way to Holland, staying long enough to snatch a few gnats, diving and twisting to skim the surface of the Broad in graceful flight. As spring passes into summer the first young waterbirds make their appearance, among them baby coots bobbing on the water like tiny black corks. After a swim they struggle ashore to stand unsteadily on their black lobed feet, while they preen their bedraggled down, their bald foreheads and scarlet faces making them look like grotesque little clowns.

Quite different are the teenage herons of Fishley Wood. Still too young to fly but too old to remain in the nest, they clamber awkwardly about the topmost traceries of the tall ashes of the heronry. Their stilt-like legs were hardly made for a tree-top existence, but they climb shakily from one bough to another and, when all else fails, grasp the branches with their dagger bills and haul themselves upwards amidst much wing-flapping. The struggle over, they regain their dignity, standing upright to await their parents' return with the next meal of fish. A heronry is a noisy place, particularly when the young are being fed. Then their raucous squawks carry far out over the water.

Coypu breed all the year round, although most litters are born in early summer. This animal is without doubt one of the strangest newcomers to the Broads. It was originally imported from South America and farmed over here for its fur called nutria. During the Second World War a number escaped from time to time and those fortunate enough to reach the Broads soon made themselves at home. Here was a habitat remarkably similar to their native swamps, but with one great advantage, no predators save man. So the coypu settled down and multiplied, moving far and wide throughout East Anglia following the river system. In moderate numbers they are harmless, but having virtually no natural enemies they soon became too numerous and started to raid farm crops, being especially fond of sugar beet. Though not really great burrowers large numbers of them began to cause damage to river banks with their scratching and digging, as well as eating down huge areas of reed-bed. Something had to be done and so in 1962 the Ministry of Agriculture started its coypu campaign with the intention of exterminating the poor animal. Personally I hope they never succeed and I don't think they will. Having watched and filmed coypu in the wild, kept them as pets and bred them, I have a soft spot for these much-maligned creatures who have even been exhibited in country fairs as "giant sewer rats." Apart from his unfortunate tail, which is nevertheless most useful to man as a means of catching hold of the animal, the coypu is not at all rat-like. His large hind feet are webbed, his fur is dense and soft, his face is rounded, and above all he has long stiff white whiskers and large orange-red incisor teeth. He is really more like a beaver than a rat. When a wild coypu is cornered he will put up a good fight and his long teeth can cause ugly puncture wounds in a dog. But the coypu is basically tame and confiding and even a wild-caught specimen soon gets used to being handled without attempting to bite. The softest fur is on the belly and for this reason coypu for the fur trade were skinned by cutting the pelt down the centre of the back not along the stomach as in other animals.

Perhaps one of the most curious things about coypu is the position of the female's teats. These are high up along each flank and, when the animal is afloat, the two rows of teats are just above the water line. The baby coypu, who can swim well within a few hours of birth, are thus able to swim up to their mother while she remains floating and suckle in the water like submarines alongside a depot ship. I was lucky enough to film this and when they had finished feeding, some of the babies climbed on to their mother's back and she carried them ashore into the reeds while the rest of the litter swam close beside her.

Another strange thing about the coypu is its weird wailing cry which is mostly heard at night, making the marsh sound eerie and forbidding.

Like all aquatic animals the coypu is always grooming his

coat. Then he looks like a huge water vole, for he has the same way of pulling his front paws over his head from behind and brushing his whiskers. Sitting up on his hind legs, he will carefully groom the fur on his belly, combing it with his front claws and pausing now and then to scratch. This is sometimes accomplished by bringing up a hind leg to scratch the flank and back of a front leg, just as a dog does.

Coypu are wonderful swimmers and are able to remain under water for a remarkably long time. This is their chief means of escape and, if not being hustled, they are able to lie submerged for at least ten minutes. While this is the longest I have timed one, I shouldn't be surprised if they could double it. Like seals and other aquatic mammals, coypu are able to slow up their whole metabolism when under water, their pulse rate drops sharply and they require far less oxygen than normal to keep going; but if they are chased they are forced to surface much sooner. Propulsion is provided by the webbed hind feet, whether swimming above or below the water, while the long tail helps to balance the animal and to steer it. In clear water you will eventually see a chain of bubbles rising from the animal's nostrils and shortly afterwards it is bound to surface for air. It is, as it were, a sign of the tanks running out of oxygen.

Well-marked runs show the routes taken by coypu from the water to their feeding grounds or to resting places, sometimes burrows, more often under dense vegetation or a fallen tree. They frequently make platforms by the water's edge in reeds or sedge which are just places where they rest and groom after swimming, and it is from these platforms that you are most likely to disturb a coypu as you walk round the Broad. If taken by surprise it will dive into the water head first with a loud splash, otherwise it will slip quietly over the side and swim away unseen.

Nobody seems to know why the coypu's four front teeth are such a vivid colour. I can only think that it is an added deterrent to any would-be attacker, since the coypu on the defensive holds his head high and gnashes his orange-red teeth in a most disconcerting way. Unlike ours, the coypu's teeth grow again should he break them, and in captivity it is important to provide twigs and branches for them to gnaw otherwise their teeth will grow too long. A litter of empty mussel shells along the high-water mark of certain Broads puzzled me for some time and I attributed them to the activities of rats. The shells of the large fresh-water mussel had been gnawed open and the contents cleaned up. Now rats are fond of water and often scavenge river banks, but I could not quite understand how they got the mussels out of the water in the first place. One evening as I made my way round a disused gravel pit I found the answer, for there in the beam of my torch sat a large coypu, a mussel held firmly in its front paws. The following day a closer examination revealed the presence of large numbers of empty shells all along the edge of the water and unmistakable tracks and other signs of coypu. Up to that time I had been firmly convinced that the coypu was completely vegetarian. Despite its liking for shell-fish, I have found no other evidence to the contrary. Early one spring I was searching a sheltered bay for signs of toads breeding, for it had been a favourite spawning ground for a number of years. To my surprise I found the remains of toads all along the shore; every one had received the same treatment, the skin rolled back and left lying attached to the two hind legs. At first I thought coypu might once again be responsible, but it turned out that the culprits were rats.

Although coypu are seen by day, it is under cover of darkness that they really become active. For this reason few people have watched them courting but I was once lucky enough to film the whole performance. Basically it was just a case of the male pursuing the female but although she was not ready to accept him and could easily have swum off, she appeared to enjoy his attentions and so the two of them swam round and round and in and out amongst the clumps of reed and water iris. Sometimes she would disappear one side of a clump while he went the other; then they would meet face to face and start a mock fight with mouths open and orange-red teeth flashing in contrast to their stiff white whiskers. The splashing of the water and their weird screams all adding to the effect as they circled round and round as if caught in a whirlpool. First one then the other would dive, only to continue the battle when they both surfaced. If the male appeared to be losing interest, the female swam up to him and rolled over under his nose rather as a puppy will do when trying to induce an older dog to play. Sometimes she went ashore and the male followed her and tried to mount, where-upon she turned on him screaming and drove him back into the water. She also had another trick to entice him; she swam rapidly away and quite suddenly stopped dead; then the moment he swam towards her she crash-dived with a splash and reappeared somewhere else. The whole display lasted nearly an hour before the male tired of it and retired to the shore where he sat grooming his coat, paying great attention to the soft fur on his belly. Having watched the courtship I could not help feeling that the bright colour of the teeth had special significance in this particular display. The other strange thing was their ability to stop dead in deep water when swim-ming along quite fast, so that ripples faded away in front of the stationary animal.

The coypu has only one other serious enemy apart from man in Britain and that is frost. Coming from a sub-tropical climate, it is unable to withstand prolonged spells of severe weather and, when they occur, as in the early months of 1963, the coypu are among the first creatures to suffer—many die of exposure or as the result of eating frozen food. The lucky ones survive with the tips of their tails raw and bleeding from frostbite.

No Broad would be complete without its pairs of great

crested grebes. These magnificent birds were once brought to the verge of extinction in Britain by Victorian ladies who used their skins as muffs until bird protection stopped this folly. Nowadays the grebes remain to build their floating nests of aquatic vegetation firmly anchored to the reeds. Although the eggs are chalky white when they are first laid, they soon get stained a dirty brown, which blends well with the nest. Despite this camouflage, the sitting bird, if disturbed, carefully covers the eggs with nest material before slipping into the water and diving to swim away unseen. If this precaution were not taken, crows or gulls would soon rob the eggs, and in spite of it many clutches of grebes' eggs are taken by black-headed gulls on the Broads every summer. Great crested grebes are among the most beautiful and spectacular of Broadland birds. Their courtship displays are well known and have been described in detail by several observers, but most thoroughly by Kenneth Simmons, who has spent many years studying them.

I watched the first grebes' nest I filmed being built. A narrow belt of reeds extended about ten yards out into the water and the nest was twelve feet from the shore among the reeds. When I first found it the platform would scarcely support the weight of a bird, but the pair worked hard adding more vegetation until a substantial nest was formed. During this period I often saw the birds displaying out on the open water beyond the reeds; sometimes one bird would dive and swim towards the other just below the surface, causing a ripple which the second bird would watch. Upon surfacing to continue the display, the grebe would find its mate facing it with wings spread and head held back. Then both birds would perform the head-shaking ceremony which is the commonest form of display. They face each other with necks stretched up and head tufts raised; then they shake their heads from side to side, sometimes in unison, pausing only for mock-preening which is itself part of the display.

The sexes are not easy to distinguish by appearance and the fact that both build the nest, both incubate the eggs and both tend the young, makes it no easier to tell them apart. Once, before the eggs were laid, I watched the birds mating, they arrived at the nest together and one immediately jumped up on to it and squatted low with its neck stretched out. The other bird swam up and down facing the nest, hesitated as though not sure of itself, and then jumped up and mounted. After mating both birds indulged in head shaking. Even after this, I could not be absolutely sure that the soliciting bird was the female, since even this role can be reversed with the great crested grebe, when the female will sometimes, possibly very rarely mount the male, a complete reversal of the sexes. After the eggs have hatched the parents carry their chicks about on their backs. This is one of the most attractive things about grebes and I was keen to film it. As incubation starts with the laying of the first egg or soon after, the hatch is staggered, which should have given me greater chance of success. I spent several days in the hide and saw the parents carrying their tiny striped chicks, but each day was duller than the one before and filming in colour was out of the question.

Another curious thing about grebes is that the chicks are given feathers to eat by their parents. It is thought that this may aid digestion of fish and aquatic insects by enabling the bird to make a pellet. The fish bones would then lodge in the pellet and be cast by the bird. Once on the nest and incubating, the grebe was rather a dull subject, but fortunately for me a sedge warbler had his favourite song-post on a twig of willow within a few feet of my hide. One morning I set the camera up with a telephoto lens and waited, a microphone concealed close to the willow. In less than half an hour and in bright sunshine the little warbler returned and I was able to film him in full song, his wings lowered and quivering with ecstasy as he sang. It was from this hide that I filmed a bittern quite by chance; the grebe was on her nest sitting very still, almost asleep. Nothing had happened for more than an hour, when I heard a rustling in the reeds only a few feet away. As I watched, a bittern came out into the open, pausing to stare at the camera before disappearing again with a considerable commotion into the tangle of alder and willow at the water's edge. The young grebes are dependent on their parents for two months or more and, if the brood happens to be a large one of three or four chicks, the adults often divide their responsibility, each taking sole charge of half the brood. This quite often happens when there are only two chicks; each parent will then only look after its own particular youngsters and will have nothing to do with those in the care of its mate. Late-hatched young are still attended by their parents in October or even November, following the adults and keeping up a continuous high-pitched querulous call for food.

As midsummer approaches the marsh flowers are at their best. Sweet gale, marsh orchid and valerian are in blossom, while the tall spiky flowers of the sweet sedge stick up like erect caterpillars from the broad crinkled leaves. When crushed the leaves smell sweet, as the name suggests, something like a freshly cut canary cake. They were the rushes strewn on the floors of churches and houses in medieval times.

Milk parsley is one of the commonest plants and is the only one upon which the caterpillar of the swallowtail butterfly feeds. This large and magnificent insect is still found in the Broads, although it is never numerous. After feeding all summer on the milk parsley, the green and brown-striped caterpillar climbs down to a sheltered position in the vegetation and spins a cocoon firmly attached to a twig or the stem of some plant. Here it pupates, remaining dormant all winter, a shrivelled, hardened green or brown chrysalis. Towards the middle of May or later there is a sudden change; the pupa begins to swell and soften and becomes almost translucent. Soon the yellow and black markings of the butterfly's wings can be seen through the casing and within forty-eight hours the perfect insect will hatch.

The process now becomes one of gradual change, the pupa swelling still more, becoming softer and even more translucent. The dark markings on the abdomen can be seen through the casing, the wings are very visible and the pupa starts to change colour, a green one becoming much darker. The eyes of the butterfly can now be seen and there is a slight movement of the insect within the pupa once in a while. Over the next hour or two the colour of the abdomen seen through the casing may change further to golden, the transverse dark bands disappearing. The slight movements at long intervals continue.

Then suddenly and without warning the front of the case splits open, rather like the nose of a freighter aircraft, and the butterfly struggles to be born. It emerges rapidly and straight away climbs to the tip of a twig to dry its crumpled wings. As it clings there it passes a jet of fluid from its abdomen, the same fluid which it pumps through the veins of its wings as they unfurl in the sun. Within an hour or so the perfect insect in all its splendour of blue and gold is ready to fly away. All the pupæ I have watched and filmed hatched between 11 a.m. and 4 p.m. B.S.T. The most difficult job was to guess just when this was likely to happen, so the camera could be running from the start and miss nothing. There were many false alarms and many butterflies emerged when I was not expecting them; but in the end, after three whole days of concentrated watching and waiting, I managed to film one hatch from beginning to end.

Most birds are very shy when actually building their nests, but house martins are among the easiest to watch. Not only do they allow a reasonably close approach while they are gathering beakfuls of mud with which to build, but their nests are conspicuous and the birds themselves are unafraid of human beings. One spring we had an exceptionally long dry spell and at the beginning of June two pairs of house martins started to build under the eaves of our house. They seemed to make slow progress and it occurred to me that they might be finding difficulty in obtaining mud, so I ran the hose on to a nearby cart track, making several large puddles.

A couple of days later I noticed quite a flock of martins collecting mud. Up to twenty birds would arrive over the area and start pitching in at the puddles in quick succession and then, after a few moments of feverish activity scooping up mud in their bills, all would leave at once. The curious thing was that out of the twenty birds only two pairs were building their nests nearby; the rest were travelling to the nearest houses, almost half a mile away. Despite this all the birds would congregate in the air over the puddles and start pitching in at the same time and leave a few moments later all together. They were most active from noon B.S.T. to about 2.30 p.m. and I was able to film them from a hide built on a farm trailer parked by the puddles.

The following summer five pairs of martins started to build under the eaves of a friend's house facing south. Once again there was a period of intense activity between 11.30 a.m. B.S.T. and 1.30 p.m., after which there was a sharp decline, although odd birds continued building all day. They worked in spells of about twenty minutes, leaving off for half an hour for the mud to dry before beginning again. Three of the nests had only just been started and were like shallow kidney bowls attached to the house. I set up the camera to film them building, only to find them in heavy shadow cast by the eaves of the house. However, a large mirror from a friend's dressing-table solved the problem, for with it we were able to reflect the sunlight right on to the nest. The birds took no notice provided we waited until they had swooped up and alighted at the nest before illuminating it. Both sexes did their share

"Wind in the Reeds." Above: left, bittern in a reed-bed; right, coypu, one of a species which broke bounds and found paradise in Broadland waters. Below, a hide for filming

Limpet exploring her favourite backwater—and demonstrating a typical
otter posture in the clear water of her pool

of the building, often working together, pushing beakfuls of mud on to the rim of the nest and working them in with their open bills. Just as a bricklayer lays one course of bricks at a time, so the birds built up their nest with successive courses of sun-dried pellets of mud.

The reed warbler employed quite a different technique in weaving its cup-shaped nest round three or four stems of reeds. I found the nest soon after it had been started when it was little more than a frail platform slung precariously between three swaying stems. From a hide I was able to watch and film the work in progress. Only the female built, the male singing continuously nearby and even accompanying her to the nest to go on singing while she worked. The female arrived hopping from stem to stem carrying a long piece of grass or reed top in her bill. Once at the nest she quickly settled down in the half-built cup and started weaving one end of her piece of grass into the structure. Working with lightning speed she seized the other end and passed it round the outside of a reed stem; ducking back into the nest, she leaned right out the other side of the reed to reach for the grass with her bill, passing it back round the stem to knot it. The speed of her actions surprised me, punctuated as they were by quick shuffling movements when she would press her breast right down into the cup as if to mould it round her. During a spell of building she arrived with fresh material every three to five minutes. The reed warblers' nest has an exceptionally deep cup to prevent the eggs or chicks falling out when the reeds lean over in a strong wind; yet I have known one of these birds to complete the whole structure in just under forty-eight hours.

Like the coypu, the Canada goose is a newcomer to the Broads, having spread here from privately-owned flocks kept full-winged in various parts of Norfolk. Now they have settled down with the flocks of feral greylags which also breed on some of the Broads. Even that quarrelsome bird, the

Egyptian goose, has wandered from private collections and breeds in a wild state in some areas, often choosing a hollow tree in which to lay its eggs.

The story of the marsh harrier in Norfolk is a sad one, as it no longer breeds in the Broads. Every year one or two birds have appeared in the spring, but no attempt at nesting has been made. This is all the more surprising in that several pairs breed annually on the Walberswick and Minsmere marshes in Suffolk. Both these marshes are strictly preserved, the former privately and the latter by the Royal Society for the Protection of Birds; it is entirely due to this protection that the harriers remain. Hickling Broad is also preserved by the Norfolk Naturalists Trust, but unlike the Suffolk marshes the Broads all have public rights of way and are visited by countless pleasure craft which makes effective control far more difficult. Add to this the fact that not all neighbouring landowners or their keepers are in favour of harriers and one has to seek no further for the reasons for their decline in Norfolk. Fortunately some keepers are more enlightened and not only respect the law but take a genuine interest in birds other than pheasants and partridges.

Some years ago a keeper came to see me in a considerable state of anxiety. He had with him a sack and in it an adult female marsh harrier. He had been trapping rabbits on his beat some distance from the marsh, but by some ill chance the harrier had been caught and one leg had been virtually severed. The man was very upset and brought the bird to me hoping I could do something for it. It was quite obvious that the leg would have to be amputated, so I took it off and dressed the stump. The following day the bird ate a small chicken and within a week was putting the stump to the ground. I kept it for a month to make sure the leg had healed and then released it, but not without misgivings. I couldn't help wondering how it would manage to catch quarry with only one foot and whether it would stand any chance of survival.

Nearly six weeks later a farmer telephoned to ask if I had lost a trained falcon for he knew I kept and flew hawks. I told him that I had not lost one and asked what he had seen. He then described the marsh harrier accurately and added, " the strange thing was I saw it flop down and grab a young bantam chick. It flew up on to a gate with the chick in its foot but seemed unable to balance properly, then it toppled off and flew away." So I knew that so far my one-legged harrier had managed to fend for herself.

Apart from their extremely graceful flight one of the most fascinating things about marsh harriers is the food pass. I have witnessed this a good many times and yet it never fails to intrigue me. While the female is incubating or when the young are small, the male does the hunting and brings the quarry back. On seeing him the female leaves the nest in the reeds and rises in the air to meet him. Then they both fly round, the male well above the female. Suddenly he drops the quarry which she catches in her talons, often turning over on her back in the air, and flies on with it to the nest. I once saw quite a large grass snake brought by a male harrier and passed to his mate; as it fell the snake was twisting and turning in the air. Marsh harriers are difficult to photograph at the nest and easily desert; so I have never attempted to film them there, being content with shots of birds hunting away from the nest.

Another Broadland rarity is the natterjack or running toad, now confined to one or two localities. It is quite easily distinguished from the common toad by the narrow golden line which runs down the centre of its back, and by its legs which are much shorter. So instead of crawling like the common toad, the natterjack runs for a short burst, then stops and runs again and so on. Although chiefly nocturnal, this toad often comes out in daylight after a summer shower to look for worms. The one I filmed belonged to a friend who very kindly loaned it to me, and we became attached to it. During the day it remained asleep buried underneath some loose earth, but in the evening it came out to look for food. Its nightly ration was two medium-sized earthworms or one large one, and even under the glare of powerful lamps it could see a worm two feet away. The moment it spotted its quarry it turned towards it and ran quickly to the attack. When close to the worm it stopped, gazed at it intently and then suddenly reared up on its hind legs and pounced, seizing the worm in its mouth and worrying it like a terrier with a rat. Having grasped the head of the worm, it soon started to swallow it in convulsive mouthfuls, pushing it down with its front feet. The last of the worm gone, it wiped its mouth on the backs of its hands—a most human gesture. Finally the toad worked its meal down into its stomach with a series of convulsive heaves of its body, often accompanied by a most expressive closing of its huge eyes. The natterjack was certainly a gourmet who refused to hurry over his food.

On warm summer evenings the marshland vegetation is alive with the cheeping of bush cheeps. The noise is like the rasping of a cricket and is made by rubbing together the serrated edge of the horny wing covers. The males keep up these stridulations to attract the females which look something like large brown grasshoppers. They clamber about the undergrowth but if disturbed can leap like grasshoppers with the aid of their powerful hind legs. The female has a large sickle-shaped ovipositor at the end of her abdomen and when ready to lay her eggs she descends to the ground and, choosing a suitable spot, thrusts the ovipositor down into the soil whereupon the egg passes down it and is left safely buried. Bush cheeps are well camouflaged and therefore difficult to see in the light of a torch, added to which they leap out of sight if disturbed and so are not very easy to catch, especially as they like to live among brambles and stinging nettles. Oddly enough these insects have a twilight rival and a bird at that, for the continual churring of grasshopper warblers fills the gloaming in many parts of the Broads. These tiny elusive warblers, who love to skulk in the thickest vegetation, are not uncommon in Broadland. Their nest is one of the hardest to find, so well is it hidden deep down in the luxuriant growth of marsh plants.

Perhaps the most difficult British mammal to watch, the otter, is nevertheless still common in the Broads and I have seen several. Although they catch and eat some fish, otters prefer eels and warm-blooded creatures like water voles, moorhens and wild duck. They are intelligent and soon get to know where they are safe and then lose much of their shyness. A bitch otter and her three cubs frequented a mill pool belonging to some friends of ours and could be watched from the bridge almost any evening as they fished in the river below. The otter's method of catching a waterbird is to launch an underwater torpedo attack, approaching the quarry unseen and grabbing it from below. Eels are caught by diving deep and searching the bottom for them. Even in the muddy water of the Broads, the otter can locate his prey by means of his highly sensitive whiskers. They are long and bristly and each is connected at its root to a large nerve area. The result is that any disturbance in the water made by the quarry is instantly picked up by the otter who can continue the chase in the murkiest conditions.

As the days shorten and the leaves start to take on that dull grey-green look which denotes the fading of summer, the marsh falls silent. The reed and sedge warblers are already across the sea, journeying south to warmer climates. The nights are cold now and a chilly mist rises from the surface of the Broad at dawn. The magnificent guelder rose turns blood red in the autumn sun and golden hops overhang the water. Soon the alder carr will echo the harsh chuckle of fieldfares, freshly arrived from the north. With the approach of winter, wildfowl become restless and even the home-bred Canada geese gather in flocks to fly noisily from one Broad to another. The wintering flock of mute swans dotting the open expanse of Hickling Broad grows larger daily as fresh arrivals swell its ranks. They sweep low over the swaying reeds like great white angels out of a churchyard, their pinions humming a mournful tune as, with black paddles down and necks outstretched, they swing round to settle on the water. Once more the boats are laid up for the winter and the holiday-makers have gone leaving the Broads deserted. Only the reed-cutter remains poling his punt homewards in the dusk along the narrow channel from the marsh and its great reed-beds to the cottage in the wood.

After three years of watching, waiting and filming I had shot something over ten thousand feet of colour-film, depicting most of the scenes I have described as well as a good many more. Now the work of making the film really began. Once again Ted Ellis proved invaluable. I had provided him with a list of every shot together with the month in which each was taken, and from this list Ted produced a story. All the film was copied, and the recordings transferred on to sprocketed magnetic track. Everything was ready for the editor to start cutting. I was very lucky in having the services of a young editor called Raoul Sobel who had never cut a natural history film before—this was perhaps a great advantage for he had no preconceived ideas. We worked together in the cutting-room in London for many weeks and I learned a great deal about making films from watching Raoul at work. Eventually the ten thousand feet had been reduced to sixteen hundred, the sequences had been built up and followed the pattern of Ted's story, while two sound tracks of effects—natural history sounds—had to be " laid " and synchronised with the picture. Where there was no natural sound, music had to be used and this is where Raoul came to my rescue, for he knows about music and has a good ear for it and must have listened to hundreds of records in the process of selecting the appropriate piece for each sequence. When he had made his choice we listened to all the recordings together and made the final decision. In the meantime Ted had seen the cutting copy and had written the commentary to fit the picture.

At last the day came when we were ready to record the commentary and " mix " all the tracks so that commentary, music and sound effects would all be on one track synchronised with the picture. I read the commentary in the studio at the film laboratories, watching the cue marks on the picture which was projected on to a screen in front of me. Finally we all went into the dubbing theatre where once again the film was projected on to a screen. This time all five sound tracks, two for music, two for effects, and one for commentary were running together synchronised to the picture. The sound-mixer sat at his desk faced with a row of knobs and, while he watched the cue marks on the film, he faded the various tracks in or out as necessary until all five were amalgamated in one correctly balanced sound track. This is a highly skilled job demanding concentration and a good memory on the part of the mixer.

For a long time I had been wondering what to call the film and finally decided on *Wind in the Reeds*. The title had been superimposed over an attractive shot of reeds swaying in the wind and now the film reached the final stage in its production. The cutting copy was sent to the laboratories and there the original material was cut to match the cutting copy exactly frame by frame. From this original the first " married " print was produced with an optical sound track down one side of the film. *Wind in the Reeds* was ready for its première. After a successful Press preview in London we decided to hold the première at the Royal Festival Hall and to give the proceeds to Cancer Research. *Wind in the Reeds* was supported by two shorter films I had made and the star of one of them, Bokhara, a trained golden eagle, sat on his block at the front of the vast stage, while Bubo my tame eagle owl sat the other side.

I well remember the worries which preceded that April afternoon in 1961. All our family, friends and relations had bought tickets but what of the rest of the three thousand seats? Supposing nobody else turned up, and why should they? I was an unknown quantity and so was the film. It is said that the things you fear most rarely happen and the hall was not empty. To my astonishment it was packed full.

10. On Tour

The following autumn I took *Wind in the Reeds* together with Bokhara and Bubo on a prolonged lecture tour to most of the major cities in Britain, starting with the Colston Hall in Bristol. If the effort involved was arduous the results were well worth it for the appreciation of wildlife shown by the general public. I subsequently showed the film in full on Independent Television and since then it has been seen on television in no less than twenty-two foreign countries; for this purpose the sound track is re-dubbed with commentary in the appropriate language.

Before the tour began we decided to have a trial run, using some of my older films, at the Theatre Royal in Lowestoft. I decided to take Bokhara with me because he never failed to arouse interest. He was still very obedient and well behaved and we thought it would be interesting to fly him across the theatre for the audience to see him on the wing.

For the trial run I stood on the stage with all the lights up, while Pat took him up to the front of the circle and unhooded him. I then asked for the auditorium lights to be put out as I felt that Bokhara would then be able to see only me and there would be less chance of things going wrong. I blew my whistle and held out my hand with a large and tender haunch of hare; Bokhara sat quite still and refused to move. We had all the lights put up and he flew to me without hesitation. We tried him again to make certain it was no fluke, and again he flew.

It now only remained to be seen whether he would do the same when all the seats were occupied. After introducing him and showing the audience how he was hooded and unhooded and why, Pat came up and collected him. Once again she stood at the front of the circle. A great hush fell in the theatre as everyone sat tense and expectant, all heads craning round to look at Bokhara. My heart was thumping like a steam engine. Suppose he refused to fly at all or worse still blundered off and crashed on some balding head? I held out the piece of hare, Pat slipped off his hood, I blew the whistle and called his name. He saw me and bobbed his head then turned to survey the sea of faces below him. I whistled again and he half opened his wings before once more looking round at the people; suddenly he jumped, swooping straight down low over the stalls so that his impetus carried him upwards again to land on my fist. I have never been so pleased to see him.

His next public appearance was at the Royal Festival Hall when he came with Bubo, the eagle owl, for the première of *Wind in the Reeds*.

Both these birds have since travelled thousands of miles on tour with us, living for several days at a time on their perches in the back of a specially fitted Land-Rover. I try to find a quiet place where I can put them out on their blocks for a spell either before or after the day's journey. Sometimes the only place is a hotel garden and the management is usually most co-operative over our somewhat unusual request. I remember the astonished looks on the faces of some elderly ladies drinking their afternoon tea in the lounge of a large provincial hotel when our little procession marched through. It was led by the manager carrying a large bunch of keys for some reason the garden was kept locked); next came two pages each carrying a massive stone-topped block with a steel spike a foot long for pushing into the ground; and behind them followed Pat with Bubo sitting on her fist while I brought up the rear with Bokhara.

It was during my lecture tour that I began to realise just how much Bubo took in despite her inscrutable gaze—she came out of her shell as it were and used to greet me whenever I returned to the Land-Rover after an absence by bobbing her head and walking along her perch towards me, squawking and raising her ear tufts. Her true ears are hidden beneath the plumage on each side of her head and the so-called ear tufts are merely feathers which can be raised or lowered at will, and very expressive they can be.

I made a point of feeding her last thing at night when we had finished the day's journey. We always left home with several dead rats and when these ran out I used to buy rabbit or hare and cut it up into chunks for her.

During the show Bubo used to sit on her block at the front of the stage on one side, while Bokhara sat on his on the other side. They were a tremendous success, especially Bubo who never misbehaved unless occasional bouts of hooting and squawking count as misbehaviour. The audience never thought so and used to love it if she interrupted while I was talking. In some strange unfathomable way Bubo seemed to like being on the stage, so much so that if she could see her block when I was carrying her on, she would jump off my fist and try to fly to it. As soon as I realised this I made use of it and always ensured that her block was on the far side of the stage. When I was certain she had seen it I would let go of the leash and she would fly silently across the stage and land on her block—a manoeuvre which always pleased the audience.

During that particular tour one of the three films I was showing happened to be about the training of Bokhara the eagle for falconry and one sequence towards the end showed him pursuing and catching a wild rabbit. Despite the fact that she was so close to the screen and to one side of it, that sequence never failed to interest Bubo who would watch it intently, bobbing violently and swaying from side to side.

She took absolutely no notice of the other two films, which showed numerous animals and birds, so presumably it was the sight of such a gigantic eagle in flight which excited her. A human observer from her position could hardly distinguish the picture on the screen and if she could see the eagle, it must have seemed to her to have a twelve foot wing span.

Her complete tameness and confidence make Bubo a favourite with children and many times she has sat quietly on my fist while up to a hundred hot little hands have reached up to stroke the feathers on her back.

Most people are genuinely interested in the birds and ask intelligent questions, but there are always the cranks. One old man gave me a long lecture on what the world would be like without " all the eagles, owls, hawks and vultures." The countryside, he assured me, " would be a mass of stinking meat and we should all be overrun with flies." I could think of many reasons for protecting our birds of prey, but this was a new one to me. Usually the cranks are of two kinds, there are those who harangue *me* for being so cruel as to keep two poor birds tied up by their legs, apparently failing to appreciate that both Bubo and Bokhara are so tame they have no desire to escape or I should not be able to fly them loose. Then there are those who condemn all birds of prey because *they* are so cruel, killing and eating other birds. One man even wrote me a long letter explaining how he was sure, given sufficient time, he " could accustom an eagle to thrive on grass and other green vegetables." It was all a matter of progressive education, so he said, a sort of yoga for eagles I suppose.

Then of course one hears some priceless remarks from time to time. A friend came to one of our shows and was sitting in his seat when three old men came in and sat in front of him. Bubo and Bokhara were already on their blocks on the stage. For a time the men talked of this and that and then one suddenly said to the other two, " Is that old owl alive?" " 'Course it isn't," said the second, " it's stuffed." " No, it

isn't," said the third, " 'cause I've just seen the beggar move."
" Oh, I know," replied the second, " but that's all done by
the 'lectric."

The interesting thing is that one never knows quite what
will happen next. I was once bringing Bokhara back from a
television programme in the West of England; he was sitting
on his perch in the rear of the shooting brake, and was therefore rather visible to passers by. Driving through Oxford
I happened to notice a large and expensive motor car behind
me with an elderly woman at the wheel. At the next traffic
lights, which were red, she suddenly leapt out of her car and
ran towards my door; fearing the worst I immediately put my
window up, the lights turned amber and I quickly let in the
clutch and shot away. Unfortunately I was stopped almost at
once by another lot of lights also at red. Again the big car
pulled up behind and the woman leapt out and ran up; there
was nothing for it, I should have to listen. To my relief she
was not insane, but simply fascinated by the sight of a golden
eagle riding in the car and wanted to know if she could ever
see him fly. I invited her to Norfolk, and a few days later she
appeared at our house.

It is said that eagles usually become more aggressive and
difficult to handle as they get older, and I think there may be
something in this. Bokhara at five is certainly far more likely
to strike out at strangers than he used to be and has lately
taken to grabbing at my legs when I set him down on his
block. Nevertheless he was always perfectly behaved on tour
with one exception. The stage at Birmingham was old-
fashioned, large and very high, with a sheer drop of six feet or
more to the stalls. Before the show I put Bokhara on his block
at one end and left Bubo's block ready for her at the other.
When I came on she flew to it as usual, and Bokhara was sitting
quietly with his hood on, he sometimes pulls it off by getting

a talon underneath the back of it and wrenching it forwards over his head. Even so I never worry, as he just sits unhooded until I have an opportunity to pick him up and put it back on again.

During the films, which have their own sound tracks, I always go to my dressing-room back-stage until it is time to introduce the next item. That night we were sitting having a quiet drink with a friend during the second film when there was the sound of running feet in the passage outside. A stage hand burst in to announce that the eagle was hanging itself. Awful visions went through my mind as I raced to the wings. The theatre was in darkness, the only illumination being the reflection from the screen. I could just see that Bokhara's leash led from his block to the edge of the stage over which it disappeared. I went over as quietly as I could and hauled Bokhara up feet first like a fish dangling on a line. Down below in the inky darkness of the stalls people were shuffling and muttering. He was still hooded and quite unperturbed, and had apparently jumped off his block and walked about. Being hooded he had no idea where he was and had walked straight over the edge of the stage.

During the interval one or two people tried to make out that I had been very cruel and that the eagle had been close to death. They refused to accept the fact that, had he felt so inclined, Bokhara could easily have climbed back for himself and doubtless would have done so had I not arrived within seconds. As it was it taught me to make sure in future that his leash would not reach the edge of the stage. Trained birds of prey are often tied to a screen-perch in their mews at night, this is a padded perch from the underneath of which hangs a sheet of thick canvas or hessian well weighted at the bottom to keep it taut. Should a bird jump off, it can only hang by the length of its jesses—a matter of inches—and it can very easily turn round and flutter up the canvas to regain its perch. A falcon will perform the whole movement so quickly that it is back almost before it is down, but eagles are much slower and sometimes hang for several minutes before bothering to clamber back.

The strangest assignment which Bokhara and I ever undertook together was to appear in the initial shooting of *Cleopatra*, or the film that never was, at Pinewood Studios. As is often the case, this occurred quite by chance, the film company happened to need a tame golden eagle, its handler to act the part of Cæsar's standard bearer. Tame eagles are not found very easily and after exhaustive inquiries they heard of Bokhara. The fees arranged by my agent seemed attractive and so, although it was a job for which I had no enthusiasm, I agreed to go.

The first thing I discovered about feature filming was that everyone is expected to start horribly early in the morning. My instructions were to be on the set with the eagle by 8 a.m. For a production of this size I expected things to be done on a grand scale, but I was not quite prepared for the vast sets which had been built inside and out to represent Cleopatra's palace in Alexandria. One of the indoor stages contained a replica of the approach to the palace with a raised roadway winding past a life-size sphinx which must have stood over twenty feet high at the shoulder and three times as long. Behind it stretched the roof tops of Alexandria against a wonderful deep blue sky. Another even larger stage contained the throne-room with magnificent fluted pillars of shining marble rising thirty feet into the air and approached by marble steps wide enough for ten men to march abreast and longer than a cricket pitch.

The construction of the marble interested me; it was most realistic, but inspection behind the scenes showed that it was plaster of some kind smoothed over a framework of slats and wire. The outside plots covered several acres and were dominated by a model of Alexandria harbour with water ten feet deep and of dazzling Mediterranean blue. Enormous buildings larger than St. Martin's in the Fields towered sixty feet to the sky with flights of stone steps and lofty colonnades, life-size ships of war and merchant vessels lay at anchor in the harbour.

Tremendous trouble had been taken to see that every detail of furniture, architecture and dress was a faithful reproduction of the period. Among the conglomeration of buildings were offices where qualified architects redesigned in plaster and plywood the treasures of old Alexandria. The whole huge area was a scene of bustling activity and noise; several thousand carpenters, plasterers, painters and electricians were busy erecting scaffolding or taking it down, hammering, sawing and painting, so that slowly but surely the majesty of ancient Egypt rose again in all its splendour under the cold grey autumn sky.

When I first arrived I was informed by a little man in charge of the " animal department " that a cage had been prepared for Bokhara. I hastily explained that he had never been in a cage in his life and all I needed was a place where he could sit on his block in safety when the weather was fine; for the rest of the time he would remain on his perch in my Land-Rover. After some deliberation I was told to go to the animal enclosure, where I discovered that two tame lions, a tame leopard and a number of reptiles were already in residence. The two lion handlers were most helpful and soon had a place cleared for Bokhara within the chain-link compound where he would be quite safe.

Feeding Bokhara at Pinewood presented no difficulty as the two lions and the leopard were given prodigious quantities of raw beef which the handlers collected from the stores every day, and one of them always kept a choice piece of lean meat back for Bokhara. Of the two lions, one was a good deal more docile than the other and it was this one which they decided to have loose on the set for a certain scene. It would

Fennec, five years old and still as docile as the family cat

Rollo and his mate play in the snow

Badgers are "one man" animals. Grumpy still plays with me although
she is five years old

The bedroom window of the underground sett

have to lie by Cleopatra's throne and get up and follow her as she walked off, the handler standing in the wings calling it at the right moment. All this had to be rehearsed and one day I was asked if I would mind giving a helping hand during the lunch break. I readily agreed and arrived at the animal compound just in time to see the lion being loaded into a chain-link travelling crate which stood on a flat trolley.

It was being a little difficult and the usual crowd of curious spectators, mostly props men, had collected to watch. Lions urinate like tom cats, lifting their tails and sending a powerful jet straight out backwards, and this one eventually rushed into the travelling cage, swung round and sent a gush of evil-smelling liquid straight through the netting on to one of the spectators. Naturally everyone roared with laughter, especially the man's mate who stood next to him doubled up with mirth. At that moment the lion swung its rear and let go another gush which, to the accompaniment of fresh roars of laughter, went straight down the mate's neck.

On arrival at the set where the rehearsal was to take place, the trolley was pushed up to the enormous sliding doors which were parted just wide enough to admit the side of the travelling cage. Four of us went inside, watched by the usual mob which gathers on those sort of occasions. They were all craning their heads through a narrow gap between one of the doors and the end of the trolley.

The handler opened the cage and, after some hesitation, the lion jumped down on to the floor; whereupon the man took hold of the chain around the animal's neck and half-led, half-heaved it up the long flight of shallow steps. Once on the stage proper he made the lion lie down beside the throne. I was given a sheet of hardboard six feet by four and told to stand at the top of the steps; should the lion try to go back down them I was to stand in its way, " Then just shake the sheet of hardboard so that it makes as much noise as possible," they said. The other two guarded the remaining exits in a similar manner. The handler walked across the stage and called the lion, slapping his thigh; the great beast growled and refused to budge. He went back and kicked its backside; it hardly bothered to look up. After a lot of cajoling, he managed to get it up; he called again and walked off; the lion padded slowly after him. Taken back to the throne again to repeat the movement, it was a little better this time, but still rather lazy. At the third attempt the lion refused to obey and walked slowly round the set. As it advanced towards one of the exits I noticed that the man who had been guarding it had disappeared.

The handler had also noticed this and ran across to head the beast off; slapping its rear end, he tried to coax it back towards the throne. But the lion had other ideas. It had plainly done all the rehearsing it was going to do for that day and padded purposefully towards the top of the steps where I stood behind my sheet of hardboard.

Three feet from me it stopped to survey the situation. It looked enormous. I retreated just one step down and it promptly looked bigger still. Then it opened its jaws and emitted a fearful roar from the depths of its belly. Try as I would I could not shake that piece of hardboard; not a muscle in my body would move. I just stood frozen to the spot as immobile as one of the great stone pillars. The lion had made up its mind. Walking casually past me, it bounded down the steps and jumped back into its travelling cage where it promply flopped down to sleep.

In the early stages of the film there were about a hundred extras taking the part of Roman cavalry; later the number increased to several times that figure. I had to wear the same uniform, so joined the crowd in the props department to be fitted out. It was an enormous warehouse with a long counter round three sides and the central area packed full of wooden boxes of equipment, stacks of shields, helmets and swords. The rows and rows of garments hanging from racks down the middle would have stocked Peter Robinson's several times over. Apart from the fact that the boots hurt my feet when I walked and rubbed sores which I tried to pad with cotton-wool, the uniform was reasonably comfortable. It consisted of plum-coloured tunic and tight-fitting breeches, both made of cotton jersey, calf-length lace-up leather boots, stout leather jerkin, a leather belt and scabbard containing a short sword, and leather gauntlets studded with brass. A loose cape of the same plum colour hanging from the shoulders and a rubber helmet painted to look like bronze, enclosing one's head except for one's face and lacing across the throat, completed the outfit.

When the extras marched off somewhere I was left standing about holding Bokhara. His seven pounds balancing on my fist grew steadily heavier as time passed and so I walked up to the assistant director and asked what he wanted me to do. He looked me over, then the eagle. Somebody asked if it really was a golden eagle because it did not seem golden enough. Perhaps they could spray it to improve its colour? His hood, it seemed, was not the sort of hood a Roman eagle would have worn; could they get the props department to make another in the shape of a Roman helmet? Patiently I explained that making an eagle's hood to fit took a great deal of practice and knowledge which nobody in their props department would be likely to possess. So we compromised and in the end they were content only to paint his hood golden and add some leather trimmings to make it look more Roman.

My position as eagle handler-cum-standard bearer was rather unusual, so I was regarded as a specialist. This had several advantages, not least of which was that I did not have to arrive quite so early in the mornings. Bokhara only took part in scenes in which Cæsar himself appeared and my job was merely to march close behind Peter Finch who was playing the lead at the time.

All the extras appearing in Cæsar's army had been picked

for height, most of them being about six feet tall, and all the helmets must have been made for men of similar stature. Mine was far too big for me and I felt more like a man in a space suit than a Roman cavalryman. I think I must have looked a little odd. Once, when I was trying to push my way through a crowd of extras to reach my place with Bokhara, one of the men shouted, " Out of the way, chaps, here comes Noddy with that bloody eagle again!"

During filming most of the time is spent standing about, or sitting, if you are lucky enough to find anywhere to sit, waiting for something to happen. As virtually every shot had to be relit, delays were frequent and prolonged while the one enormous camera (Todd AO) was set up and the lighting rearranged and tested. In the middle of the second morning the director himself arrived on the set and we were told that shooting would shortly begin. Most of us were sitting on some benches behind the scenes when the loudspeakers announced that the director would like all artists, technicians and staff to assemble on stage where he wished to talk to them. Finally the crowd assembled and the great man delivered his speech about the privilege of directing one of the greatest epics the world had ever seen, the need for team spirit, etc. etc.

Not wishing to subject Bokhara to the crush outside, I remained sitting behind the scenes. On other benches two Nubian slaves lay prostrate on their backs fast asleep. The director's voice droned on, punctuated by stentorian snores from the sleeping slaves. I came to feel rather sorry for the Nubians, if indeed they were Nubian. They were of magnificent physique, tall and well-proportioned. They always looked rather cold and out of place and I felt that, like Bokhara, they were being subjected to a certain loss of dignity in those phoney tinsel surroundings. My sympathy was probably misplaced, for they seemed entirely relaxed and would casually blow their noses by placing an index finger against one nostril while blowing hard down the other—a signal for two little men with mops to come running on to the set to polish up the marble floor.

Who could have foreseen that all the film shot at Pinewood in the days that followed would be scrapped or that the vast expenditure of time and money on the fantastic sets would be utterly wasted?

11. Limpet the Otter

Suddenly it was there, a flattened brown head, broad muzzle and two beady eyes looking at me from the depths of the tree-lined pool. Just as suddenly it sank from view, leaving scarcely a ripple. Limpet my tame otter was enjoying an afternoon out, swimming in a flooded gravel pit.

I used to enjoy those summer days sitting quietly on the bank watching her antics in the water. Wild otters are usually extremely difficult to watch, for not only are they cunning and secretive, but for the most part they are creatures of the darkness, being most active in the hours before midnight and sometimes around dawn. Comparatively little is known of the lives of otters in the wild, and most of the information available has been gained from the study of their droppings or spraints and from observations made over the years by fishermen and followers of otter-hounds.

More recently an enthusiastic band of naturalists in the west country carried out a survey of the numbers and movements of their local otters aided by an electrical device, which when placed near a holt recorded the time at which the otter passed that way and touched the wire trip. Despite all this work, nobody really knows the gestation period of the British otter; how long the cubs stay with their mother; what happens to them when they finally leave her; what, if any, contact the dog otter has with his family; whether each otter has an individual territory and, if so, its size, and so on. The otter in the wild is an enigma.

Apart from one or two records in the latter part of the last century, otters have not, so far as I know, been bred in captivity in this country.[1] The Canadian species, *Lutra canadensis*, is, however, bred regularly by at least two naturalists on the other side of the Atlantic. Both these breeders have written to me and have given me much useful advice and information. One of them, Mr. Art Hoffman of Kansas City, has sent me several otters, including Limpet, the first otter I ever kept.

The Canadian otter is very closely related to our native species and, having kept both side by side, I have had ample opportunity to compare them. On the whole Canadian otters are larger and bulkier with broader and deeper heads and thicker rudders. Their coats are inclined to be darker and they have a characteristic pale band across the top of their muzzles. Rolo, my Canadian dog otter, has pale-grey markings each side of his muzzle rather like an old Labrador dog; but, as I do not know when he was born, perhaps he is just getting grey with age. He weighs twenty-five pounds and so is a good deal heavier than the average British otter and certainly far bigger than any I have kept.

It is curious that most authorities put the gestation period of the British otter at about sixty-three days, though they have very little evidence to support this figure. Both Liers and Hoffman, who breed the Canadian otter, have told me independently that their captive otters have a gestation period varying between nine and twelve months owing to the phenomenon of delayed implantation of the fœtus. I shall be surprised if so close a relative as our British otter turns out to have such a vastly different period of gestation. Nevertheless, it does appear to have different breeding habits. Newly born otter cubs have been found in every month of the year in this country, whereas my American friends tell me their otter cubs are usually born in the late winter or spring.

[1] One of my Canadian otters gave birth to three cubs in March 1965 and reared them all successfully up to the time of going to press.

Some five years ago I was sent a young pair of otters from Bulgaria. Now the European otter is supposed to be the same animal as the British, but these two were much paler than any I have seen in this country. Whereas ours are the colour of plain chocolate, the Bulgarians were the colour of milk chocolate. They were not very large, the male weighing 15 lb. and the female 12½ lb., but their age was unknown.

As the result of the Ministry of Agriculture's campaign to exterminate the coypu, many hundreds of traps have been set along the waterways of East Anglia. Basically these traps are elongated wire cages and, when an animal enters and puts its feet on a treadle platform, the spring-loaded door at the end claps shut. The traps are set in well-used coypu runs made where the animals are in the habit of leaving the water to graze or to reach cover where they can lie up. No attempt is made to camouflage the cages and although they may sometimes be baited with carrots or sugar beet, quite often no bait is used at all and yet the coypu will still blunder into them. On two occasions I have been brought bitch otters caught on the River Wensum in these traps. It is difficult to understand why such an intelligent and shy animal should enter such an obvious cage. I can only think they go in out of curiosity.

The first bitch was brought to me in mid-July in lovely condition, but unfortunately the shock of capture proved too great and she gave birth to one still-born cub four nights later, the foetus being found floating in the pool. Despite veterinary attention and penicillin, pituitary extract and vitamin A, she died a week later. The next female otter arrived in mid-September and she soon settled down and started to eat well.

The following winter a largish dog otter was caught in the peat store of the Norfolk School of Agriculture not far from the Wensum. A student saw the animal and chased it into a poultry crate. He then brought it to me in perfect condition and we released it into the pen with the wild-caught female. They soon settled down together and I hope they may eventually breed. Nobody seems to know why a wild otter should leave the river and wander a mile or two into a peat store. But the weather was unduly severe at the time with rivers and ponds frozen over and the country-side snow-bound, so it is possible that the animal was hungry and attracted there by the smell of chickens.

Much has been written about the attractions of tame otters and perhaps I have been unlucky in never having had a really tame one, if by that one means a creature that can be picked up and fondled. Limpet was certainly tame in that she would feed from my hand, follow me about and allow me to stroke her. She would certainly not permit anybody to pick her up and was always slightly aloof. I gained the impression that she tolerated rather than liked human beings. The same could be said of all three of my tame Canadian otters.

Anyone who is thinking of keeping an otter as a pet should consider the facts. In the first place only really young cubs are likely to become docile enough to handle, and they are hard to come by and even harder to rear. Otters are extremely active and intelligent animals who, by their nature, are given to roaming over large areas. If they are to be kept in captivity they must either have really large enclosures with adequate water in which to swim and play, or else they must be given some liberty. Those that try the latter course nearly always lose their pet, either by accident or because it fails to return. In addition, otters are not easy to keep alive in captivity for any great length of time; in this respect they rather resemble their relative the stoat—indeed otters are not unlike huge aquatic stoats in many of their ways.

When Limpet was sent over from the States, her breeder supplied me with the food formula he always used. It consisted of raw minced meat, hound meal, a little bran and rolled oats, some bone meal, yeast, a raw egg, cod-liver oil, milk and grated carrot. I have used it ever since and my otters have never failed to thrive on it. As a luxury now and then I give them an eel or a dead day-old chick. I think that one of the reasons for the short life-span of otters in most zoos is the unsuitable diet of raw white fish.

I learned much of the habits of otters from watching Limpet, especially when I used to take her to the gravel pits and study her in comparative freedom. She never liked to stay too long in the water and after twenty minutes or half an hour she would climb out and rub herself dry by lying on the ground and pushing herself along with her hind feet, turning first on one side then on the other. Then she dried her neck and chin by sweeping her head from side to side on the earth and completed her toilet by carefully nibbling and grooming her coat. One of her favourite attitudes was to lie on her back with all four feet in the air wriggling with pleasure and then, without moving her hind quarters, bend forward in a complete circle to nibble and groom the soft fur on her tummy. After a spell on dry land, lying curled up either in the sun or hidden among reeds and sedge, she would get up and explore along the water's edge, eating all sorts of small creatures. Frogs were a great delicacy which she ate by holding them in her front paws and chewing them in the side of her mouth.

Back in the water she swam powerfully, propelled by her webbed hind feet and using her rudder to turn quickly. She had four distinctly different dives and each had its purpose. The most usual was a shallow dive. She would swim across the pool on the surface with only her head showing and leaving a V-shaped wake; then suddenly she would slip her head under the water and disappear, swimming on unseen save for the chain of tell-tale bubbles rising to the surface.

When hunting eels, one of her favourite pastimes, her approach was quite different. To reach the bottom in twenty feet of water she had to dive deep, and this was when she employed the " rolling over " dive. It was very porpoise-like as she rolled over and down in one graceful curve, her rudder following her body in a perfect arc. An almost stationary group of bubbles would rise to the surface from these deep-hunting activities. I could imagine her down there in the murky twilight nosing about amongst the stones and mud, her sensitive whiskers responding to every movement of her slippery quarry, so that even if she could not see it, she could sense its whereabouts. Having captured an eel she broke surface and swam for the shore, with it in her mouth, method-ically chewing as she swam and always starting at the head end. Having climbed out on to a patch of grass between the sedges she continued her meal, holding the eel between her front paws and chewing it in the side of the mouth, reminding me of a child eating a stick of rock, and making a rather similar crunching noise. The eel gone, she would go through the elaborate ritual of rubbing herself dry and grooming her fur.

If strangers appeared when she was in the water, or if I did something which she suspected, she would adopt the " I'm watching you " position from the centre of the lake. There she would remain motionless, upright in the water with her head and neck well above the surface as if to get a better view. From this position she would sink silently straight down, leaving scarcely a ripple to show where she had been. The fourth type of dive was only used when something frightened her badly. Then she crash-dived with a mighty splash.

One afternoon I had been lazing on the grass beside the pool watching Limpet, when the activities of a pair of reed warblers drew my attention. They were nesting in a very small patch of reeds no more than half a dozen yards long by two yards deep and I was just able to see the female as she built her nest. I had a special interest in these birds since over the years I had watched them colonise this particular gravel pit. No gravel had been extracted for ages and vegetation, especi-ally willows, sedge and alder had covered all the old scars, so that it appeared to be a natural lake. But the reeds had taken longer to become established and had started with a patch, appearing in a shallow working adjoining the main pit.

The following spring the first pair of reed warblers arrived and took up their territory in this still small area. Five years later, little pockets of phragmites had sprung up in the odd corners and shallow bays all round the main pit and no fewer than five pairs of reed warblers were breeding. A sixth cock bird sang incessantly all the summer in a new clump of reeds scarcely the area of a billiard table, but he never succeeded in attracting a mate.

When at length I looked for Limpet, there was no sign of her. The surface of the lake was still and she had vanished. To begin with I was not worried as she often hid underneath a clump of sedge overhanging the water's edge or she might well be curled up asleep amongst the tangle of alder and willow thicket. I called her, but nothing happened. Then I began to worry and started to search along the shore where I had last seen her. There was no trace of her. I ran to the top of a huge pile of gravel, now overgrown with thistles and grass, from here I could see in every direction; but there was still no sign of Limpet.

As I returned to the water's edge I happened to glance back at the little patch of reeds where the reed warblers were building. A moorhen skittered out from their shelter and settled on the water thirty yards away. There was something about the bird which made me watch it. Clearly it was uneasy for it swam to and fro constantly dipping its bill in the water as though it could not quite make up its mind whether it wanted to drink or not. Without warning there was a commotion right beside the moorhen as a flat brown head rose from the depths and made a lunge at the bird. Before it could lift itself into the air, Limpet had grabbed it by the tip of one wing. The moorhen retaliated by pecking hard at the otter's nose. This was too much for Limpet who let go and submerged again; but before the moorhen had gathered its senses she returned to the attack, and this time she succeeded in seizing the unfortunate bird in her mouth. She swam for the nearest cover carrying it as a Labrador retrieves a duck; the two of them disappeared amongst the sedges and I ran round to look for them. As I approached the spot I was astonished to see a moorhen scurry out and take flight across the water. There was Limpet rubbing herself dry in the grass while her victim flew off apparently none the worse. I can only imagine that her attack was in play and not with intent to kill.

It may be wondered how I could recapture Limpet after one of these outings and transport her back home. That was usually much easier than it might seem. In her pen she had a wooden sleeping-box to which she was very attached and in which I put her dish of food. She was always transported in this box and, having let her out, I used to put it down by the water's edge with the door open. When the time came to go home, I would put an eel or some food just inside the entrance and Limpet usually went in without any trouble.

One evening she decided to play me up and every time I approached her she slipped out and dived into the water. It took me half an hour to coax her in again when exactly the same thing happened. The light began to fade and I was getting desperate; then I remembered that there was some string in the car. I ran back and collected it and soon had one end securely attached to the door of the box. Threading the other end through the staple on the side I hid in the sedge and waited. Limpet emerged from the water and walked over to the entrance; there she sniffed the piece of eel and finally went in to get it. With a feeling of relief I gave a mighty heave on the string and the door slammed shut. But I pulled so hard that the string snapped and Limpet, feeling herself trapped, barged the door open and crash-dived into the water. I re-set the trap and this time put a whole eel well inside, rubbing it along the floor from the doorway to lay a scent trail. Having once failed to catch an animal in a certain way, it is very difficult to succeed a second time, for unlike us they rarely make the same mistake twice. In the wild the penalty of such foolishness is often death.

It was pitch dark when, about two hours later, Limpet cautiously left the water and approached her box. I could just discern her as she stood close to the doorway sniffing, and I could plainly hear her snorting with suspicion. When curious or suspicious, otters have a habit of exhaling sharply, making a characteristic noise rather like someone puffing out of the side of their mouth. At last she went in and this time I gave a steady heave on the string and held on to make sure she did not barge the door open again. Still keeping a steady pull on the string, I walked up and slid the bolt across—Her ladyship was safely recaptured.

Limpet remained with me for just over a year and I lost her in a rather stupid way. Her pen was an exact replica of the ones used so successfully by her American breeder. It was roughly thirty feet long and half as wide; the floor was constructed of large stones laid to a depth of a foot, with several inches of sand on top. A concrete pool three feet deep and nine feet across was built towards one end, and the whole pen was surrounded by a steel frame to support the galvanised wire-netting which also formed the roof. Otters do not dig very much and the sand and stone foundation, being free-draining, keeps the pen dry, Limpet's wooden sleeping-box stood at the back. I had been warned that otters had exceptionally powerful jaws and that one must use heavy-gauge netting to be sure of keeping them in, so the pen was surrounded with seventeen-gauge wire-netting of one and a quarter inch mesh.

For months all was well. In August we took our children down to Sussex to stay with my mother and had only been there a couple of days when there was a telephone call early one morning. It was our foreman, to say that when he came to work he noticed a large round hole in the netting covering Limpet's door. He had gone inside and looked in her box, but she had disappeared. After searching the nearby hedgerows for any sign of her, he had returned and put a dish of fresh food in the pen leaving the door open in the hope that she might return.

As soon as we got home I reinforced her old pen and the one next to it with chain-link fencing—a classic example of shutting the stable door after the horse has gone. But I felt I had to do something and in any case I was determined to go on keeping otters.

About a fortnight after Limpet had gone the otter hounds arrived in our area and were due to meet the following day at Lyng bridge on the River Wensum, scarcely a mile away. I felt certain that Limpet was clever enough to find her way to the river, especially as it was in the general direction of the gravel pits which we had often visited. Furthermore, I knew she would not understand the danger she would be in should the hunt find her, for she had always been quite friendly with our dogs. The thought of her turning to play with hounds, only to be done to death, haunted me.

The next morning I went to the meet and explained what had happened to the Master. He asked if I would recognise my otter and what I thought she would do. He was extremely helpful and promised to do his best to stop the hounds the moment I gave the word. When they set off they started to draw up river towards the gravel pits, the hounds were huge and powerful animals; they needed to be since they spent most of their time swimming, usually (it seemed) against the current. I was told that most of them were old fox-hounds chosen for their size and stamina; they had a wonderful deep ringing cry when they started to hunt.

There were many coypu about and hounds were for ever chasing them instead of looking for otters. Most of the time it was difficult to tell what they were hunting as the river was deep and muddy and the quarry could keep out of sight fairly easily. I hoped that if they came across Limpet, she would show herself. Early in the afternoon they reached a place where the river widens and flows either side of a tree-covered island. It looked just the place for an otter.

Hounds were spread out on either bank, some of them splashing along in the river. The followers too had divided so that some were each side of the stream. All at once something shot out from under the left bank and dived, the nearest hound gave tongue, and within a few moments the whole pack had rallied and was swimming in a straggling line for the island, their heads held high and baying as they swam.

Upon reaching the island the pack surged ashore and raced into the middle where they quickly killed their quarry. All that could be seen was a circle of hounds, heads to the centre and waving sterns on the perimeter. The huntsman, a young man called Rodney, gave a toot on his horn and called to them but with no effect. Taking off his coat and dropping his whip he waded into the water and struck out in his shirt sleeves for the island. The followers lined either bank gossiping. They were an odd assortment of young and old; some in hunt dress, blue jackets and knickerbockers with deerstalkers, were leaning on tall ash staffs; others displayed a remarkable diversity of muftie.

The huntsman, still wearing his hunting cap, was swimming slowly but surely for the island. A heavily built man with a beard was announcing in a loud voice that the hounds had killed another coypu. Now Rodney was on the island and wading amongst his hounds. Retrieving the pelt of a large coypu, he called his pack together and, surrounded by them, started the long swim back, carrying the pelt in his mouth.

Allowing for the island, the river here is almost a hundred yards across and he was making for the far bank. When he still had a dozen yards to go, I noticed that he was no longer making any headway and indeed seemed to be slowly sinking. At that moment a hound appeared to be in difficulties and in its fright endeavoured to put its front feet on Rodney's shoulders, pushing him under. I realised they were both caught in the weeds. Rodney reappeared for a moment, but he was no longer swimming, his bare arms flailed the air wildly. Nobody moved, so I shouted across the water that I thought he was drowning. People looked at me in horror as though I had spat in a first-class railway compartment.

By now Rodney had gone under and the people his side of the river realised the situation. Once more his pale hands groped despairingly from the dark water as he finally went down. A woman in her sixties, a regular follower, leapt into the water and grabbed him before she too was entangled in the weeds. Others jumped in and soon a human chain was formed. At that moment there was a heavy thud on our bank, I looked round to see Arthur, the whipper-in, flat on his back, in a faint: apparently he and Rodney had been brought up together.

A moment later Rodney had been hauled to the bank and was lying on the ground, his lungs emptying of water. Somebody produced a flask of cherry brandy and put it to his lips. After ten minutes or so he got to his knees and finally staggered to his feet. A woman with a loud voice shouted, " It's all right, Arthur, you can get up now; Rodney is all right." As if recalled from the dead Arthur stirred and sat up. Within a few minutes a very wet Rodney once more called his hounds and the hunt moved on.

The river here meanders through low-lying water meadows intersected by narrow ditches. Successive dredging operations have left the silt piled on either bank, resulting in a luxuriant growth of thistles, nettles and willow herb. There is no tow-path and fallen willows and rough spinneys of alder and thorn clutter the bank. Hounds worked slowly upstream, leaving the gravel pits which Limpet knew so well on their right, sometimes they followed one of the ditches leading away from the river but without success. As the afternoon wore on, it began to look as though no otters were to be found on this stretch of the river. Two or three hounds were splashing about in a small ditch which divided two meadows, when suddenly an otter dashed out of a clump of thistles and dived into the river.

I happened to be standing less than ten paces away and knew at once that it was not Limpet, this otter was too small and pale. Hounds rushed into the water in full cry, swimming back down the river; the followers ran along either bank leaving one or two elderly members of the field leaning on their staffs and gazing down into the water. There they remained quite still, watching, reminding me of herons waiting for a fish. The pack left the river and hunted through a rough alder spinney, then they seemed baffled and fanned out on the meadow beyond. The huntsman called them and led them back to the river, casting on downstream. Suddenly one of the silent watchers upstream caught sight of the otter as it dived under the opposite bank leaving a tell-tale line of bubbles. He holloa'd and the huntsman ran back with his hounds. So the hunt went on; twice the otter took to the land, but it was always forced to return to the river after a few hundred yards. Several times hounds were at fault and it looked as though their quarry would slip away, but somebody always spotted either the otter's head as it came up for air or the trail of bubbles as it dived.

After more than an hour it became obvious that it was beginning to tire. Its dives were of shorter duration, it was forced to surface for air more frequently, and it was only swimming from one bank to another downstream in an attempt to find safety. Once it took refuge under the roots of a fallen tree but was dislodged by several men poking about and rattling their sticks under the straggling limbs. Finally in desperation, half-drowned and exhausted, the poor creature dragged its sodden body ashore. Twenty yards out in the meadow it met its end—a young bitch otter weighing fourteen pounds.

To me it was all rather pointless, the otter was so much more beautiful and interesting alive. While I agree that traps are even more cruel than hunting, I can see no excuse for wanting to kill otters at all. They are enchanting creatures who by their specialised requirements of food, habitat and living space are never likely to become numerous. Furthermore any damage they do to fishing interests has always been exaggerated and in any event would never be a thousandth part of the destruction caused by pollution, detergents and chemical insecticides. Add the fact that nobody has yet proved that otters do more harm than good, bearing in mind the large numbers of eels and small rodents they kill, the more logical course would be to give them total protection.

From that day to this I have had no clue as to Limpet's whereabouts. If she had been caught or killed locally, I think I should have heard as so many neighbours and friends knew her. Sometimes when I lie in bed on a summer's night with the moon up and my windows open, I fancy I hear her far-off whistle down by the river, and in my mind I see her flat head rise from the depths of the gravel pit and swim away, the ripples shimmering in the moonlight to mark her going.

12. *Foxes and Badgers*

Hunting is a sport which always arouses strong feelings and although I personally can find no possible excuse for hunting otters, there may be practical reasons for accepting fox-hunting. Of course hunting is cruel, but of all the methods of killing foxes, I firmly believe that hunting them is less cruel than most. It is certainly less cruel than shooting, where many foxes are wounded and die a slow and agonising death, and it is far less cruel than poison and trap. Nearly all killing is cruel, but wild creatures know neither sentiment nor humanity, these are virtues which only man is privileged to understand, and how often he abuses them.

I admire the fox, I think it is one of the most beautiful, graceful and intelligent creatures we have, and that it should be allowed to live in peace. But unfortunately, man's greed and economics have to be reckoned with. Foxes do on occasion attack and kill poultry and devour sitting game birds, so that a large section of the community would like to wipe them out. Now the easiest time to kill foxes by gun, trap, gas or poison is during the breeding season when the vixen is hard put to find food for her cubs; that there is a truce during this time of the year is due entirely to the influence of the hunt. Abolish hunting and the truce will be over whatever the law may say—foxes would soon be wiped out as a native species. Although it is some years since I gave up hunting, I hope, for the sake of the fox, that the sport will continue.

Shooting men on the whole dislike foxes for fear they

will kill some of their precious pheasants. It so happened that seven years ago the keepers on a large Norfolk estate caught a vixen in a gin trap in May. The estate was well outside country visited by the foxhounds so they had no qualms, despite the fact they knew she had a litter of cubs dependent on her for food.

The night the vixen was caught, she succeeded, in her frantic efforts to free herself, in pulling up the peg which anchored the trap. She crawled back to her earth dragging the gin whose steel teeth had clamped firmly on to one hind leg. This much the keepers knew by following the trail of the dragging trap with its splashes of blood from the mutilated leg. They naturally assumed that the cubs would starve to death and were surprised some days later to find signs of life within the earth; they decided to dig them out and kill them with the assistance of a local rat-catcher. When they reached the end of the burrow they found four cubs in fair condition three of which they killed with their spades, the fourth was larger than the others and they put it alive into a sack. Also in the earth was the vixen's body or what remained of it, for the starving cubs had stripped it of every vestige of flesh except for the leg held in the jaws of the trap.

The surviving cub eventually came into my hands, we called him Fennec because at that age his ears were so large he looked almost like a Fennec Fox from North Africa. He still lives here sharing a large pen with a vixen from Northumberland, and despite his age he is as tame as he was as a cub. I can go into the pen at any time, walk straight up to him and pick him up like a cat. He knows his name, will come when called, and is a magnificent specimen standing taller than many wild foxes.

We have also reared a number of other cubs which have been brought to us from time to time; two of them, Topsy and Loopy, still live with us, sharing a large open-topped enclosure. They are both extremely tame and always pleased to see us, rushing up and wagging their tails with delight. Like all foxes they whine with pleasure, just as some puppies do. Perhaps Topsy is the more intelligent of the two; I have twice watched her catching sparrows in a remarkably clever way. Near her feeding trough is a large hollow tree trunk lying on its side which we put there for the foxes to play in. Her method of catching birds is to leave some food in her bowl, either by accident or by sheer cunning, and then lie in wait behind the tree. The sparrows, ever on the lookout for something to eat, fly down and while they are busy eating, she springs. They invariably see her coming and fly up at the last minute, but she is too quick for them, snatching one in the air with a snap of her jaws. Not long ago I saw her running round the enclosure with two cock house sparrows in her mouth while an envious Loopy watched where she was going to bury them. Topsy is a hill fox from the border country but she is not a typical long-legged rangy type, being a good deal smaller than old Fennec and with shorter legs. She has a beautiful white tip to her brush and the reddest of red coats.

Foxes become so tame and attached to their owners that I believe they would soon become domesticated were it not for the fact that our red fox, unlike the North American silver fox, is very difficult indeed to breed in captivity. People always seem to expect foxes to smell, but if they are kept clean and in the open air, there is very little odour. Their droppings have an unpleasant fetid smell but the foxes themselves smell rather pleasant, like fresh hay. If they are suddenly frightened it is another matter for, like the skunk, the fox has two anal glands either side of the base of the tail from which, if alarmed, it can expel an evil-smelling oily secretion. It is this which gives rise to the notion that all foxes smell disgusting. When Fennec was a cub he provided me with a perfect example of the working of a fox's scent glands. Some friends had come to dinner and were entranced to see a tame fox cub playing round the room. After dinner Fennec jumped on to my lap and snuggled down for a nap. One of the guests begged to be allowed to nurse him, but I explained that, not knowing him, Fennec would probably be very frightened. Nothing would convince him so in the end I handed the fox over; there was a struggle and a terrified Fennec leapt for the floor, at the same time releasing his scent, several drops of which fell like a fine oily mist upon the spectacles of another guest sitting nearby. The smell of fox in the warm room was almost over-powering.

Fennec never made a mess in the house and needed no training, but he had a weakness for electric light flex and if he suddenly became silent somewhere out of sight I had to check up on him quickly. On several occasions he had almost chewed his way through a live wire and was therefore never left alone in a room where such wires existed.

Perhaps the most extraordinary attachment of a fox to its human foster-parent happened to some friends of ours living in Norfolk. They were hunting people and had been given a small fox cub when an earth had been dug out and the rest of the litter destroyed in the interests of game preservation. They reared the cub in the house until it was almost full-grown, when they decided it was time to let it go to fend for itself. There was a wood on their farm not far from the buildings and they decided to release their fox there and to put food down for it each evening until it showed by not returning for a meal that it no longer needed their help. To their amazement the fox stayed around the wood and every evening when they took its food out they called and it came running through the trees wagging its tail in delight. This state of affairs continued into the hunting season and they had to arrange with the hunt not to visit that particular wood for fear of hunting their fox. Finally towards Christmas the food was not disappearing so regularly and with the turn of the year the fox disappeared in search of a mate.

Fox cubs are frequently kept as pets by people who soon grow tired of the novelty, or who have no suitable accommodation for them when they start to grow up and every summer we are asked to take on unwanted cubs. To turn them away is in many cases to condemn them to death or to a life in a tiny run, or worse still chained to a kennel like a dog, and so whenever possible we take them.

It would be quite impossible to keep them all and if the cubs are strong and able to fend for themselves I often let them go in suitable country where they will stand a good chance of survival.

One July evening I took two large cubs to a wood about six miles away and released them. As I watched them trotting off together through the trees I wondered what fate held in store for them and I hoped and prayed they would avoid contact with people until they had learnt the way of the wild. They were active and not particularly tame so I felt their chances were at least reasonable. The dog fox was big and rangy while the vixen had a white tip to her brush; both had come from the same litter.

I knew if they were shot I was likely to hear about it and as the weeks went by with no news I felt they were probably safe and they soon passed from my mind.

The following January Gordon left a young pointer dog with us for a few weeks while he moved house, and one Sunday I took it for a walk. It immediately ran away and started to work a strip of kale on a neighbour's land not far from our boundary. I knew it would be useless to shout at him so I walked quietly along the edge of a small wood intending to wait at the end of the field for him to come out. I still had eighty yards to go when a fox left the kale and trotted across the open plough towards the trees. I froze in my tracks and almost at once a second fox broke cover and trotted after the first. Suddenly it saw me but instead of running away it sat down on its haunches and stared purposefully at me. For perhaps a minute or two neither of us moved then it got up and walked towards the wood passing within forty yards; as it went I noticed the white tip to its brush.

Had the two cubs returned to their one time home or were they perhaps visiting my tame foxes? I have no proof they were the cubs but somehow I felt I knew those foxes and I believe they knew me.

Badgers are just as easy to rear as fox cubs and they also become delightfully tame, but in my experience they have entirely different personalities. They are even more " one man animals " than foxes and they remain aloof and less demonstrative. While still young they are tame and confiding, but as they grow older they become very independent and apt to bite if thwarted. This particularly applies to boar badgers. I have had two and both grew into really fierce and decidedly ill-tempered creatures.

Several years ago we were given three hand-reared badger cubs, all females and all very tame. They lived outside in a large loose box where they spent the day asleep under a vast pile of straw. They slept soundly and soon made it very clear that they were not to be disturbed in the day-time; if anyone was foolish enough to try, they would growl and snap. In the evening they woke up and started to play, chasing each other and rolling over and over and biting each other's stumpy tails. I used to go into their box, switch on the light and sit down on the straw to watch them. They would soon come running over and start to play with me but before indulging in any games every badger went through the same ritual. It started by smelling my shoes, then quickly turned round and squatted for a second or two over my foot with tail raised. This process is known as " musking " and results in the depositing of an oily secretion from the anal glands at the base of the animal's tail. Unlike the fox's scent, the badger's musk is virtually odourless. It was just visible, a few minute mist-like drops on a clean shoe. Several times I took my shoe off and smelt it, but there was scarcely any scent to my sense. This does not mean that the musk is odourless to a badger. I suspect the reverse, and that to them it is a powerful and recognisable smell. One would assume that this musking is chiefly used as a means of marking out the animal's territory, but I believe it is also a means of immediately recognising an object which has been examined and found to be harmless and friendly. A badger's sight is probably very limited, whereas its sense of smell is highly developed; hence this method of recognition. I noticed that my young badgers would quite often anoint each other with musk during their games. For a nocturnal animal the badger has tiny eyes; but since it lives by grubbing about on the ground and is constantly burrowing, large eyes would be both unnecessary and incon-venient. Having inspected my person and passed it by musking on me the young badgers would start a rough-and-tumble. One would stand on its short hind legs and plunge its cold wet little nose in my ear, while another got hold of my trouser leg and pulled it like a puppy and the third rolled over and over on its broad back, four stubby feet sticking in the air, to have its tummy tickled. This was something they all loved and it appeared to have a most soothing effect upon them.

Of the three the smallest, Pearly, was the least forthcoming and the quickest-tempered. She was a shrewish little thing and not to be trusted. The other two, Grumpy and Greedy, were quite different and would let me pick them up and nurse them, holding them upside down in my arms and rocking them like babies. They used to like this treatment when they were full-grown. Although they lived outside I liked to have at least one of them in the house during the evening; I never chose Pearly because she always bit me if I tried to pick her up. One night I had a bath before supper and put on my pyjamas and dressing-gown. When I came down our old housekeeper reminded me that I hadn't brought in any of the badgers; so pulling on a pair of rubber boots I set off with a torch to their box. Two of them immediately came up to me but the third, obviously Pearly, stayed back. Neither of the other two ever showed signs of biting, so I seized one of them by the scruff of the neck, not an easy thing to do since a badger has virtually no loose skin, and hoisted it under my arm. With the torch in my other hand I set off back across the lawn to the house. Half-way there my thumb was suddenly bitten to the bone and I dropped the badger in a hurry; I remember seeing its black and white form running off down the drive.

Rushing to the barn I grabbed a big net which we use for catching animals and large birds if we want to move them. On the way past the kitchen window I yelled to the house-keeper to come and help me and went off after the badger. Fortunately the drive is flanked on each side by the wire-netting fence of the waterfowl pens so it was bound to be ahead of me. I was just in time to see it disappear through the gate and out on to the main road. Luckily it kept to one side and, being fat, it was not moving all that quickly. I ran as fast as I could in dressing-gown and rubber boots and at last managed to thrust the net over it; not wishing to be bitten again I rolled the badger up in the meshes and carried it back to the loose box.

When I switched on the light to release it, I realised it was Pearly after all. Several cars passed during the chase and I often wonder what their occupants thought of a man in pyjamas, dressing-gown and rubber boots carrying an outsize landing net and running down the main road in the dark.

A popular misconception about badgers, constantly repeated in books on natural history, is that the scent from their anal glands smells obnoxious to humans, whereas I repeat it is virtually odourless. In certain mammals, notably skunks, the stink glands have been evolved to a remarkable degree, so much so that other animals shun the owners of these very efficient weapons of self-defence. Such animals are conspicuously marked with black and white which shows up in the dark and warns other creatures not to molest them. In badgers it is the head which is conspicuously striped black and white and not the body, for the simple reason that the head is the dangerous end of the animal owing to its terrific bite. Their droppings certainly smell very unpleasant and I suspect that this is where the inaccuracy originated. Also a badger's bed, after it has been in use for some time, smells very strong and so does the badger itself after it has been lying in it all day generating body heat. But then a dog smells none too sweet when it has been lying in its bed all night and the same might be said for most human beings. Hence the expression " to stink like a badger."

Badgers are essentially clean animals. They have latrines, shallow excavations, where they deposit their scats, and they change their bedding at regular intervals, dragging the old out of the set and bringing in fresh in the form of dry bracken, grasses and leaves. When a badger has collected enough material for a new bed it drags it down into the set by moving backwards, pulling an armful of bedding with it which it holds in place with its chin.

One of the first things a badger does when emerging from its set in the evening is to have a thorough and prolonged scratch to groom its coat. I don't know whether they often bathe in the wild, but in captivity they love a bath. My tame sows have one nearly every night in the summer and a most amusing sight it is, for their bath is also their water trough, a cast-iron bowl some eight inches deep by fifteen inches in diameter. Into this the badger sits with a splash, then raises itself so that it is sitting on its rear-end while it scratches and rubs its large tummy for all the world like a fat woman enjoying a hip bath.

Badgers are known to dig out wasps' nests in order to eat the grubs and I have always wanted to see how they set about this hazardous task. A nest had been found in the bank bordering a nearby field and to it I took the tamest of the three sows. I showed her the entrance hole which she sniffed and promptly ran off to dig and root elsewhere in the hedge bottom. Calling her back I tried again, but she was not in the least interested. Thinking that being hand-reared she failed to recognise a wasps' nest, I popped some pieces of raw meat just inside the hole. She then started to dig and soon an angry cloud of wasps appeared; some of them landed on her body and, climbing on her bristly coat, began to sting her. She left off digging and ran away to roll in the grass to rid herself of the insects. Nothing would persuade her to return to the nest. Presumably young badgers learn from their parents that succulent grubs are to be found just below the ground wherever the black and yellow insects have made their hole. Most of them are dug out at night and it may well be that wasps are dopy during the hours of darkness and less inclined to sting.

Having three sows we needed a boar, and one day a friend who had seen our badgers wrote to say he knew of somebody with a young hand-reared boar for which they needed a good home. They lived in the south and since I was about to take the children to Bexhill to see their grandmother, it was arranged that the badger would be brought over while we were staying there. I naturally expected them to bring the animal in a box of some kind and was therefore rather surprised when they came to tea with the badger lying comfortably over the woman's shoulder. " Oh, don't worry about a box," they said, " Digger is perfectly tame and loves riding in a car."

The badger seemed tame enough and while we had tea in the loggia it lay under its owner's chair. After tea it trundled off to inspect the garden and when it had had enough it came back to us. Suddenly it became rather upset and rushed to and fro along the side of the house until it found a down pipe and drain, where it squatted and carefully deposited its scats in the open drain—apparently it always did this when outside

in their garden. Shortly before it was time for our visitors
to go Digger ran off and lay under their car. I tried to call
him out but failed and, not wishing to be left with a loose
badger over which I had no control, I suggested that the owner
should extricate him and that we should shut him up. We
really had nowhere suitable which was also badger-proof,
so in the end decided upon the outside lavatory which with its
concrete floor and heavy oak door would have held a lion
had it been bigger. I put a bed of old sacks in one corner, a
bowl of water and another of food and Digger was securely
bolted inside. Later that evening I went to see him but he was
not pleased to see me and snarled angrily.

The only box I could find was a rather flimsy orange-box
and as we had to leave early the next day I set about strengthen-
ing it with any odd bits of wood I could find. Luckily I
discovered an old piece of chain-link fencing and I nailed it
over the top of the box leaving a third of it loose so that I could
get the badger inside. I was up very early next morning and
took the box and the garden fork to the lavatory all ready to
confine Digger for the journey. He had plainly had a bad
night and was glowering angrily in a corner when I opened
the door a little and peered inside.

My plan was to take the box in, turn it on its side, push the
opening opposite Digger and hope that with the aid of a minor
prod he would nip inside. The first discovery I made was that
since the door opened inwards, only just clearing the front
of the lavatory seat, there was virtually no room for the box;
and even if I got it inside, it would be quite impossible to shut
the door. Digger too was crouching in the corner opposite
the door ready to make a dash for freedom. It seemed to be
a case of stalemate, but fortunately my mother had a most
resourceful cook called Alice who came to my rescue. It was
decided that we should open the door just wide enough to get
the box in on its end and that we would then lay it across the
lavatory seat. Hastily I would squeeze inside and stand on top

of the box on top of the seat, thus giving Alice room to close the door. While this was going on she was to block the entrance with the flat surface of the garden fork to prevent Digger's escape.

All went according to plan, so that I was shut in with the box and Digger. He was no longer a tame badger where I was concerned but an extremely disagreeable boar determined to bite me if he could. There was no room to manoeuvre the box and once I had got it on the floor it took up all the space, so that there was no room for me to stand. After much struggling I managed to get the opening opposite the badger, but the lavatory bowl prevented me from pushing the box any closer. Alice still had the garden fork which I now needed but she could not open the door because the box was wedged right up against it. More struggling from my unsteady perch on the seat and the door opened just wide enough for her to pass the fork through. Finally with a prod from behind Digger shot into the box.

I hastily pulled the chain-link across the top and down over the end where I fixed it over three nails I had driven in to hold it. Once more came the problem of opening the door. The box had to be stood on end but now it contained a furious badger who would bite off any finger he could reach. When I at last stepped out into the open air Digger showed how strong he was by very nearly forcing the netting off the top of the box. It had to be reinforced quickly. There was only one answer, the steel door-scraper. I grabbed it and together we wired it over the top. Finally a still protesting Digger was carried to the brake in his somewhat rickety box and stowed amongst the family luggage. One side was firmly wedged against the body of the car, the end against a trunk, and another case was pushed up to the remaining side. Once the car started he soon settled down and slept most of the way home, waking up only whenever we stopped.

Digger seemed to approve of his three wives but as he grew

175

older his temper grew worse. Pearly was given away to a friend who was keen to have a badger as a pet and had built a nice enclosure in which to keep one. For two years Digger, who had grown large and powerful, lived peacefully with Grumpy and Greedy. One December afternoon I heard strange little whimpering noises coming from their loose box and, on going in, found that one of them had given birth to cubs in a chamber burrowed out from beneath the pile of straw. I was uncertain which of the two sows was responsible and wondered whether to remove the boar, but as all seemed in order I decided to let well alone for fear of disturbing the mother and her newborn family. My decision was wrong for at eleven o'clock that night the box was silent and there was no sign of the litter. They had all been eaten and I suspect Digger was the culprit.

My suspicions were strengthened when some months later we were sent a hand-reared sow for which the owner wished to find a home. I felt sure that Digger would not object to another wife, so put her in with the rest. The two original sows were perfectly friendly towards the newcomer, but early next morning one of our staff looked in to see Digger biting her repeatedly. He at once got the new sow into another pen, but it was too late; within a few hours she was dead. Digger's method of attack was particularly vicious. He had torn her stomach between her hind legs and virtually disembowelled the poor animal.

Few people can have seen badgers actually mating, but in June last year we watched Digger serving one of his sows at eight o'clock in the evening. We had transferred the trio to another pen by the house which had an open run attached to the sleeping quarters. It was in this run that mating occurred. The two animals remained coupled for fifty-five minutes, during which time the boar repeatedly bit the back of the sow's neck. Several times the other sow wandered over and musked on them. Digger would attack anyone entering the pen to feed them and in the end we became rather tired of his aggressive nature and decided to let him go. One morning early this summer we took him to a nearby forest and released him on a bracken-covered slope overlooking the river. He trundled off without a backward glance and within five minutes we heard some small creature squealing from beneath the bracken. Digger had made his first kill.

We often wondered how the old rogue was faring and then six weeks later one of our staff saw him. It was late on a summer evening and the boy was cycling home. As he rode along the lane, less than two miles from the wood where Digger had been set free, he was surprised to see a badger coming towards him in the twilight. He kept going and the animal passed within six feet of him without taking any notice. He was easily able to recognise the powerful form of Digger for badgers are uncommon in this part of Norfolk. After passing him Digger blundered noisily through the hedge and away into the night.

Although over five years old Grumpy and Greedy are as tame as ever with me and will still allow me to pick them up, but if anyone else tries to touch them they will bite, and they even attack members of our staff who feed them. As I said, badgers are apt to be " one man " animals.

13. Roe Deer

Few people can gaze upon a fawn a few days or weeks old without feeling some strange protective instinct. Put two baby fawns in an enclosure and listen to the remarks as people pass them. Nine out of ten will say, " Oh, look, aren't they sweet? "

There is something about the helplessness of a fawn which arouses some of our better qualities, but it goes deeper than that and is, I think, largely due to three things. First, the fawn is covered with nice warm fur; secondly, it has exceptionally large doleful eyes; and thirdly, it has big and mobile ears which are themselves capable of considerable expression. What I find odd is that none of this, with the possible exception of relatively large eyes, is found in our own newborn offspring. Why then do we all feel so protective when we see a tiny fawn? Perhaps it is a primeval instinct going back into the dark recesses of time when our own offspring were covered with fur. Then, from nursery days we have all been brought up on the idea of the fawn being the supreme example of helpless wide-eyed innocence, the Bambi of all time. It would be interesting to discover if primitive people, unfettered by this nursery propaganda, feel the same good-will towards baby deer. I think it quite likely that they would, even though they might hunt and kill adult deer for food.

Of our native deer, the tiny roe is to my mind the most fascinating. The red deer may be far more majestic, especially the huge stags of Thetford Chase with their enormous spread of antlers, while the spotted fallow is perhaps the most beautiful of the three and certainly the most docile. Nevertheless, there is something about the sylvan charm of the roe which I find irresistible. Less is known of the life of the roe than of the other two, partly because it is a creature of the dense forest and partly because it is solitary or at most lives in family groups and never in a herd. Fortunately this small deer is on the increase throughout Britain, chiefly because of recent large-scale afforestation. The roe requires extensive woodlands if it is to thrive.

The buck chooses his territory in the forest and remains there most of the year. During the rut he defends his territory rather than any particular doe; and during the period of the year when he has his antlers he spends much of his time patrolling the perimeter of his domain marking it by rubbing his antlers up and down on the bushes and saplings, fraying the bark in the process.

During the rut the buck chases the doe of his choice until she finally stands and allows him to mate. Very often she will run in circles round some conspicuous object such as a gorse bush or tree stump and when this happens so-called " roe rings " are made with the animals' tracks clearly defined. The rings are often made in a clearing in the forest or even outside in more open country. Favourite rings are sometimes used year after year.

Roe deer drop their kids during May and June, choosing a secluded place amidst bracken in the depths of the wood. After three or four weeks the youngsters are able to follow their dam and they remain with her for a year. Twins are common and usually of opposite sexes.

One tiny pair was brought to us by a keeper only a few hours after they were born, the dam having been shot by poachers. They were no bigger than large hares and the two of them arrived curled up on some bracken in a cardboard box. It was late in the evening and we spent nearly an hour trying to persuade them to take a little warm milk and water from a fountain pen filler. We finally succeeded, though the amount they took was pathetically small. The male seemed a good deal stronger than his sister. Pat got up at five o'clock in the morning to feed them again. She is remarkably successful at hand-rearing baby animals and they all grow up to adore her. To her dismay the little female roe was already dead and the male, although alive, was very weak. He revived after a good feed with a few drops of brandy added and we had learned our lesson, which was that for the first two or three weeks of their lives baby roe must be fed every three hours, day and night.

We christened the fawn Bracken and he spent the daytime out in the garden, coming into the kitchen at night or in wet weather. He too soon learned to disregard the dogs and would even push his way past them to get a place on their bed. In a few days he had graduated from the fountain pen filler to a baby's bottle, and after a couple of weeks Pat had taught him to drink from a bowl. We gave him a mixture of half cow's milk and half water with a teaspoonful of glucose, fed at blood heat. His method of drinking was to plunge his nose to the bottom of the bowl so that the milk went up his nostrils, then he would draw back spluttering and snorting and settle down to drink properly. Even so, at the end of his meal his face was covered with milk.

Our old labrador Rufus takes a keen interest in any new arrival and he plainly disapproved of a baby deer with a dirty face. As soon as Bracken had been fed, Rufus would walk over to him and lick his face clean. The deer may not have liked this procedure, but he put up with it. Rufus was so enormous compared with him he probably felt it best not to argue. The washing over, Bracken would lie warm and snug between the dog's paws; he was growing fast and we both became very fond of him. I think perhaps he was the most confiding of any young deer I have ever known.

One summer evening Pat took Bracken for a walk round the garden. He followed her closely until he saw the large expanse of lawn, then he rushed off at full gallop round and round before skidding to a stop in front of her. In a moment he was off again at full speed. This went on until he had let off all his steam, then he returned to Pat to be petted and trotted back into the kitchen at her heels. That evening he drank his last feed greedily and settled down on his bed by the stove for the night, the picture of health. Next morning I was awakened by Pat standing by my bed with tears in her eyes. Bracken was dead.

She had gone down to feed him at the usual time and to her horror had found him just as she had left him, curled up peacefully on his bed; he must have died in his sleep without a movement. We could scarcely believe it had happened and were at a loss to understand what had gone wrong. He was a boisterous and friendly little animal and the house was strangely quiet without him. It seemed to me that we must find out what mistake we had made and so I telephoned an old friend at the School of Veterinary Medicine at Cambridge, and explained what had happened. He said if I sent Bracken's body to him he would see that everything possible was done to discover the cause of this sudden death.

In a few days he telephoned with the answer: Bracken had died of calcium deficiency. His reserve of calcium was being steadily used up on the diet we had been giving him, and galloping about the evening before he died had made fatal inroads into what little was left. Since that day we have never mixed cow's milk with plain water, but with lime water from the chemist. One learns the hard way, especially when trying to rear unusual babies.

One June some years before a newborn roe kid was picked up by a forest keeper who found it lying near its dam. She had once again been shot by a poacher the night before and near her lay the body of her female fawn, the poor little thing having died of hunger and exposure. The male, though weak, was still alive and soon recovered when placed in the care of a friend of ours. Some weeks later he was handed over to us and what an enchanting little creature he was; Pat fell for him straight away. He was christened Misty and put on the dogs' bed under the kitchen table. At first our dogs, two pointers and Rufus the labrador, could not understand the new arrival, but within a few days all were lying together under the table.

In fine weather Misty spent the day on the lawn outside the kitchen window in his pen. This was really an enlarged version of a child's play-pen, ten feet square and three feet high, constructed of wood and wire-netting. The four sides were bolted together at the corners and the whole thing could easily be moved daily on to a fresh piece of grass by one person. At first he was fed a mixture of cow's milk and water every four hours, the last feed being given at 11 p.m. and the first at 6 a.m. He was fed from a baby's bottle which he sucked greedily. After feeding, he would find a shady corner and lie down, but as the next feeding time came round he became more active, racing round and round and bleating rather like a small lamb. Pat used to take him for a walk in the evenings and he would follow with no lead, better than any dog. Sometimes he would gallop wildly round and round the lawn as if to let off steam, always charging full pelt back to Pat and coming to an abrupt stop in front of her.

All British baby deer are born covered with attractive pale spots and they spend the first days of their lives lying still amongst the bracken or heather awaiting the return of their dam for their next feed. At this time they give off very little scent, so that foxes and other predators do not easily discover them. Misty still had his baby spots when he came to us, but as he grew they slowly disappeared. One of the minor snags of

a deer indoors is that it never becomes house-trained, so Misty
was kept in the kitchen as much as possible. This was easier
said than done since he disliked the rubber flooring upon
which he was inclined to slip. He much preferred to gallop
round the drawing-room ending up with a flying leap on to
the sofa where he would lie down, his forelegs bent beneath
him, and quietly snooze.

Visitors were sometimes surprised at meeting a deer indoors,
especially if we had forgotten to warn them. This happened
to a couple home on leave from Hong Kong. Their first
evening they came down to dinner before anyone else was
ready and went into the drawing-room to help themselves
to a drink. They had just settled down when Misty charged
into the room and leapt up on to the sofa and lay down as
usual. They were both so fascinated by him that when we
found them they were talking in whispers for fear of frighten-
ing him away.

As he grew bigger we added a well-known baby food to his
milk diet and tried to persuade him to nibble hay, but with
little success; he seemed to prefer dock leaves, dandelions
and plantain. He had grown too big for his play-pen and
spent the day in a small enclosure near the house. We gave
him a little hut for shelter and, as the summer nights were
warm, we started to leave him out. One day we noticed he
seemed to be getting rather thin and soon after he began to
scour badly. We sent for the vet who gave him antibiotics and
some medicine, but after several days on the treatment he
was worse. Though he still drank his milk he was losing
interest, still scouring badly and getting visibly weaker. We
discontinued the docks and substituted hazel and sycamore
leaves, but without any improvement. Nothing we could
think of seemed to help and it became increasingly obvious
that Misty was going to die. In desperation I telephoned
Ted Wilson who had given him to us. The only thing he
could suggest was that he should have him back and see if the

change would improve his condition. He volunteered to meet me that afternoon in Newmarket and take Misty back to Madingley. The best way to transport a small deer for a short distance is in a sack with its head sticking out and the top of the sack tied loosely round its neck. Misty travelled thus on the back seat of the car and in due course I handed him over in the middle of Newmarket. As he was driven away I could not help wondering if I should ever see him again.

Three nights later Ted telephoned to say that Misty was no worse. He had been almost sure he was going to lose him the first night and had gone out at 3 a.m. and given him warm milk and a little brandy. He had put him in a large rough grass enclosure where there were trees and bramble clumps and Misty was beginning to totter round eating leaves and shoots of various kinds. The improvement continued and six weeks later we went to Madingley to bring Misty home. To our delight he was a changed animal; he had grown quite a lot but above all he had filled out and had a beautiful sheen on his coat. Roe deer, being browsers, are difficult to keep fit and healthy in captivity unless one has a semi-natural paddock with trees and bushes growing in it. It may well have been these conditions as well as Ted's nursing which finally saved Misty from an early death.

By the autumn he had the same coat as an adult roe and two protruding horn buds on his head where his first antlers would grow the next spring. He was still very tame and enjoyed two feeds of milk and Farex a day, though he now drank from a bowl; he had also developed a liking for calf nuts.

During the closing months of the year we started to make a short film for children about the adventures of a little girl with her tame deer. Naturally Misty was the star, and our eldest daughter Sonia, aged nine, took the part of the small girl. While much of the film was shot at home, the story made it necessary to shoot a number of scenes in the forest and it was there that Misty demonstrated how tame and dependent upon us he really was. Sonia led him about on a cord, and when she took it off and turned him loose he merely wandered away and nibbled the bushes and rough grass, never straying far. All she had to do when she wanted him back was to walk up and he allowed her to slip the rope over his head again.

The closing scene of the film was supposed to show the "escape" of the tame deer and its return to the forest. My idea was to show the child running along a ride with Misty trotting beside her; just as she was level with a pile of freshly trimmed timber she would trip and fall headlong; the deer would leap the pile of logs in fright and dash off, never to be seen again. We set up the camera and tried the shot, Sonia fell quite naturally in the right place; but Misty, far from leaping the logs, merely ran on for half a dozen yards then stood and waited for her.

Something had to be done, so we took a twenty-foot pole and stood it on end opposite the pile of timber. Pat balanced it there and, as Sonia reached the place where she would fall, she pushed it over. The timing was perfect, the crash of the pole coincided with the child's fall and so alarmed Misty that he leapt the logs in fine style and dashed off into the forest. After going thirty yards through the trees he stopped and lay down waiting for us to collect him.

It was only with the appearance of his antlers that Misty's temperament changed. It started during his second summer when he proudly displayed his first set of small antlers. As soon as he had rubbed the velvet off in the spring he developed from a docile, timid youngster to a fierce little buck ready to charge anyone who entered his pen. At first it was difficult to believe this sudden change, but not for long. We kept some breeding pheasants in the same enclosure and Misty took to attacking the man who went in to feed them every morning. On my orders he armed himself with a dustbin lid, but I had underestimated the impetus of Misty's charge and the first day he used the lid the deer hit it with such force that the shock almost broke his wrist.

During his third summer it was no longer safe for one man to enter Misty's enclosure. He attacked everything on sight. He even went so far as to charge a tractor which was used to cut the grass in his pen. In doing so he broke his left antler and damaged the pedicle, the base of the antler where it joins the skull. I was worried that this would result in a peruke head, a horrible cauliflower-like growth in place of the proper antler when the new one was due to grow the next spring. But although his left antler has always been rather misshapen, it has never been too unsightly and improves each year.

Misty is still with us and is now a fine buck in his prime. His temperament changes almost to the day with the growth or dropping of his antlers. After he has shed them, usually about November, I can walk up to him and pick him up like a great big dog. He remains friendly and docile until the spring. Then one day, his new antlers having completed their growth, the blood supply to their velvet dries up and he starts to rub the dead velvet off. From that day until he drops them in the autumn, Misty will attack any intruder, although his temper is at its worst during the rutting season in July and August.

It has for long been my ambition to breed roe deer and I still hope to succeed. At the time of writing we have three lovely bucks, Misty, Bimbo and Fern. Each is in sole possession of a sizeable paddock and each awaits the arrival of a wife.

14. A Sun Bear grows up

"Definitely not a bear cub," said Pat as we parked the car. We were outside an animal dealer's shop in North London, not far from the Zoo. It was a place well known to both of us because we often called there on our way home to Norfolk. I had telephoned the proprietor to ask if he had any tame animals which we could add to our collection; after a moment's thought he had replied, "I haven't much that is really tame at the moment unless you want a bear cub I have recently imported, it's pretty tame."

Once inside the shop we stood looking at rows of cages stacked all round the walls from floor to ceiling with another tier running down the centre. Many of them were full of tiny birds. Other cages contained hamsters and rabbits, guinea pigs and pigeons, while a solitary capuchin monkey occupied one corner. It sat huddled against the front of its cage, a pathetic picture, its tiny arm thrust imploringly through the wire mesh. I wished we could take it home, but we had nowhere suitable to keep it. The proprietor beckoned us through a door at the back of the shop, which led to a smaller room lined with cages containing more delicate tropical animals.

But it was the large steel cage against the end wall that interested me for in it, standing erect on her bandy little hind legs, was the most adorable bear cub imaginable. Her owner opened the cage door and put his hand inside. The cub instantly started to play, cuffing his hand with her black paws and wobbling her head from side to side as she danced round. She was three months old and stood thirty inches tall on her hind legs, her soft coat was coal-black except for a large pinky-orange patch emblazoned on her chest like the rising sun. Hence her name, for she was a Malayan Sun Bear. Two tiny black ears topped her head and even at that age her yellow teeth were remarkably large when she opened her mouth to play.

The owner had left the room to attend to another customer.

" We can't leave her here."

" I know," said Pat, " but where can we keep her ? "

" We'll find somewhere," I said. " I wonder what he wants for her."

So it was that we left London half an hour later with a baby sun bear firmly nailed down inside a large tea-chest which had been reinforced with wooden slats. As soon as we started, " Baby Bear," as she was already called, began to object, scuffling about inside her chest scratching at the sides and growling like a disgruntled terrier. But, as with most animals, the motion of the car seemed to soothe her and she soon fell asleep. On the way home we discussed where we should put the bear. Although quite small she showed signs of being destructive and she was already good at climbing. We had one or two empty loose boxes but they would be useless: she would soon climb up to the roof and I could picture an avalanche of tiles clattering down as her little curved claws got to work prising them apart. Then we remembered the dog kennels. There were two of them, side by side, made of heavy gauge chain-link fencing on a wooden frame, each with a warm shelter of stout timber. In one kennel lived two pointers and in the other our old yellow labrador Rufus. It was clear that he would have to be promoted to the house, sleeping under the kitchen table at night, while Baby Bear took over his kennel. There was still the problem of a roof for the open run, something would have to be done about that.

I carried the bear's crate into her run and levered the lid open, she clambered out and ran straight into the wooden shelter. Though not particularly big as kennels go, her new house and run was many times larger than the cage in the shop and gave her plenty of room to move about. She soon discovered to her delight that chain-link netting was ideal stuff for climbing and it was not long before she was rushing up one side and crossing the roof, hanging on upside down by her curved claws. That night she ate a large bowl of fresh fruit with some boiled tripe and hound meal.

We dislike keeping animals entirely confined to their cages and try whenever possible to give them some form of liberty. Plainly Baby Bear could not be permitted to roam loose, she was far too mischievous for that. So I hit on the idea of attaching her by a chain collar to a much longer chain pegged down on the lawn. This I thought would give her a certain amount of freedom and a change of scenery each day. It was a comparatively simple task to slip a short length of chain round her neck and join the two ends with a split link, leaving enough slack to allow for her growth. Nevertheless one had to be fairly nimble as she resented any restriction and could bite quite hard even at that early age. She hated being chained up right from the start and though we persevered for a fortnight it was no use. She looked unhappy and spent the whole time straining to escape, tearing up the lawn in her fury. The moment she was released she calmed down and I used to take her back to her cage in the evening by putting my hands under her arms and carrying her with her hind legs dangling, as one lifts a small child. Pat saw me doing this one night and suggested the bear would follow me if I put her down. I thought it just as likely she would bolt in the opposite direction but we tried it and to my surprise she trundled along happily beside me back to her pen.

This was the beginning of far greater freedom for her since we discovered that she hated being left alone. We abandoned the chain and took her for a good walk at least once, often twice a day. She quickly formed a strong attachment to Pat and would play beside her by the hour when she was gardening. We felt that she could not go through life as Baby Bear and so we christened her Pooh.

Just as she had objected strongly to being chained, so she now refused to be led. The moment we attached a lead to her collar she would growl and try to bite the legs of whoever was leading her. We began to realise that we had an extremely determined youngster on our hands. The dogs were puzzled by the strange animal in the next run and rushed at the wire barking whenever Pooh appeared. She took no notice of them until she discovered that she could bait them by climbing the chain-link partition. This was something the poor dogs could not stand. Then she started to play with them through the wire, waiting until a dog had its back turned within reach and then stretching her arm through the netting to prod it. Sometimes Rufus spent the day in the kennel, and Pooh instantly fell in love with him. It is curious that nearly all baby animals seem to trust him unerringly from leverets and fawns to kittens and squirrels, and now a bear cub. Unlike the noisy barking pointers, Rufus stood placidly sniffing at her through the wire, his tail waving from side to side.

Her daily walks were something she looked forward to now she had Rufus as playmate and companion. Wherever he went she followed. When he started to dig out a rat in the hedge, Pooh would join in. Being much shorter in the leg than the dog, she would dive in between his hind legs and start excavating at the same place. Her method of digging was quite different from his and far more effective, while the dog scratched away in frantic haste with his front paws, biting through roots and kicking the soil away with his hind legs, Pooh worked slowly using her front paws as hands, reaching down into the hole and pulling up large handfuls of earth. Tiring of digging she would wait for Rufus to run on, then launch a mock attack from behind, rolling herself into a tight ball she would somersault into him, nipping his legs in play. The two of them would then start a rough-and-tumble and if it got too rough Rufus would snap at her and growl; this always had the desired effect for she regarded him as the boss. His status has not changed with the years and to this day she will run away if he goes for her despite the fact that she could easily kill him if she wanted to.

Mother bears must cuff their youngsters frequently to restore order, for Pooh's instant reaction to a playful slap is to cover her head up with her front paws and she does this whenever Rufus snaps at her. She could never resist his long waving tail and would wait until he was lying down in the shade before padding up quietly behind him to seize the tip between her front paws, this rarely failed to result in another game. Should he pretend not to notice and go on lying there, she tried a different approach. Standing erect on her hind legs she would waltz up and prod him with a front paw, immediately jumping back out of range only to repeat the movement. If all this still failed to get a response she would walk up and, turning her back, sit down with a bump on top of him; this always roused him and she would roll over on her back trying to grab his legs with her hands, and so the game would start all over again.

Most bears are born comics and I am quite sure Pooh has a real sense of humour, even if it is of the slap-stick variety. She was always intrigued with the hose used for washing down her concrete run and would start to play with it as soon as it was turned on. The water comes out in a fairly powerful jet and, having sniffed it and pushed the end of the hose about, she grabbed hold of it and stood up on her hind legs only to receive a gush of water straight in her face which knocked her over backwards. As if to make sure that nobody was going to laugh at her, she was up in a flash, seized the hose and directed the jet straight at the dogs next door.

Malayan sun bears have a well-earned reputation for being

highly dangerous. Although they are quite small as bears go—
a full grown adult stands about four feet on its hind legs—
they are nevertheless extremely savage. An old animal
collector who had spent a life-time out East once told me that
he would sooner meet a tiger in the forest than a sun bear.
He maintained that the tiger would almost certainly move off
on hearing his approach, whereas the bear would stand its
ground and charge the moment it saw him. Having once
heard Pooh roar in anger, I can imagine few things more
terrifying than to be suddenly confronted in thick jungle with
a charging bear out to kill. Their ferocity and uncertain
temper are the main reasons why sun bears are hardly ever
used in circuses. Unlike the big cats, bears give no warning
when they are going to attack; they have no tail to start
nervously swishing and their facial expression never changes.
They remain poker-faced and deceptively cuddlesome, real
live Teddy bears one instant and charging murderous demons
the next.

We were soon to have a foretaste of what even a tiny cub
can do if thwarted. We wanted to film a sequence of Pooh
climbing on to a table out in the garden to steal some food.
Pat was encouraging her to climb up for the feast while I was
behind the camera, the scene was watched with interest by
Bubo the eagle owl sitting on her block beneath the apple
trees and by Lionel, my father-in-law, reclining nearby in a
deck-chair. For a time all went well, Pooh enjoyed climbing
on to the table, playing with the mincer and drinking milk
from a bottle. She was very clever at that. Having knocked
the milk bottle off the table, she climbed down, took it in her
forepaws and, holding the top to her mouth, rolled over on
to her back drinking the contents. She got the last drop by
putting her hind feet under the base of the bottle and then
stretching her legs to tip it up.

We still had one more shot to take, but Pooh got bored
and wandered off towards the apple trees. Pat called her back

in vain. Lionel thought he would help, so rising from his deck-chair he grabbed Pooh under her arms whereupon she bit his hand. As he dropped her she slashed out with her claws making tramlines down his forearm and across the back of his hand; at the same time she barged into his legs and tripped him up. The free-for-all was too much for Bubo who jumped off her block and joined the mêlée so that for a moment Lionel, the bear and the eagle owl formed a struggling mass of arms, legs and wings. A better cameraman would have secured the shot of a lifetime, but I was too worried to think about that. Fortunately the damage to Lionel's arm and hand was not serious, and on his return to London he made the most of his Whitsun adventure. He delights in telling the tale of how he lunched at his usual restaurant in the City the following week. The waitress saw his scarred hand and asked, " Oh, Mr. Polgreen, whatever happened to you over Whitsun?" "Oh," said Lionel casually, "I was mauled by a bear in Norfolk." "Coo," replied the waitress, "I wish someone would maul me like that."

If Pooh Bear regards Rufus as companion and boss, she looks upon Pat as mother-substitute. The moment anything frightens her she rushes back to Pat for protection. We used to tease her by taking her for a walk in a cornfield where she would find all sorts of interesting smells to investigate, and while she was busy grubbing we would lie down and hide in the corn. Suddenly it would dawn on her that we had dis-appeared and she would rush to and fro in a panic until she found us. This attachment is all-important, for without it we should have no control over her whatever.

Being forest dwellers sun bears are natural climbers and Pooh had no fear of heights from the start. Her bandy legs with feet turned inwards might look awkward on the ground but once in a tree it is another matter. She is perfectly adapted to climbing, her long curved claws hook into the smallest crevice so that she can run up the bole of the stoutest oak faster than a man can run upstairs, her arms spread wide across the trunk. She comes down like a man on a ladder, hind feet first.

I should like to be able to say that we often had Pooh in the house sharing the hearth with the dogs, but it would not be true. Bears are about the most destructive animals you can imagine and, although Pooh often got as far as the kitchen, we managed to stop her there. She has an unerring nose for what in the Navy was called the " the gash bucket," and once inside the kitchen she invariably went straight to the sink and turned out the contents of the garbage pail underneath. It was no use putting things up high out of her reach for she always smelt them and simply climbed up or pulled the table over.

Sudden noise has always been the one thing she cannot stand and the only way to get her out of the kitchen was to grab a saucepan or bucket and hit it with a tablespoon, making as much clatter as possible. This nearly always drove her out into the garden again.

Running for the back door as soon as she was let out began to get rather a habit and we used to take care that all the doors into the house, and windows on the ground floor, were tight shut before opening her cage. Even so she would go round on her hind legs tapping at windows and doors with her front claws as if to check they were all securely shut. At that time we had an elderly housekeeper who, hearing someone banging on the front door one day, opened it only to be confronted with Pooh Bear standing up on her hind legs waiting to come in. She recovered from the shock in time to shut the door firmly in Pooh's face.

Although sun bears come from the tropics, they acclimatise fairly readily and I hoped Pooh would get through her first winter without additional heating in her house. Having a wooden kennel she had done her best to demolish it, and had succeeded to the extent she had ripped off a number of boards on the front. We always made sure she had a deep bed of dry straw, but even so she was rather exposed. Half-way through January we had a sudden and severe frost. Early one morning, soon after our foreman had arrived, he wondered why Pooh was not out in her run to greet him. He went inside and there she lay on her straw bed, apparently dead. She was still warm, and he thought he could see faint signs of breathing. He fetched one of the other men and they carried her into the incubator room. There was a radiator and they spread some sacks on the floor near it and laid her down; she was quite unconscious and her tongue hung limply from her mouth. They gave her additional heat by hanging an infra-red brooder lamp from a beam so its warming rays fell on her, then they covered her with a horse blanket.

Immediately we heard the awful news we rushed out with two rubber hot-water bottles which we put against her back. The vet soon arrived and examined her, he was at a loss to explain her condition but said that her circulation was almost non-existent; amongst other things he gave her a shot of Coramin to stimulate her heart. Two hours later the warmth seemed to be having some effect; her breathing was stronger and her tongue less blue, showing that circulation was return-ing. We tried spooning a little warm milk and brandy into her mouth, but she refused to swallow it. One of us stayed with her all the time, renewing the hot-water bottles and turning her over every hour or so to prevent pneumonia. Our secretary was exceedingly fond of Baby Bear, as she always called her, and was distressed when she came that morning and heard how ill she was. She remained with her all the morning and by lunch time had managed to spoon the milk and brandy mixture down Pooh's throat.

The crisis seemed to be over by the middle of the afternoon. Her breathing was much stronger, she could move her legs a little, and would take small quantities of warm milk. On his second visit the vet gave her further injections and told me to call him at once should Pooh look any worse. He would come again in the morning. When I went out last thing at night to feed her again she was trying to get up, though she lacked co-ordination and kept falling over. I knew it would be fatal if she got cold again in the night, so I built a barricade of wooden egg boxes round her to keep her under the warmth of the infra-red lamp. After another feed of warm milk I covered her up and left her lying comfortably beneath the heater on a bed of dry straw.

Early next morning I went out to see how she was. As I approached the barn I heard a tremendous roar and the noise of splintering wood. At least she is still alive, I thought, and apparently much stronger, but I was not prepared for the sight that met my eyes as I peered cautiously round the incubator room door. The place was a shambles. Most of the egg boxes had been reduced to splinters and thrown about the room. A table which had been near the window had been pulled over and torn to pieces, while the front of the large incubator had been gashed by her claws. Pooh herself crouched amongst the wreckage and was obviously in an ugly mood; flecks of foam dripped from her mouth and as soon as she heard me at the door she roared in fury. Then she charged or rather tried to, only to swerve violently to the right, roaring and slashing the air with her front claws. The slightest sound set her off again circling in a paroxysm of rage and always to the right. She was obviously completely unbalanced and highly dangerous.

Many of the broken egg boxes were lying about with nails sticking upwards and I was worried that she might tread on one and drive a nail through her foot. Clearly they had got to be removed. Fortunately there are two doors to the incubator room and one of the staff went round to the other door with a broom for protection and opened it slightly. While Pooh's attention was distracted I nipped in through my door and swept as many broken boxes as I could reach towards me. After several attempts I managed to remove all the more dangerous debris. Soon after breakfast the vet arrived and we went to look at Pooh. She was still frothing at the mouth, roaring and charging her own shadow. She frequently gnashed her teeth, snapping at imaginary objects and flailing the air with her claws. To approach her in that state was out of the question, but there was a more sinister reason for keeping out of her way.

The vet had come to the conclusion that not only was she mad, she showed all the symptoms of rabies. Nobody seemed to know whether bears could contract this disease, but since dogs and cats can, and since Pooh had been imported from the East where rabies is common, it was no use taking any chances. Rabies is nearly always fatal to human beings unless a particularly unpleasant course of injections into the stomach is started without delay, a procedure which has to go on for several months. I had awful visions of the whole family and staff having to undergo this ordeal. In the meantime the vet said he would have to inform the Medical Officer of Health in Norwich of the possibility of the disease being present.

Since human lives were at stake, particularly those of our children, I suggested that Pooh should be destroyed at once so that a post-mortem examination could determine whether she had really got rabies. If she had, then the injections could be started that much sooner. The vet explained that this would achieve nothing, since the changes in the brain tissue of an infected animal do not appear until after the victim has died of the disease, so that we should not know for certain until after Pooh had died. If she had rabies, she would probably die within four days. I asked how the disease was transmitted from animal to man, to be told that it was usually via mucus from the animal's mouth either when it bit somebody or licked someone's hand which had previously been cut or scratched. Suddenly I remembered the day before she was taken ill I had been playing with Pooh who had unexpectedly shot out her long tongue and licked my face. Not a very comforting thought!

It was hopeless to try to feed Pooh, but during the afternoon I spent nearly an hour watching her. She seemed to me to have quietened down a little but she was still dangerous and circling to the right. That evening Pat and I discussed what we should do. Two of our children had just gone back to school. Ought we to inform their respective headmistresses? and what of the injections; ought we all to start having them straight away? It looked as though there was nothing much to be done but wait four days to see if Pooh died. The vet had been again and agreed with me that she seemed a little quieter. There was little sleep for us that night; next morning I hurried out to the barn, half expecting to find Pooh dead. Instead she was looking rather better and although she still snarled and snapped at shadows, her movements seemed more controlled and once she even circled to the left instead of always going to the right. The vet was not so sure there was much improvement and warned me again not to go anywhere near her; but on his second visit that day he too was sure she was better, for during the afternoon she had eaten some fruit I threw to her and had stopped the perpetual circling and snarling.

Next day she appeared to be back to normal and all our hopes began to rise. Even the vet took a less serious view of the situation although he could still find no explanation for her odd behaviour. Nor did we ever discover what was really wrong with her. To our immense relief it was obviously not rabies and I can only guess she was suffering from the effects of exposure and intense cold. Under such conditions a tropical animal might well lose consciousness and suffer from lack of circulation and it is even possible that her brain was temporarily damaged giving rise to a brief bout of madness as she recovered.

During her second summer Pooh spent a great deal of the time every day going for walks with Pat and the dogs or playing with her old favourite Rufus while Pat was busy in the garden. When working outside Pat always wears stout rubber gloves, especially when gardening, and Pooh often goes up to her to be fondled. She has developed a special approach when in need of affection; standing on her hind legs she walks backwards until she is able to lean against Pat, she then holds on to her by putting her front paws round behind her back, at the same time looking up at Pat and expecting to have a fuss made of her. So it was that we discovered Pooh's mania for sucking rubber gloves. One day, while playing with her, Pat took off a glove and handed it to Pooh who immediately grasped it between her front paws and started to suck the fingers. She appeared to become quite entranced, frothing at the mouth and making a contented humming noise the whole time. No doubt she derived a feeling of security from the rubber fingers which she must have associated with her mother's teats or more likely the artificial teat on the bottle used to rear her. This addiction to a rubber glove has proved useful on more than one occasion as a means of persuading Pooh to do something or other, but one thing has to be remembered at all times and that is never to try to take the glove away from her. To do that would be to court disaster for, as I have said before, a thwarted bear is a very dangerous animal.

Fortunately for us we have a kind and understanding neighbour on our boundary. He farms a considerable area and allows us to take Pooh for walks across his land where she is unlikely to meet any people. Not that she would attack anyone; rather the reverse, for she mistrusts strangers and will either run back home or disappear into thick cover. Buzz, as his friends call him, is not only a good farmer but keen on forestry as well and during the last decade has planted up odd corners and little spinneys all over his estate.

One particularly attractive copse is right on the boundary and has become one of Pooh's favourite haunts. She always goes that way on her walks and as soon as she is within a hundred yards of the wood she dashes in and disappears to grub in the gloomy light beneath the close-planted trees. Sometimes she is lucky enough to find the remains of a wood-pigeon somebody has shot and failed to pick up, or perhaps a dead rabbit. If the carcass is not too putrid she eats it, otherwise she turns it over and greedily licks up the maggots and beetles underneath. She is always busy digging in the soft sandy soil or picking off pieces of rotten bark in search of insects. For Pooh it must be like returning to the tropical jungle she has never known. Yet despite the wood's appeal and Pooh's apparent independence, she keeps one eye on Pat and if she thinks she is getting left alone she soon emerges and comes lolloping back to her.

In the autumn of her second year we decided to start taking some more film of Pooh with the idea of showing just how intelligent she was. Our plan was to devise a series of simple tests and then to film her reactions the first time she was confronted with them. We should need a set of some kind, a place outside away from distracting influences where she could be taken and put through her paces. In one of our fields an oak tree had been split by lightning and a huge limb had fallen against a sandy bank. It was one of Pooh's favourite haunts and in an ideal position for filming for it faced south and the fallen tree would provide an attractive natural background. Having agreed a series of tests we took all the necessary paraphernalia in the form of a water tank, buckets, poles, ladder, boxes and so on down to the set to get it ready.

In the majority of cases it is useless to set a problem for an animal which is completely outside its normal scope. For example one could not expect a bear to retrieve an object without being trained and we did not want to train Pooh; we wanted to discover her natural mental ability. By the same token one could not expect a dog to prise open a tin, though many will retrieve without training. How many would be able to solve a particular problem concerned with retrieving as cleverly as Rufus subsequently proved he could, s open to question; but more of that later. When endeavour-.ng to film the results of tests of this kind, it is necessary to run he camera the first time the animal is confronted with a par-icular problem. This can be wasteful since one has no idea twhat the animal's reactions will be, nor when it is going to succeed. If one waits until it has solved a problem with the idea of filming it next time, the result is often most disappoint-ing. Animals are not fools and, having once discovered the clue, they will nearly always repeat their initial success quickly and easily. The interesting thing is to watch how they find the clue in the first place and quite often luck plays an important part.

The first test we tried on Pooh involved taking an egg out of a large pail. When it was empty, except for the egg, Pooh put her head in and collected the egg in her mouth. We then put about ten inches of water in the bucket and dropped the egg in. Pooh promptly put her head in again to retrieve it, but the water went up her nose and into her eyes, making her draw back coughing and spluttering. She walked round the pail for a few moments, sniffed the water again and then put her paw in and picked up the egg. Now we filled the bucket brim full of cloudy water so that the egg was not visible but we allowed Pooh to watch it being dropped in. Without hesitation she plunged her arm in up to her shoulder and felt about until she was able to lift the egg out in her claws. As she swung round she transferred it to her mouth and carried it as gently as any gun-dog before rolling it on to the grass. Then she held it down beneath the claws of one foot and carefully cracked open the shell with the other, while her long tongue cleaned up the contents.

Sun bears are naturally clever at manipulating things with

their claws, which they can move almost like fingers; and the next test for Pooh took the form of an empty golden syrup tin with the lid hammered on. Both ends of the tin looked superficially the same and yet, after a moment's examination, she hooked her claws beneath the flange of the lid and sent it spinning through the air. We repeated this several times and not once did she attempt to open the wrong end of the tin.

Most animals need an incentive in the form of a tit-bit before they will attempt to solve a problem and Pooh was no exception. She loves both raw eggs and bananas, so these were usually the prize. For one test we put a banana at the top of a large galvanised-steel pipe driven into the ground like a fence post and about five and a half feet tall. Pooh tried to climb the slippery pipe without success so we put an orange-box close to the bottom. She immediately climbed up on to the box and standing on tip-toe could just reach the banana. We moved the box back a mere six inches and replaced the banana; she tried to reach it the same way but failed. We hoped she would understand that she had to move the box closer to the pipe but, though we repeated the test on many occasions, this was something she never managed to do, not even by accident. I have since learned that not all chimpanzees would be able to solve this particular problem, and they are usually rated high in the animal intellectual scale.

There was one test in particular which was obviously right in her world and I believe that many human beings would have earned fewer marks. We hung a banana on the end of a piece of string eight feet long. The other end of the string was tied to a bough of the fallen tree so the banana dangled just high enough for Pooh to be unable to reach it when standing on tip-toe. Bears cannot spring, but Pooh did her best to hook the banana down. Finding she was unable to reach it, she ran to the main trunk and climbed up the bough to which the string was tied. There she made her first miscalculation, for the banana was still swinging eight feet below her. She promptly tried to climb down the string which slipped through her claws so that she fell to the ground with a bump, landing on her back, the bough springing upwards with the banana still swinging wildly at the end of its string. Picking herself up, Pooh climbed the tree again, going out along the bough hanging upside down and moving hand over hand. Once at the string she leant down and hooked up a loop with one paw holding on to it in her mouth while she hooked up a second loop, putting that in her mouth in the same manner. After the third loop had been successfully gathered, the banana was almost within her grasp. She grabbed at it and in so doing the loops of string slipped from her mouth, and she was back where she started. I felt she would give up but, after a moment's pause, she put an arm round the string so that it dangled between her upper arm and her flank. She then went hand over hand along the bough, upside down, with the inevitable result that the banana was drawn steadily upwards until she was able to seize it in her mouth.

At the end of each session Pat walked home with Rufus carrying a bucket, his head held high to stop the bottom of it bumping on the ground, and Pooh running beside him. It was on one of these occasions that she turned to me and said, " You may think Pooh is clever at solving problems but I think old Rufus is just as intelligent."

" So he may be," I replied, " but can you prove it? "

" We can try, and it might make an interesting piece of film," she said.

Her idea was to put two plastic food-bowls on the ground and send Rufus to fetch both at once. The bowls had no lip and tapered from the edge down to a fairly small base. I set up the camera and decided to film his very first attempt. " Go on, Rufus, fetch those bowls," she ordered. He got up and ran to them taking the nearest in his mouth. " No, both bowls, Rufus, fetch the other one as well." He looked puzzled and, putting his bowl down to pick up the second, he started to come back. " No, Rufus, fetch BOTH bowls," she repeated. He seemed to understand and, dropping his bowl beside the other one, he attempted to pick both up at once by grasping the two edges in his mouth, just as we can pick up two glasses together with a thumb in one and an index finger in the other. Unfortunately the bowls were tapered and slippery and immediately slid out of his mouth. Picking up one of them he deliberately placed it inside the other, then let go of it and transferred his grip to carry both triumphantly back to Pat.

This was the very first time either of us had ever thought of testing him in this way and we were both astonished at the result. Of course it cannot be denied that luck may have been on his side. It could have been luck that he put one bowl inside the other, but even so he was clever enough to perceive at once that he could carry them both that way. The whole action is recorded on film without a cut and everyone who has seen it agrees that it looks as though his action was deliberate. Since then we have often repeated the performance for our friends to watch and he soon learned to pick up three bowls at once, putting one inside the other to carry them. While this may not be an outstanding feat for a retriever, I feel it does demonstrate that Rufus is highly intelligent in his particular sphere. The point I want to emphasise is that we have never trained him to carry things and that his ability to solve this problem was entirely due to his innate brain-power.

Bears are well known to be heavy sleepers and Pooh spends the night curled up in a tight ball in the deep straw of her den. Nor is she an early riser, particularly during the winter months when it is often eleven o'clock in the morning before she gets up. Then she appears at the entrance to her den with short pieces of straw clinging to her coat. Sleepily she sniffs the morning air, then she yawns, putting out her tongue to its full length and curling the end under into a complete circle. Being tropical animals, sun bears do not hibernate but remain active throughout the winter. At the same time we have noticed that Pooh puts on a good layer of fat every autumn and she seems to do this automatically without eating any extra food. Then her shiny black coat ripples over the rolls of fat beneath. Her diet has remained much the same all the time we have had her, a basis of cooked tripe and hound meal served hot with plenty of gravy, two or three oranges, half a dozen bananas and any other fruit that happens to be available with lumps of fat, bones or raw meat for a change. Melon is perhaps her favourite fruit and once or twice each week she gets raw eggs, yeast and a vitamin supplement added to her usual meal.

When Pooh was two years old Pat went abroad for a short holiday with her parents and I took over the job of taking the bear and dogs for their daily walk. There was nothing very new in this. I often accompanied Pat when she took them and indeed Pooh was always pleased to see me and regarded me as a sparring partner. We used to have great games, shadow boxing and a general rough-and-tumble, things which she never attempted to try with Pat. In consequence I was not prepared for the sudden change in her demeanour on the first day I tried to take her out. Picking up Pat's rubber gardening gloves, two bananas and some sweet biscuits, all of which are Pooh's special favourites, I called Rufus and went out to her cage. She seemed quite pleased to see me and I handed her a banana. The trouble started as soon as she walked out of her cage door. She stopped, stood up on her hind legs and looked for Pat; finding she was not there, she immediately ran back into her cage. It took me half an hour to persuade her to come out again and this time I got her to follow me forty yards when suddenly she panicked and ran back once more. I felt sure she would come with me if only I could get her right away from the buildings and out into the countryside, but how? The last thing I wanted to do was to upset her and run the risk of being attacked.

Eventually I enlisted the help of three members of the staff, each of them carrying an empty bucket or tin can with an implement of some kind with which to bang it like a gong. They hid behind the corner of the hay barn and waited. At last Pooh consented to come out of her cage and follow me hesitantly down the path. Every familiar object which she had passed hundreds of times seemed to scare her, a gate post became a ghostly spectre waiting to pounce on her, while behind every bush lurked a terrifying enemy. I dropped pieces of biscuit as I walked to lure her on and after many stops we eventually reached the slip rails into the horses' field. Rufus and I went under them and on down the field, Pooh reached the rails and stood up to examine them, then she turned and started to run for home. That was the signal the others had been waiting for and the three of them lined the way, banging and crashing their pails and tins and making an awful din. It was more than Pooh could stand; she turned and fled back to me. As she approached I called Rufus and we both ran down towards her favourite spinney. Pooh followed behind and for the rest of the walk was no trouble. Once safely out in the country, I thought she would behave normally again, climbing trees, playing with Rufus or having mock battles with me. Instead she loped along in a melancholy mood, keeping aloof from both of us. Nothing would induce her to play and, when I handed her one of her beloved rubber gloves, she stood up and sucked it half heartedly for a minute or two, then dropped it and ambled off. As soon as we retraced our steps up the horses' field towards home, Pooh scampered ahead to the safety of her cage. It was the same all the time Pat was away. Every day I had an awful job to get her to come with me and when she did she walked along in a vacant mood, taking not the least interest in anything.

It was snowing the day Pat came home and one of the first things she did was to take Pooh out for a walk. I went with them and the change in Pooh's behaviour was astonishing. She was full of life, digging in the hedges, climbing trees and rushing up to me for a game. All her interest in life had returned and she was as inquisitive as ever. I have no doubt that she missed Pat during her absence but not, I think, in the sentimental way one might imagine. For Pooh it was something more basic. Without Pat's familiar figure she felt insecure and lonely, her protector had gone and the only really safe place was inside her cage, her own familiar territory upon which nobody ever trespassed. Even her old friend Rufus was no substitute. As for me, I was merely an irresponsible male without the least idea how to protect a frightened bear who could so easily kill a man!

I have only once ever felt in any real danger from Pooh and it happened during the terrible winter of 1962-3. As is usually the case with animals, the incident arose largely through my own fault. For weeks the whole countryside had lain beneath a sheet of frozen snow. Life had been a battle for survival in temperatures usually confined to polar regions. Every day was one of ceaseless toil to provide food and water not only for all our animals but for ourselves. As fast as we hacked holes in the ice for the waterfowl, otters or coypu, it froze again so that in the end the little drop of open water was at the bottom of a shaft of ice over a foot thick. There was the danger that birds or animals might get in and be unable to get out again. There were oil heaters to tend in some of the more distant pens and all our stock had to have extra food against the cold.

In spite of the weather Pooh went for her daily walk unless the blizzards were too severe. One afternoon she gave Pat the slip and ran round the house and on to the lawn. We had hung some large lumps of fat from the boughs of an apple tree near the kitchen window and Pooh soon noticed them. She was up the tree in a flash and reaching for the fat. She managed to hook the string of the nearest piece and soon ate it, then she tried to get the next one, but it was beyond her reach and the boughs were too thin and whippy to support her weight. She struggled in vain and in true bear fashion she lost her temper and started to roar and shake the boughs to try to knock the fat down. Hearing the noise Pat went on to the lawn carrying Pooh's hot dinner steaming in a bowl. She called to her to come to have her food and Pooh obediently climbed down the tree and started off towards her. At that moment I arrived from the opposite direction, carrying a stiff broom, to see what all the fuss was about. Just as she reached Pat, Pooh changed her mind and ran back towards the apple tree and the swinging fat. I ran to try to head her off, waving the broom and shouting at her, but the moment she saw me she changed course and with a dreadful roar came straight for me.

In a flash I realised this was a full-blooded charge and that she meant business. I don't think I have ever run as quickly despite the fact I was wearing rubber boots and running on ice. Dropping the broom I sped for the gap in the blackthorn hedge leading to the vegetable garden. There was a sharp turn to negotiate and the path was frozen and slippery but in my panic I grabbed the hedge with my bare hands and never even felt the thorns as I used it to swing myself round the corner. Down the path towards the barn I fled with Pooh emitting a series of short roars more like barks close on my heels. There is quite a steep slope at the end of the vegetable garden and it was covered with ice; as I reached it I realised too late what would happen. The next thing I remember was falling heavily on to my right shoulder and skidding head first along the ice.

I thought that this was the end and that I should be lucky to escape with a bad mauling if not worse. As I slithered across

Growing up.   Pooh at twelve months old, out for her daily walk

Above: left, the golden pheasant, common in captivity yet its nest and eggs in the wild remain undescribed; right, the common koklass, first bred in Britain by the Trust. Below, perhaps only a few hundred mikado pheasants remain alive today

the ice I tried frantically to get to my feet and, though it seemed to take an age, I was actually up and running on before I had stopped sliding. Making for open country as fast as I could go I became conscious that I was no longer being followed. I glanced back and Pooh was nowhere to be seen. Very cautiously I retraced my steps and was just in time to see her going back through the vegetable garden. Apparently Pooh had come a cropper too. As she charged down the slope she skidded sideways, rolling over and over, and by the time she recovered I was twenty yards away and she had lost the impetus of her charge. Some who have heard this tale have said, " Why didn't you stand your ground and ward off her attack with the broom?" They have no conception of the determination and power behind a real charge. Nothing but a bullet would stop Pooh once she had room to gather speed and, as for the broom, it would either be knocked from one's grasp or splintered like a matchstick.

We have tried Pooh with a number of toys; some she has ignored, others she has destroyed, but over the years we have learned the sort of thing that is likely to amuse her New toys are apt to prove a novelty at first but are soon forgotten for, like a child, Pooh has certain old favourites; chief among these is a hefty piece of bog-oak five feet long and too hard for her to chew but just the right size for her to wrestle with. Tins never fail to intrigue her, especially if they have previously contained some sweet substance. Buckets, old saucepans, brooms and a rubber car tyre also figure high on her list. One particular saucepan is a special favourite. It is made of heavy steel and has two handles, one at each side of the rim. Sometimes she hooks a claw through one of the handles and walks upright round her pen with the saucepan dangling nonchalantly from a front paw. At other times she wears it on her head like a hat, dancing round on her hind legs swaying from side to side and generally playing the fool. Rain never seems to bother Pooh and in warm weather she loves to sit out in a storm, looking up at the sky with her mouth wide open to catch the rain drops.

During her third summer there were scenes of unprecedented activity at Great Witchingham, gangs of men and noisy machines worked seven days a week. From the roof of her den Pooh watched it all with interest and during her walks would be taken to inspect the progress. Little did she know that within a few short months all this activity would start a new chapter in her life with us, but that is another story which must wait a little while.

15. *The Rarest Pheasants in the World*

It was half past eleven on a wet night in October 1957. John Yealland and I were walking up the Brompton Road towards Knightsbridge when he suddenly said, " If somebody doesn't do something, a good many breeds of pheasant will soon be extinct."

John is curator of birds at London Zoo and we had known each other for many years. I too was concerned for the future of many species of pheasant, for of the 150 forms known to science only one, the rare Congo Peacock, is found outside Asia. I do not, of course, include the various mixtures of game pheasants turned down for sporting purposes and now feral in many parts of the world.

Throughout almost all Asia the human population is expanding at a terrifying rate, forests are being felled, grasslands ploughed and scrub cleared to make way for cultivation for more villages, towns and roads. Add the fact that pheasants are good to eat and most of them highly colourful and it is not difficult to understand their swift decrease in a world where firearms are rapidly replacing more primitive weapons.

On top of all this many species occupy a very restricted range in the wild and are therefore even more vulnerable. Some, like the beautiful Mikado Pheasant, of which the male is a deep bluish purple with red wattles and a purple and white barred tail, are found only on one particular island, in its case

Taiwan, or Formosa as it used to be called. There the Mikado inhabits the bamboo and juniper thickets of the mist-enshrouded mountains above five thousand feet. It has never been common and is now considered almost extinct.

Also in Taiwan, but living in the central mountains at lower altitudes, is another beautiful species, Swinhoe's Pheasant, named after a British Consul there, who discovered the bird in 1862. Like the Mikado, Swinhoe's has never been common on the island and it too is in danger of disappearing for ever. The male Swinhoe's is a magnificent upstanding bird, his neck, underparts, rump and outer tail feathers being a dark metallic blue; a white crest tops his head and there is a white patch on his back; his scapulars are bright maroon set against the greenish sheen of the wing coverts. Curving gracefully in an arc in the centre of his deep blue tail are two large white feathers, these, with his crimson wattles and legs, contrast with the darker hues of his body.

Several other species were known to be in similar plight and the question was how to set about saving them. The obvious answer was to breed large numbers in captivity and then to return young birds to their native land where they would be released to augment the depleted wild stock. But there were difficulties to be overcome.

In the first place nobody knew just how many species of pheasant existed in captivity in Britain or what their numbers were. There had been very few importations since the war owing to stringent fowl pest regulations imposed, quite rightly, by the Ministry of Agriculture. These regulations require all imported pheasants to spend a minimum of four weeks in quarantine at the approved quarters of an urban zoo. During this period they are subjected to various tests by the Ministry, and if any bird reacts to the blood test for fowl pest the whole consignment is slaughtered without compensation. At that time I was on the Council of the Avicultural Society, as were John Yealland and a number of other prominent aviculturists whom I knew. We discussed the problem at length and eventually it was decided to send a questionnaire to every zoo and known breeder of pheasants in the United Kingdom. Every member of the Society received a copy with the request that, if they did not keep pheasants, they should pass it on to anyone they knew who did. In this way a complete coverage was made and the response was excellent.

Several months later I was able to compile a summary of the nation-wide census which was published in the *Avicultural Magazine* of January 1959. One thing emerged with startling clarity: there were even fewer pheasants in captivity than we had thought. Twenty-seven species were represented and of these ten consisted only of odd birds and no breeding pairs. Of the remaining seventeen species only a dozen exceeded twelve pairs in the whole country. But the position was even worse than the census showed, because nearly all the rarer forms consisted of old birds which had been inbred for generations and were thus infertile.

Large importations would have to be made before numbers could be propagated up to even pre-war level, let alone to the scale we hoped for. This was something outside the scope of the private individual and it seemed to me that a trust would have to be formed which, aided by public funds and goodwill, would be in a position to carry out the work.

It may be wondered why this could not be done by a group of private enthusiasts, but unfortunately any such scheme is doomed to failure from the start. Most aviculturists like to keep a number of different species and, as their accommodation is usually limited, it is not possible for them to maintain more than two or three breeding pairs of one particular form. An accident or a run of bad luck can soon wipe out such a small breeding stock. Again, rare species are usually worth a lot of money on account of their scarcity, and the temptation to sell a few pairs each year at fifty to a hundred pounds per pair is one few private breeders can resist. So it goes on, and a potential breeding stock of rare birds is frittered away. A classic example is that of Temminck's Tragopan, one of the most beautiful members of this family and the easiest to keep in captivity.

Quite large numbers of Temminck's were bred in one or two pheasantries between the wars and even as recently as the nineteen forties. The young birds commanded a good price and found a ready market, many of them being sent abroad. Most of them ended up in private collections run by people who had no idea how to look after them, with the result that only a handful of breeding stock remained and they were too old and inbred to be of much use. This is what happens when commercial interest takes precedence over good husbandry.

Finally I raised the matter at a council meeting of the Avicultural Society. Having explained the position I suggested that a trust should be formed under the patronage of the Society for the express purpose of saving those species of pheasant and other game birds threatened with extinction in the wild by breeding large numbers in captivity. In those days I kept a small collection of pheasants numbering about fifty individuals of eleven species. I offered to present them all to the trust as a nucleus.

As no financial help was possible it was agreed that the new trust would have to be supported by its own membership and by donations. In addition a certain proportion of the trust's council would have to be drawn from the members of the Avicultural Society. I left that meeting with a nasty feeling that I might have bitten off more than I could chew.

Towards the end of 1959 the Ornamental Pheasant Trust came into being. I disliked the word " Ornamental" and still do because it seems unnecessary. Most birds are ornamental without having the word as a tag. But it was felt that without it the public might think the trust was concerned with shooting pheasants instead of protecting them.

As for the birds themselves we were to have three pieces

of luck during our first year. The first was the presentation by Arthur Prestwich of a pair of Swinhoe's Pheasants which had been caught in the wild in Taiwan and sent to this country. They were probably the first wild Swinhoe's to be imported into Europe in this century and provided a much needed change of blood. Though very nervous when they first arrived, they settled down in a large pen well planted with flowering shrubs and the hen laid a number of eggs from which two male birds were reared. Both of them are still alive in the collection to-day and their influence on our stock of these pheasants has been most marked. Until their arrival nearly all the Swinhoe's in captivity had been bred from one pair imported into Europe in 1866 with the result they were all highly inbred.

Then a friend of mine, Ken Searle, had a medical practice in Hong Kong and was prepared to procure birds for us from various parts of the Far East. That year he spent his annual holiday in the wilds of British North Borneo in the Sandakan River area and after several weeks of intensive trapping in the forest he had caught a trio of Bornean Great Argus and several Greater Bornean Crested Fireback Pheasants as well as a number of the rare Chestnut Flanked Bornean Tree Partridges. In spite of numerous hazards he managed to get them all safely to Hong Kong by sea and, as soon as they had become accustomed to captivity, they were packed in specially padded boxes and flown to this country.

The Bornean Great Argus has very rarely been imported and none had been seen alive in Britain for many years. The male is a remarkable bird, large as pheasants go, and though not brilliantly coloured, his plumage is unique. He carries his tail parallel with the ground and the two central feathers are of enormous length, delicately patterned and twisted at the ends. His wings are even more fantastic for, while the flight feathers or primaries are of normal length and width, the secondaries are very much longer and square tipped; an individual feather may be as wide as five inches at the end. Nor is this all, for each feather is a marvel of intricate design and each has a chain of superb *ocelli* set like precious stones along its entire length just below the shaft. These *ocelli* or " eyes " are a delicate shade of blue-grey shading to greenish-blue with golden centres so that they appear to change colour according to the light. Below the line of *ocelli*, the broad web of the feather is a complicated pattern of dark brown and white wavy lines running lengthwise like tide ripples in the sand. Above the shaft the design changes to a multitude of dark brown spots set against a pale background shading to whitish along the upper edge. Finally the broad tip of each feather is brown spangled with hundreds of tiny white tsarlets.

In the wild, Argus are shy and retiring birds inhabiting deep forest. Each male takes up his own territory where he makes his presence known by his loud and persistent call. Somewhere within his territory is his display ground, a circular area of the forest floor four or five yards in diameter, which the bird has picked clean of every leaf, twig and small stone. During the nesting season the Argus stays near his display ground and when the hen bird comes into breeding condition she goes to find him aided by his frequent calls. It is then that he performs his incredible dance which culminates in his wings being fully spread and arched over his back to form a huge circular fan above the centre of which the two long central tail feathers stand upright. During this display the bird's legs are bent and his head held back, hidden by the wings through which he peers at the hen from time to time.

Two of the three Argus caught by Ken Searle are still alive in the collection and the male's plumage seems to grow more fantastic after every moult. Last summer the hen appeared to come into breeding condition, so perhaps we shall be lucky enough to breed them before long. The Firebacks from

Borneo also settled down despite the difference in climate and last year one of the females laid several eggs which unfortunately were infertile. All the tropical pheasants are kept in large pens, each of which has a sturdy wooden hut heated either by electricity or oil lamps in the winter.

Soon after Ken returned to Hong Kong he met a Chinese who had contact with Peking and who offered to get several pairs of the very rare Cabot's Tragopan for him from Szechuan. Like all tragopans, and there are six known forms, Cabot's is a most beautiful bird. The male is large and his plumage is a complicated yet delicate pattern of red, black and pale buff. His head and neck are black, with the sides and tip of the crest and the sides of his neck bright orange-red. On each side of his face is a large area of bare skin, bright orange-yellow in colour and reaching round under his chin.

The most extraordinary thing about tragopans is their display. The males have two fleshy horns which are normally hidden beneath the feathers of the crown. Under their throat is a lappet of skin which is usually shrivelled up and hardly noticeable. But during his display the bird erects the two horns on his head and at the same time lowers his lappet so that it hangs like an apron over his breast. This lappet is really a thin flap of brilliantly coloured skin. The male Cabot's tragopan has pale blue horns, while his lappet is bright orange with purple spots in the centre surrounded by vivid blue with greenish-grey patches. Fully extended it measures as much as five or six inches in depth and nearly three inches in width. Despite its size it can be retracted in a matter of seconds.

Cabot's tragopan are not easy to establish in captivity, but of the five males and two females to reach this country a pair is still alive and doing well in the trust's collection. From them we have bred ten young birds in the last three years. These are the only Cabot's to have been reared in Britain since the beginning of the century and, if we are lucky enough to import a few more birds from the Far East, there would appear to be a reasonable prospect of establishing this rare species in captivity.

Soon after sending the tragopans, Ken chanced to visit the premises of a bird dealer in Hong Kong. Amongst a jumble of bamboo cages and wicker baskets he noticed a large white bird which at first sight he took to be a chicken. He was about to leave the shop when something about that bird made him look again and to his amazement he found it was a beautiful specimen of the White Eared Pheasant from Szechuan. Naturally he bought it at once and it soon joined the collection where it proved to be a female. From that day to this we have sought a mate for her without success, and as the years go by our solitary White Crossoptilon grows no younger and remains the only representative of her race in Western Europe.

White Eared Pheasants are also found in Tibet where they are, or were, given complete protection in the vicinity of the monasteries. They are large and powerful birds, chiefly white in colour but with bright red legs and a large patch of scarlet skin each side of their face. The top of their head is covered with black velvety-looking feathers, while the white ear tufts, so prominent in other species of eared pheasants, are short and barely noticeable. The snow white plumage shades to greyish-purple on the wings and the beautifully disintegrated tail feathers curving over like miniature ostrich plumes are a glossy shade of greenish-purple at their tips. With the single White Eared the trust has representatives of all three species of crossoptilon, White, Blue and Brown, which come from China.

One further instance will suffice to show what an important part luck plays when one is trying to collect a breeding stock of rare animals of any kind. This time Pat and I were returning from a visit to London, just as we were on the day we found Pooh Bear. We made our usual stop at the same animal dealer's shop and I asked whether they had anything which might interest us. In reply I was shown a cage containing a pair of pheasants which had recently arrived from India amongst a large consignment of small birds and mammals. I recognised them at once as Koklass Pheasants, though at the time I was uncertain to which form they belonged.

Koklass are high mountain birds and come from the western Himalayas and North Eastern Tibet across to Eastern and Northern China. There are ten distinct forms, but they are distinguished from each other only by comparatively slight plumage differences. Like many birds from high altitudes they had acquired a reputation for being difficult to keep alive in captivity. They had never been bred in Britain and had long since died out in Europe where very few were bred in the closing years of the nineteenth century.

The prospects of keeping this pair alive seemed rather poor. Nevertheless I decided to buy them and give them to the trust. The cock was in good condition, but the hen was terribly thin and I felt sure she would not survive for long. Back in Norfolk I put them in a large enclosure and gave them a variety of food including our standard pheasant breeders' pellets, whole wheat, chopped fresh fruit, live maggots and minced raw meat. Although it was in the middle of winter it was soon apparent they preferred fresh grass to anything else. They cropped it short just like geese and only ate fruit when snow covered the grass. Raw meat was ignored, though they took some maggots and seemed to like the pellets. After a month, to my great surprise, the female had put on flesh and both birds looked very well.

Having studied the literature and read of the extraordinary difficulties attendant upon keeping Koklass alive in captivity, I hardly expected to breed them. To keep them alive and well for several years would be an achievement since it would enable us to study their behaviour, display and food preferences, besides giving many people a unique opportunity to see living examples of a very unusual species.

Our pair continued to thrive but one evening in May when

I was going round the breeding pens I could not find the hen. The cock was much in evidence but the hen seemed to have vanished into thin air. It is surprising how easily a pheasant can vanish in a pen nine yards wide by twenty long with a few shrubs growing in it. Even the long grass round the edge against the netting has to be searched yard by yard. Eventually I found the hen Koklass squatting under some fir boughs close to the hut. When I put my hand in to disturb her, she fluffed out her feathers and pecked but she dd not run away as I had expected. I lifted her gently and thiere to my delight was a nestful of shiny eggs. There were seven in all, richly blotched with different shades of reddish-brown against a creamy buff background.

Exciting though this was, there was no guarantee that they would be fertile. I knew that if we took this clutch and put them under a bantam hen the Koklass would probably lay again, and so this is what we decided to do. Just over a week later seven fluffy chicks hatched from the seven eggs, so the Koklass had obviously been sitting for nearly a fortnight before I found her. She laid a second clutch of five eggs later that summer and from them four chicks were hatched. Unfortunately we found those first broods rather difficult to rear, but seven youngsters reached maturity and, with their parents, were to establish the Common Koklass in captivity for the first time in history.

Since then thirty-three young birds have been reared in three years, so it has been possible to send pairs out from the Trust to join members' private collections as an additional insurance against disease striking the breeding stock at Great Witchingham.

Perhaps one of the most exciting things about keeping rare creatures is the chance to discover or observe something hitherto unknown. This was the case with the display of the Koklass pheasant. No detailed description occurs in the literature and it is extremely unlikely that the courtship of these birds had ever been observed before. Early one May a two-year-old hen laid an egg but at the time she was not mated since the one male bird available was only a year old. On the chance that he might be fertile we immediately put him in with the hen. No sooner was this done than she started to display. She was obviously in full breeding condition while the cock was too young. Despite this she did her best to stimulate him. While he walked around with his head upstretched and with the two patches of small white feathers on his cheeks standing on end, the hen circled round and round him with her tail spread fan shaped and tilted towards him. Every few moments she would smartly lower the primaries of the wing on the opposite side to the cock, so that the tips of the feathers brushed the ground, her head was held low and stretched forward during the display. She kept up a quiet clucking note the whole time, not unlike a domestic chicken.

Although in this case the hen took the initiative because the cock was not in breeding condition, the following year I was able to watch a male bird displaying to a hen in the normal way. While she stood still with her neck outstretched and head held low, he circled round her with his tail fanned and tilted towards her; his feathers were puffed out and he walked with his body leaning sharply away from the hen. He sometimes lowered the primaries of the wing away from her so that the tips touched the ground just as the hen had done the previous year. The difference was in the head carriage, for the male held his head erect and raised his long crest so that the feathers stood up vertically. The hen was silent but the cock kept up a curious clucking note and in both birds the patches of short feathers on each cheek stood out parallel with the ground.

Four years after the importation of the Swinhoe's Pheasants caught in the wild in Taiwan the number of young birds reared by the trust had reached a total of seventy-seven. The time had come when the first consignment could be returned to their native land to join their wild relatives in the mist-enshrouded mountains. The authorities in Taipeh were informed and in due course accepted our offer. They asked that the birds should remain in this country while a National Reserve was created on the island in which they could be released without risk of poaching by the natives.

That our young Swinhoe's should influence a government to create what may well be its first National Nature Reserve was beyond our wildest dreams. That is the position as I write; the birds are still here and we await further news from Taiwan. Meanwhile more young are being reared.

During 1962 the authorities in Taiwan presented a male Mikado to the trust and a pair to one of our members, John Swain. He very generously asked that they too should join the trust's collection and so three birds arrived. They had all been trapped by natives in the mountains in the interior of the island and had suffered considerable damage during the journey down to Taipeh. Both males eventually succumbed, but the female survived and to our surprise laid five eggs the following summer. From them two young birds were reared, both of them females. A small beginning perhaps, but with luck and the possibility of further wild-caught specimens we yet may be able to produce large numbers of this beautiful bird and so save it for posterity.

All these imported birds naturally had to go into quarantine upon arrival in this country; and at that time the trust had no quarantine quarters of its own. Various urban zoos came to our rescue and generously agreed to take our birds in their own quarters. Without their help we should have achieved very little in the first four years.

One other extremely rare pheasant was soon to arrive, this time because of the enthusiasm of an old friend who is also a member of our council. Fred Johnson had been talking about Hume's Bartailed Pheasant from Burma ever since I had known him. This bird had never been kept in captivity outside Burma and so was unknown in the western world other than as a museum skin. After years of disappointment Fred finally heard of an Indian willing to undertake the hazardous journey into the Naga hills on the borders of Assam and Northern Burma, an area noted for the hostility of the warlike tribes living there. Although the man asked a high price before he was willing to undertake the expedition, Fred had the courage to finance him and in due course he left Calcutta and disappeared into the blue. Nothing was heard of him for many months. Then one day a cable arrived; the man had returned safely bringing with him no less than seven Hume's Bartailed Pheasants. They all survived the journey and the following summer Fred successfully bred a number of young ones. A pair was sent to the trust.

Other varieties soon began to arrive from the East; Green Peafowl from Indo-China, Vieillot's Crested Fireback and the beautiful Malay Ferruginous Wood Partridge from Bangkok, Satyr Tragopans from India and so on. So by the end of 1963, four years after its inception, the Ornamental Pheasant Trust possessed what was probably the most comprehensive collection of game birds in Europe, comprising no less than 387 individuals of forty-six forms.

Finding the pens to accommodate a rapidly growing collection of birds on this scale might well have been a considerable difficulty but for the fact that I had so recently given up my turkey and poultry farming enterprises. Much of the equipment was quite suitable for pheasants with minor modifications, so nearly one hundred small portable pens or folds are on long loan to the trust, while a further thirty poultry range shelters have been adapted as pheasant shelters in some of the trust's larger breeding pens.

During our second year the Leckford pheasantries belonging to Spedan Lewis were discontinued and we were able to buy most of the old breeding birds. At the same time I was lucky enough to purchase all the very fine huts which had been specially built just before the war of top quality timber still in first class order. Most of them I gave to the trust since they are particularly useful for accommodating tropical pheasants which require some extra heat in winter.

Last year we reared over three hundred and forty young pheasants of twenty different forms and the number is likely to increase with each season, so we have been forced to evolve a reasonably labour-saving and efficient method of rearing, yet one which enables the poults to be kept in small individual broods of eight or ten chicks. All eggs are collected as they are laid and marked with the number of the pen from which they came. As soon as a full clutch of perhaps ten eggs of one species has been gathered they are set under a broody bantam.

At the height of the season we often have over a hundred bantams sitting on pheasant and waterfowl eggs and this necessitates keeping a flock of four hundred Silky crossed with Light Sussex bantams especially for this work. The setting boxes are arranged in long rows on top of hollow breeze-block walls three feet high. These walls are packed with earth so that the eggs lie in a hollow just as they would on the ground. Opposite each line of setting boxes and at the same height is a corresponding number of wire cages also in a long line and having automatic water and food. The whole lay-out is under cover and the girl in charge can easily handle all the broodies every afternoon. All she has to do is to lift each bantam carefully from its nest, place it in the cage opposite and leave it there for twenty minutes to eat and drink while she turns and damps the eggs. When the twenty minutes is up for the first bird in the row she starts putting them all back again and so on.

As soon as they have hatched and are dry the young pheasants are taken with their bantam and put in a small coop

A two year old roe-buck

Baby-sitting. Rufus with Bracken

A word in your ear. Rufus and Pooh on a winter ramble

Sucking the fingers of a rubber glove is Pooh's idea of ecstasy

where they have additional electric heating. They are fed on a proprietary brand of pheasant starter crumbs with the addition of such delicacies as live maggots, mealworms, grated yolk of hard-boiled egg, chopped lettuce or fruit for those that need it.

At the age of two or three weeks the poults are moved to bigger electrically heated coops without their bantam and as soon as they are feathered they are transferred to larger portable fold units which are moved frequently on to fresh grass. In some cases there is a surplus of young birds at the end of the rearing season and members of the Trust are given first chance of buying them for their own collections. In the case of some of the rarest species, one or two pairs have been deposited with members to spread the risk of loss through disease.

As the trust's collection grew, so did my own collection of birds and mammals which featured in my television programmes and films of animal behaviour. More and more people wanted to come and look round and, since it has always been our policy never to refuse anyone the chance of seeing our animals, life became a little difficult. It occurred to us that we could help the finances of the trust by opening the whole place to the public and charging admission; the only problem was where to do it. For two years we searched Norfolk for a suitable property without success. Land prices were rising all the time and the sort of place we envisaged was rarely sold, and if it was the price was out of our reach. It was Pat who discovered the answer to the problem one summer evening on our own doorstep.

16. Britain's first Wildlife Park

Hawks Hill is a small house of considerable age, its bricks have become mellowed and flaked with the passage of time, and a succession of owners has each added something to satisfy a particular need.

The requirements of a large family have compelled us to continue the process and in the past eight years we have enlarged the kitchen, turned the garage into a centrally-heated office with a studio over the top and built a separate playroom for our children. Despite these amenities and an outward appearance of character, the house remains what it is, two very old cottages knocked into one, with walls that are not true, floors that are not level, and windows and doors which do not fit. In winter the draughts have to be endured to be believed, they come up even through the floor boards, and the sight of a fitted carpet in the drawing-room heaving and billowing like a restless ocean has puzzled many an after-dinner guest.

With all its faults Hawks Hill has certain advantages, among them a main living-room of great charm, forty feet long with a large fire-place at each end and windows facing south. Despite its size this room is always warm and cheerful. The position of the house is another point in its favour. It stands at the end of a longish drive almost plumb in the middle of fifty acres of grassland divided by old thorn hedges in which mature oaks still stand. Since we came we have planted many more trees and some hundreds of flowering shrubs. The old garden has been enlarged and a new waterfowl garden laid out to the west of the drive with half a dozen pools and enclosures attractively planted with trees and shrubs. It was made to accommodate the ducks and geese which moved in when we came. In nine years the trees have sprung up, some of them twenty feet and more, while sedges, reed mace and water iris line the banks of the pools, converting what was once a thistle-strewn meadow into a most attractive shrub and water garden.

Thus was Hawks Hill three years ago. It was summer time, the countryside was a chequered pattern of greens from unripe corn, grassland, trees and hedgerow. Pat was out on one of her evening walks with Pooh and, seeing them in the distance on Whitwell Hill, I set out to join them. We met on the far slope of the little valley which runs between house and hill and almost at once Pat said, "You know, I've been thinking about finding another place and I don't believe we will ever beat this. Why don't we lay out this side and admit the public from the Reepham Road?"

I knew at once she was right. The valley itself had tremendous possibilities, running as it does from south-west to north-east, with gently sloping grassland on either side. Although bounded by the main road, the whole area is well screened with trees and hedges and the public would have an easy access from the minor road which runs along our western boundary.

It was only when we began serious planning that we realised how lucky we were to own that particular piece of land. It had been down to grass for some years, and the spot where we proposed to build the gate-house and tea-room commanded a magnificent view of rural England to the north and east. We could imagine ourselves sitting on the terrace of the non-existent building looking across the park with its enclosures, aviaries and paddocks, allowing our eyes to wander across miles of undulating countryside with its churches, fields and hamlets, watching the rooks circling and drifting above their chosen copse beyond the river. The aviaries and enclosures would, like the tea-room and gate-house, have to be made but the view would always be there, changed in season by the ploughs turning the golden stubble into rich brown earth over which the gulls would tumble and flutter like whirling snowflakes. In winter the tall oaks of Hackford Wood stand with their dark traceries clear cut against the sky-line like a Roland Hilder painting.

There were other more practical advantages of this particular site. Not only did it run up to the main road and yet have easy accesss from a side road, but it was well situated fourteen miles north-west of Norwich. No doubt, in the first few years at any rate, most of our visitors would come from that ancient city with its narrow winding cobblestone streets steeped in history and its increasing industrial population. Fourteen miles seemed just about the distance a family could be expected to drive out for the afternoon.

We decided to fence in a block of twenty-eight acres to start with. This would include the valley and what were soon to be called the old waterfowl gardens. It would still leave us with some privacy since the house and the rest of the property would be outside the perimeter of the park. The problem was how to mould the area to bring out the best in it and to use every natural advantage.

The bare essentials were fairly obvious. Water is always an attraction and we decided to make a chain of pools running down the valley which would be fed from our own bore-hole. A stout perimeter fence would be necessary both to prevent foxes and two-legged visitors from making unwanted night-time excursions and to prevent or delay the escape of any of our animals. A gate-house and tea-room combined, a car park and public lavatories were also essential and we knew where they ought to go. One important hurdle remained—to get planning permission. We submitted our rather vague applica-

*Bokhara on his weathering block
with the Island Pool beyond*

Spoonbill feeding

Pooh examines the swing in her new enclosure, which was moved away from the tree on the right to prevent further suicide attempts

Barbary sheep from the Atlas Mountains

tion and were agreeably surprised at the extremely co-operative attitude of the County Council. Within a matter of weeks they gave us the go-ahead.

We were anxious to make all the paddocks and enclosures as large as possible and to plant them with appropriate trees and shrubs; we intended to preserve an open, park-like aspect of acres of mown grass upon which it would be a pleasure to walk, and above all we were determined to avoid cages in the conventional sense. Concrete or tarmacadam paths and rows of stereotype aviaries were out as far as we were concerned. Together we worked out a master plan upon which we marked the proposed position of every enclosure, aviary and tree, even though we realised that it would take several years to finish.

One blustery March day, seven months after we began planning, a bulldozer arrived to begin digging out the series of ponds whose outline we had previously marked with wooden pegs driven into the ground. We had taken pains to place each one in a natural-looking position and to vary the shape as much as possible. The natural slope of the land was a great asset, not only because one expects to find water in a valley, but because all the spoil would be needed to build up the lower end of each pool and so there would be no unsightly heaps to cart away or spread. The bulldozer worked with staggering speed and at the end of a month seven pools had been made; the last and lowest in the chain was also the largest, covering about three-quarters of an acre and having two islands. I had miscalculated the amount of earth which would be required to build up the lower end to the correct level. This turned out to be twelve feet above ground, and to get the necessary material the bulldozer had to work deeper and deeper in the bottom of the pool, pushing the spoil up to form the bank. The result was quite an impressive-looking dam containing water over twelve feet deep.

We were determined to open on the first of August of that

year, which only left a bare five months. With the improvement in the weather towards the end of March work began in earnest. We had ordered a large prefabricated building of oiled Canadian red cedar and elm boarding to be built to our design to serve as gate-house, tea-room and shop. It was to be attractive in appearance and to have large picture windows from which people would be able to look right across the park. A firm of local builders began work on the concrete foundations and at the same time started building the public lavatories complete with their own drainage system and septic tank.

A mechanical excavator arrived to prepare the sites for the concrete enclosures which were to be sunk in the ground with only a low wall remaining in view. Pools for otters and coypu were to be constructed this way, as well as an enclosure for marmots and eventually new and really spacious quarters for Pooh Bear. While another firm of builders worked on these, water engineers had started to lay two-inch polythene piping underground from the bore-hole to feed all the new pools.

At the same time the perimeter fence was creeping slowly round the whole area. Five men on a four-wheel drive lorry drove creosoted posts ten feet long three feet into the ground to support the extra heavy gauge netting which had been made specially for us. The result was a stout fence seven feet high with an overhang both inwards and outwards across the top and strong enough to contain a stag. When complete it was nearly a mile in length and the netting alone contained over ten tons of steel. We were careful to site the fence against hedges and on low ground whenever possible so as to be as inconspicuous as could be. Up to the middle of April a forestry firm were busy planting shelter belts and clumps of ornamental trees and shrubs. It was during that month that I was horrified to discover no fewer than forty-two men were working in the park. Our own staff were kept hard at work that summer and while George, the carpenter, was fully occupied with making and hanging gates and building aviaries and shelters, the rest of us worked until dark seven days a week planting, landscaping and generally furnishing the various enclosures.

With only two weeks left until the first of August things began to look desperate. Not only was there still much to be done but the various building and landscaping operations had resulted in a trail of odd bits and pieces of equipment and material which would have to be tidied up. The gate-house and tea-room was up and most of the fittings had been installed, including a counter twenty feet long for the tea-room and various items of kitchen equipment. Plumbers and electricians had finished, but the whole building still needed decorating. Work on the car-park was going ahead. It looked enormous and little did we realise how soon it was to prove utterly inadequate. With three days to go I began to get worried. It seemed hopeless to expect any sort of order to appear out of the present chaos. I approached the builder up at the tea-room and asked him if his men would be finished in time. " I hope so," he replied, " they're going to work on Sunday. Mind you, there may be some touching up to do after you open." I hoped that that would be all left to do.

We had decided against any kind of official opening and apart from advertisements in the local papers and one or two press and television interviews, we were leaving things to chance. Perhaps nobody will turn up, I thought, and that will give us an extra day or two in which to get straight. I think Pat had the same idea, for although she had organised the whole of the catering department, she had laid in no great quantity of provisions. As each new enclosure was finished the animals or birds had been transferred from their old quarters outside the park. All the pools had been filled with water except the last and biggest, and the evening before we opened was spent in moving over two hundred pairs of ducks and geese to their new surroundings. Foxes, badgers, otters, coypu, deer, squirrels, marmots and Barbary sheep had all been transferred, together with some of our other animals and many of the birds.

The following day was reasonably fine and during breakfast the family started to discuss the number of visitors who might come. Guesses ranged from two hundred at the top down to eleven, which was my estimate. After breakfast I walked over to the tea-room to find the builders still at work painting the interior. Others were busy painting the lavatories. I asked them how soon they would be finished, just in case any visitors turned up. They said it would take most of the day, but we were not to worry as they would keep a lookout and whenever they saw a lady approaching they would hastily withdraw and wait at the back until she had gone. During the day I was amused to see this happen several times. A visitor would be walking purposefully towards the ladies' when out would file three men in white overalls each carrying a paint brush to disappear round the back; at odd intervals a head would poke round the corner to see if the coast was clear for them to continue painting.

Three hundred and fifty-seven people came that first day and most seemed delighted with what they saw. Nobody objected to having refreshments in a building which was still being painted and there were no major crises. The following Sunday was sunny and we naturally expected a few more people. A friend had come to lunch and suggested that he and I should try to catch a trout that afternoon in some flooded gravel pits which I had stocked. When we left there were about a dozen cars in the car-park and a few people wandering about, but everything was under control and our new staff in the gate-house and tea-room was well able to cope.

We had been fishing for about an hour when I noticed a car racing down the track towards us in a cloud of dust. Pat jumped out and said, " You'll have to come back, the whole place is chaotic, the car-park is packed full and there is a queue stretching down the main road as far as you can see." We followed her home, but I was still not prepared for the sight that met our eyes round the final bend. There was a queue of cars stretching in both directions and an even longer queue of people waiting to get through the entrance gate. Cars had been left anywhere. Some half on the grass verges added to the confusion by restricting the flow of traffic. Something had to be done quickly. Luckily we had made a large gate in the perimeter fence some way up the minor road beyond the car-park. Inside was a level grass field as yet unoccupied by animals. The solution was obviously to open that gate and start an overflow car-park; this would also relieve the pressure at the main gate as people would already be inside the park. For this reason their entrance money would have to be collected before they drove off the road and through the gate. Our manager and two other members of the staff were hastily summoned and provided with an old civilian gas-mask case, a child's string bag, a leather camera case and five pounds of change each. The whole outfit looked scruffy to say the least, but they took up their positions and got the cars through as fast as they could.

Half-way through the afternoon I walked up the road to see how they were getting on. A small green van of ancient vintage with a decided list to starboard had just staggered off the road and through the open gateway. Watching it stood a member of our staff roaring with laughter. He looked quite bizarre with his red face topped by a mop of hair standing on end; the gas-mask case slung across one shoulder was stuffed to overflowing with pound notes and more notes bulged from every pocket. " What's the matter? " I asked. He pointed to the little van and said, " There's *fourteen* b . . . . s in there," before going off again into peals of mirth.

Over fifteen hundred visitors came that Sunday afternoon and on Monday morning the builders were back again to make the car-park twice as big, while George started work on a second entrance gate and pay-box. It seemed to me to augur well for the future.

Up to this time the name of our establishment had been the cause of some contention. Pat objected to the word zoo since she said it would create the wrong impression, while I felt it was necessary in order to convey the idea of a collection of animals. Finally Pat suggested Wildlife Park instead of Zoo Park and I agreed; so it was that we became officially known as the Norfolk Wildlife Park. Britain's first wildlife park was away to a flying start and, to judge by the number of enterprises which have since taken the name, it must be a good one.

We did not intend to display a mixed collection of the world's fauna; we felt that existing zoos were already better equipped for that. In any case, the finance required, especially if every exhibit was to be displayed to the best advantage, would be quite beyond our resources. Both Pat and I have a horror of small zoos with their cramped quarters and lack of æsthetic design. We have always felt that fewer exhibits displayed in really large, well-designed enclosures, properly planted with appropriate vegetation, are of much greater value. Not only are the animals happier, healthier and more likely to breed, but people derive far greater pleasure and learn much more from watching them.

We both feel the conservation of the world's wildlife to be of tremendous importance to mankind and we were anxious that our collection should play its small part in persuading people that wild creatures were worth saving. It occurred to us that no zoo in Britain seemed to specialise in exhibiting our own fauna, and yet it is surely just as worthy of preservation as that of Africa or any other continent, and in just as much peril. We decided to concentrate on exhibiting British and European fauna and to lay special emphasis on species which people rarely had the chance to observe or which were becoming scarce in the wild.

There are of course a number of birds and animals in the park which are not in line with this theme such as Pooh Bear, macaws, wallabies, rheas, Barbary sheep and binturong. But I already had these and most of them were so tame that I could not possibly consider getting rid of them. The last two species are both becoming rare in the wild and we have bred Barbary sheep for a number of years. With luck we might breed binturongs as well.

The conception of a wildlife park is certainly new and I believe it will have an important role to play in the preservation of our countryside and its wild inhabitants. In the past decade more and more people have become interested in natural history, largely as the result of the many popular television programmes and the tremendous ouput of books on the subject. With increasing leisure for all, the strain on our few nature reserves from an ever-growing number of visitors may well become intolerable; and if the reserves are going to continue, there may come a time when the number of visitors has to be severely limited. If this should happen the wildlife park, falling half-way between an urban zoo and a nature reserve, will have an important part to play. Watching an animal in captivity is never quite the same as seeing one in the wild, but many people who have neither the time nor the opportunity for prolonged field study would welcome the chance to see wildlife in natural surroundings. There are other equally important functions of a wildlife park, not least of which is to remove old-fashioned prejudices, usually founded on ignorance, against such creatures as birds of prey, foxes and badgers. Children are far more likely to develop a constructive attitude towards conservation as they grow older if they have been able to watch wild animals under natural conditions.

Now that the Norfolk Wildlife Park has been open nearly

235

two years, I think I can say that it is fulfilling all these obligations as well as largely supporting the work of the Ornamental Pheasant Trust. I repeat that one of the principal aims of keeping animals in captivity should be to breed as many species as possible with a view to their release in the wild to reinforce a depleted population, just as the Pheasant Trust is doing with Swinhoe's Pheasant in Taiwan. It is a curious fact that many British and European species seem more difficult to breed in captivity than their tropical counterparts; much research is needed in this field. Foxes, badgers and otters are all extraordinarily difficult to breed in confinement; I know of only one or two successes with captive otters in Britain and not many more with foxes and badgers (see note on p. 151.)

Birds are mostly easier; wildfowl and game-birds present few problems though raptors are much more difficult. As I write our eagle owls and tawny owls in the park are incubating, while the snowy owls got as far as hatching chicks last year. It is perhaps with birds of prey and especially with owls that successful breeding in captivity is important. Poisonous sprays and seed dressings have depleted the wild populations of most of our predators and, although some species like the peregrine and sparrowhawk are extremely difficult to breed in confinement, others like the barn owl, which has suffered an almost universal decline, can be bred fairly easily and young birds might well be released in suitable areas. I should like to establish the eagle owl as a breeding bird in one or two of the large forests controlled by the Forestry Commission in England and Scotland, but this would require the co-operation of shooting interests on a scale not likely to be achieved just now. Nevertheless, I can think of no more rewarding result of breeding these magnificent birds in our park.

Many of the animals transferred to the park showed signs of enjoying their new surroundings. The foxes raced wildly

Above: left, Chogoria's crown; right, Batty, her jesses trailing behind her.
Below, Batty watches me after flying to the lure

Young eagle owls bred in the Park and sent to Sweden to help re-introduce the species there

Pat feeds two of her adopted fallow fawns

round their large grass enclosure and explored the hollow tree trunk we had provided for them before rushing back with tails wagging to whimper with pleasure as I put my fingers through the netting for them to nibble. The otters had much more space in their new pen and spent much of their time cavorting in the crystal clear water. Their pond is as large as a small swimming pool and they too have a hollow tree trunk and one or two fallen boughs as well as a warm shelter. Like the coypu and woodchucks their enclosure is built of concrete with only a very low wall separating the animals from the public. The floor of the woodchucks' and marmots' enclosure is natural turf with stout wire-netting laid underneath to prevent the animals burrowing out. The concrete has been painted in pastel shades to blend with the surroundings and we make sure that in all these pens part of the area is built sufficiently high for the animals to be able to see out over the surrounding walls. They all, without exception, make use of this facility; for the coypu it is an easy matter to see all round the compass from their central island with its sectional nest chambers; and both prairie dogs and woodchucks, supposedly terrestrial burrowing animals, spend much of their time sitting on the top of a tree stump six feet tall watching all that goes on. The otters too, climb up on their stump to get a better view. Like us, animals like to watch all that is happening around them and, when their enclosures are surrounded by solid walls or banks, it is essential for them to be able to see out over the top.

Apart from more space the herbivores like Misty the roe deer, the fallow deer and Barbary sheep noticed little change in their new paddocks. Misty soon became accustomed to the visitors and spent much of his time at the gate watching them. Roe deer are small, standing about twenty-six inches at the shoulder, and we soon realised that in a large natural enclosure they could easily disappear from view. The grass had only to grow to hide them completely when lying down fifty yards away. We overcame this to some extent by keeping the hedge-row weeds cut and the grass mown to a length of six inches or so, except for two patches near the fence.

Pooh Bear's new home was not completed until some months after we had opened. It is a large enclosure dug into the natural slope of the ground so that the wall on the outside is only three feet high as against seven feet on the inside. This is taller than is necessary to prevent Pooh climbing out, but we felt it was important people should not be able to reach down and stroke her head. There was always the possibility of her mauling a dangling hand. The centre of her enclosure is raised so that she too can see out, but in addition she has two large oak trees to climb, each in the region of eighteen feet high and complete with boughs. The trees are, of course, dead and are set in concrete about five yards apart. A hefty branch wedged in a fork of each tree connects them some ten feet above the ground and from the centre of this limb dangles a swing at the end of two stout chains. A bathing pool and a cosy den with under-floor central heating completes the basic design of her home.

We built Pooh's enclosure close to the perimeter fence and constructed an enclosed passage from the outer door to a gate in the fence so that she could still be taken out for her daily walk without coming into contact with visitors to the park.

When all was ready for her to be moved, I collected her favourite toy from the old cage, the piece of bog-oak weighing nearly half a hundredweight and about five feet long. It is so hard that even her great fangs can make no impression. She loves to wrestle with it and stands up, hauling it into an upright position, then hurls it to the ground with all her strength. While Pat took Pooh for a walk I carried the bog-oak into her new enclosure and opened wide both the door and the gate into the passage. I guessed she would try to run back to her old cage near the house and, remembering her fear of internal combustion engines, I parked the car in a strategic position blocking her route.

Pat returned with Pooh trundling along behind her; she carried a bowl of food as an added enticement and walked nonchalantly through the passage and into the enclosure. Pooh came to a halt at the gate through the fence, stood up on her hind legs, and peered down the passage. She could see Pat through the open door at the other end. Very slowly she walked on her hind legs as far as the doorway, then she swung round and rushed out again. After she had repeated this manœuvre several times it became clear that she was not going to enter her new home without persuasion. I started the engine and drove slowly down towards the gate lining the car up opposite to it. Pooh mistrusted the car and stood up to look for Pat, then walked into the passage. Revving the engine to make as much noise as possible I drove straight for the gate while Pooh fled through the open door. Pat gave her the bowl of food and stayed with her for some time while she settled down; then she slipped out leaving Pooh to explore her new domain. At first she seemed to dislike what she found and rather than sleep in her nice warm den curled up at night in the open.

She remained looking miserable for several days and we began to get used to well-meaning visitors who asked if there was " something wrong with the little bear because she looked so unhappy." Fearing that Pooh probably missed the constant contact with us to which she had become accustomed, we spent as much time as we could with her every day. Gradually she began to relax. She played with her bog-oak again and climbed one of the trees, but it was weeks before she attempted to climb the second tree. Once she had settled down Pat began to take her out again and we had no further difficulty in getting her back. In fact it is always harder to persuade her to come out.

She had been in her new home a couple of months when she

decided to test its strength. She began with the concrete covering the central mound; standing on her hind legs she went round methodically tapping with her front claws and listening intently for the sound of a hollow underneath. The moment she found a weak spot she set to work picking at it with her claws; she was remarkably persistent and within a month had opened up two or three small places large enough to get her arm through and pull out the earth underneath. Not only was this unsightly but having once started she would eventually tear up quite large areas of concrete. We decided to repair the damage and to confine Pooh to her den for a couple of days while the new concrete set. The door to her den was made of oak an inch thick and covered with heavy-gauge galvanised steel. Early one morning we shut her in; the result was electric. She roared with fury and hurled herself at the door, ripping and tearing at the crack between the door itself and the lintel. By midday she had prised up some of the steel sheeting and had started to splinter the oak underneath; she soon had a hole big enough to get her arm through and it would not be long before the whole door was torn to shreds. I thought of the still wet concrete and telephoned the vet. While we were waiting for him we started to shore-up the outside with another old door held in place by concrete blocks.

When the vet arrived I asked him if he could give Pooh a tranquilliser. He explained that the problem was to determine how much to give her; nobody had done much work with sun bears and he was not sure how she might react; also we did not know how much she weighed and such drugs are usually administered according to bodyweight. In the end we decided to try nambutol; a safe dose was slipped inside a banana which I handed to Pooh through the bars of the outer door. She ate it without hesitation and within an hour was curled up fast asleep in her straw. Next morning we repeated the dose and she remained docile and sleepy until the following day when we took down the barricade and allowed her out.

She walked straight over to the new concrete and, after examining each patch carefully, began to test it with her claws, but this time there were no flaws. I am always surprised how observant Pooh is. Recently we drove an extra staple into the round log forming the seat of her swing to strengthen its attachment to the chain; the moment we had done it she stood up on her hind legs and examined it minutely, testing it with her claws. An extra nail in here or a fresh screw there are sufficient to arouse her curiosity.

Pooh soon discovered that she could get certain reactions from a crowd of visitors by showing off to them. This has nothing to do with begging for food since the public are not allowed to feed the animals and although a few people throw her the odd sweet this is not a general practice. She has two main tricks, both of which elicit different responses from her audience. The first is the splashing game. When a suitable crowd has assembled opposite her pool she starts to play with the piece of bog-oak, wrestling with it and rolling on to her back balancing it on her four feet. Suddenly she stands up holding the baulk of wood on end by the pool, then she hurls it down with all her strength sending a shower of water over the spectators with uncanny accuracy.

The other trick is much more subtle; again she prefers a large audience although she sometimes tries it on me. The first time she had me really worried and even now I wish she would not do it. The essence of this trick is suspense. She climbs one of the trees and takes up her position standing on her hind legs on a sawn off bough some six feet above the ground. Leaning forward she can just reach the nearer of the two chains supporting her swing, she hooks her claws round it and pulls it towards her, holding on to the front of the tree with her other paw. Quite deliberately she winds the chain twice round her neck and then stands on tiptoe on the extreme edge of the stump. It is obvious to everyone that she is about to jump and hang herself; as often as not consternation breaks out and a worried visitor rushes up to the nearest member of the staff telling him to come quickly and untwist the bear before it hangs itself. Needless to say, having achieved the desired result Pooh nonchalantly unwinds the chain and goes on playing with her swing.

This trick almost had fatal results. We had a party of local naturalists to the park one summer evening and some of them lingered looking at the animals until dusk. Just as the last were going a friend's child came up to me and said, " Your bear has got her chain twisted round her neck and can't get it off."

" Oh, so she's caught you too with that trick," I replied and thought no more about it.

When it was quite dark Pat and I remembered we had left some of the birds of prey out and went to get them. As we approached Pooh's enclosure I said, " I suppose we had better just check that she is all right." Almost at once we knew something was wrong and in the beam of my torch could see Pooh huddled on her usual bough gasping for breath and quite unable to move, for the chain was not only coiled round her neck but somehow had become twisted as well.

Speed was essential if we were to save her and leaving Pat to talk quietly to Pooh to reassure her, I ran back to the house for a ladder and tools. It is curious how long it seems to take to gather a few simple things in an emergency when every second counts. Finally I returned with a ladder, hammer, pliers, a heavy screwdriver, and some raspberries.

Talking quietly all the time we climbed down into Pooh's enclosure and I propped the ladder against the bough from which the swing hung. Pooh seemed quiet enough but one never knows with a bear and my legs would be within reach of her fangs as I worked. While Pat shone the torch I went up the ladder and started to hammer away to drive the screwdriver under the large staple securing the end of the chain.

Pooh seemed to know we were rescuing her and made no move.

In a few minutes the last staple was levered out and I persuaded Pat to leave the enclosure as I felt Pooh might attack us once she found she was free.

Before going Pat scattered some of the raspberries at the foot of the tree. Very gently I released the end of the chain and leaning across, slipped it behind Pooh's neck to take out the twist, I repeated the manœuvre once again and she was free. Without hesitation she uncoiled the rest from her neck, climbed straight down the tree and began to eat the raspberries!

The last we saw of her that night she was playing with the free end of the chain and winding it round her neck again, but this time we knew she could come to no harm. Since then we have moved the swing along the branch out of reach except from the ground.

She is remarkably conservative and mistrusts anything new, being especially particular about her food bowl. When she first came to us as a cub over four years ago we gave her an old aluminium preserving pan; at that time it had two handles on opposite sides but they have long since disappeared and the pan itself is rather battered. We have tried her with several new bowls, but she has smashed them all within a few days and so we are compelled to go on using her old bowl however scruffy it may appear.

Over sixty-three thousand people came to the park the first year it was open, and it was only natural at the end of that time to discover a few mistakes and to recognise where improvements could be made. One of the first things we did was to have a large terrace built in front of the tea-room so that people could sit out and enjoy their lunch or tea in sunny weather. It has proved very popular with its attractive flooring of multicoloured tiles and tables of natural oak.

During our first winter we built a walk-through aviary

for various small British birds. It is fifty feet in length with a darkened porch at each end; swing doors allow the public to walk down the central path amongst the birds while the area on either side has been landscaped to include two small pools and planted with rhododendrons and other shrubs. The whole effect is most natural and the birds take very little notice of people, flying over their heads and perching freely within a few feet of them. We usually exhibit a dozen or more species including groups of goldfinches, yellowhammers and snow buntings and pairs of redstarts and wheatears. I quite expected children to take an interest in our native birds but was not prepared for the enthusiasm shown by many adults.

The aviary was first opened on Good Friday, George had only fitted the locks to the doors the night before and had omitted to remove a small sliding bolt on the outside of the outer exit door. During the afternoon forty or fifty people were inside when a small boy leaving by the exit porch noticed the bolt and slid it across before walking quietly away. The next people who attempted to leave found they were trapped, nor could they get out of the entrance porch as the doors only work one way and cannot be opened from inside. They shouted to passers-by outside the aviary but nobody took any notice; fortunately one of the staff heard them and went to their rescue. Since then the offending bolt has been removed. We soon discovered too that only certain shrubs will thrive under such conditions; many are destroyed by the birds constantly attacking the buds and tender shoots, evergreens of various kinds seem to do best.

One of our most popular exhibits, especially with bird-watchers, is the wader pool; covering over a quarter of an acre it has been made to represent a pool among the sand dunes of the Norfolk coast. Life size dunes run along the back and out across the centre of the pool ending in a shingle spit running out into the water. Ten tons of shingle were brought from a nearby beach and the dunes have been planted with sea-lyme grass brought from the coast. It looks something like marram grass and has the advantage, unlike marram, of growing in static sand. Sea buckthorn and brooms grow behind the dunes while scattered shells and seaweed add to the effect. Wigeon and shelduck share this enclosure with groups of oyster-catchers, common curlew, stone curlew, green plover, redshanks and godwit. Both oyster-catchers and stone curlew have made nest scrapes and display frequently, so we hope they will eventually breed.

There is much to be said for the old-fashioned ha-ha or dry ditch and, while most useful for confining grazing animals, it can be adapted in a number of ways to contain almost anything from bears to baboons. One of our most recent improvements is the construction of five new deer paddocks totalling six and a half acres with over a quarter of a mile of dry ditch, twenty-four feet wide and five feet deep. The soil from this has been pushed up to form a raised public walk on top of which is a fence four feet high. The result is that from the deers' side the ground slopes down to a very steep five-foot bank with a four-foot fence making an obstacle nine feet high, whereas visitors only have to look over the low fence to see the animals. The pathway has been grassed over and winds round in the shape of an hour-glass with the pad-docks leading off, so that straight lines and sharp angles are avoided. At the same time the path curves into each enclosure in the form of a bay which has the effect of making the spectator feel much closer to the animals. More than two thousand tons of earth have been moved in this operation, but such was the size and efficiency of the machine that the bulk of the work was completed in little over a week.

The same principle on a much smaller scale has been used for our badger enclosure, the front of which slopes down to a dry ditch with a vertical wall five feet high inside but only a foot high from the public's side and with no fence. Both the wall and the slope are of concrete, the latter coloured to look

245

like earth, but the rest of their pen is natural soil with heavy-gauge wire underneath to prevent them digging out. Mounds of earth enable them to dig freely which must be good for them, and they have a variety of hollow tree stumps in which to play. Their set is a replica of a natural burrow which can be seen through a piece of plate glass. Normally the interior is rather gloomy but anyone wishing to see in has only to press a button for a light to come on for a few seconds before switching itself off automatically. The badgers take no notice whatever of the sudden brief spells of illumination.

The director of a well-known zoo once said to me, " The railings are not put there to protect the public from the animals, but to protect the animals from the public." At the time I thought he was joking, but I have since learned that there was more than a measure of truth in what he said. If the response of certain animals to visitors surprised us, the reactions of a small section of the public to the animals was in some cases incredible.

Ignorance is always the common denominator, whether in the case of the woman who, seeing Pooh Bear, screamed to her offspring, " Charlie, 'ere, come and 'ave a look at the sealion," or of the elderly lady who marched into the tea-room and complained in a loud voice that the white owls (she meant snowy owls) had no water and that their youngsters were lying about the enclosure having died from thirst. If she had troubled to look she would have seen that the owls had water, which incidentally they have never been seen to drink, and that their dead owlets were in fact day-old chicks on which we feed them! Such people are obsessed with cruelty, yet their obsession bears no logic. They never object to seeing an owl eating a dead rat or piece of hare, but dead day-old chicks are sure to rouse their misplaced sympathy despite the fact that the chicks are humanely killed here. If we did not take them they would either be gassed or drowned by the hatchery owing to their being the wrong sex for egg production.

The other general obsession is that every animal is constantly trying to escape; the moment Pooh Bear paces up and down or round and round her enclosure somebody is sure to say "Poor thing, she wants to get out." They fail to understood that this pacing is either a perfectly normal patrolling of her territory or brought about by some external factor such as anticipation of being fed. Little do they realise that Pooh requires quite a lot of encouragement to leave the security of her home and that if she thinks dinner is due nothing on earth will persuade her to come out.

Fennec the fox is much the same; if I let him out he will rush round at first but is soon ready to go back to his enclosure, so much so that I have to keep the door shut to prevent him slipping back too soon. Not long after we moved the badgers to their new home in the park one of them, a young boar, discovered the way to climb out of their enclosure. For several months he enjoyed a nightly ramble in the surrounding countryside but dawn always found him back home safely tucked up with the others. He was seen several times by motorists trundling along the country lanes, usually on his way out. The road was to prove his undoing, for one January day he failed to return from his nightly sortie and a week later was found dead by the roadside having been hit by a car.

Accidents like this are a constant menace to wild animals which have become so-called "pets." They have lost their natural wariness of mankind; and it is a curious fact that whereas people will usually leave a bird unharmed, unless it happens to be a bird of prey, they nearly always kill a mammal, often in a most brutal manner. Both Gavin Maxwell and H. G. Hurrell have had tame otters done to death in this way.

Our hawk lawn is sometimes a cause of contention. Backed by a tall hedge for shelter and shaded by a large oak tree, it is railed off from the public and whenever the weather is fit Bokhara, Batty and Bubo spend the day there sitting quietly on their blocks. Every night they are taken into the shelter of the mews and several times a week they are flown loose. The result is that they are in perfect condition with a fine bloom on their plumage and every feather intact, a rare thing in birds of prey kept in aviaries. All this is, of course, explained in our guide; yet I have frequently heard people saying how cruel it is to keep a bird tied up in all weathers with never a chance to fly!

Our bateleur eagle, Batty, is so gentle that we often fly her in the park for people to watch and on a warm day she soars round several hundred feet above their heads in effortless flight, the tips of her primaries bending upwards as she floats on the air rocking gently from side to side before plunging down to feed on the lure. She mistrusts strangers but this does not stop her teasing them from time to time, though she would never hurt anyone. I particularly remember one sunny afternoon when she was flying round, watched by a group of youths and girls who were making quite a noise laughing and talking. Batty came sailing over their heads, then suddenly closed her wings and dived straight at them from three or four hundred feet, hurtling down with a noise like a heavy shell. They screamed and ducked as she passed harmlessly twenty feet above their heads. Bokhara is quite different. Not only is he unreliable with people, but he is inclined to attack other birds in the park; so he has to be flown out in the countryside where he can do no harm.

Few sights and sounds are more stirring than wild geese flying overhead calling. Our little flock of greylag and barnacle geese never fails to excite comment when they suddenly take off clamouring loudly and fly away only to come swinging round on arched pinions with paddles down to land on one of the other pools. Nearly all free flying birds present special problems; in the case of geese they are apt to be a nuisance at breeding time by invading other enclosures and breaking up happily married pairs, often of other species; sometimes unwelcome hybrids result or a valuable pair of birds just about to breed are prevented from nesting by the domineering greylags.

Even our macaws have one annoying habit. Though they never go far afield, they love to settle on the top of neighbouring aviaries where they set about destroying the woodwork by whittling it with their powerful beaks and even ripping up the wire-netting. This became such a habit that we were compelled to clip two or three of their flight feathers and so restrict their range; despite this they manage to get about quite well and their vivid colours are always a pleasure to see especially in the drab greyness of winter. Macaws are exceptionally hardy for tropical birds and ours stay out the whole winter whatever the temperature; only high winds and driving rain force them to seek the warmth of their shelter.

Lest it be thought that all our visitors are cranks I must emphasise that the great majority take an intelligent interest in the animals and genuinely enjoy watching them. Only a very small minority will allow their children to chase a pheasant or a duck or try to prod an animal to make it move, and in every case the underlying cause is ignorance.

The release of an animal bred in captivity is often far more difficult than it appears, if the animal is to have the best chance of survival. It is not simply a matter of finding suitable surroundings and then letting it out. I have recently heard of such a problem in Sweden where the authorities are endeavouring to re-establish the eagle owl in some of their forests from which it has disappeared as the result of shooting. They have found that young eagle owls turned out in the forest do not survive. But if an aviary is built in the woods and a pair of owls put in it to breed and their young subsequently allowed to go free, they will settle down and remain in the area. In 1964 I therefore gave the Swedish authorities a pair of young eagle owls, bred in the park, to help with this scheme.

I repeat that one of the most important things for a captive animal is that it should have something to occupy its mind. Play is often a necessity especially amongst carnivora, and I have even seen such an unlikely creature as Bokhara playing with a feather, picking it up in his bill, hopping about, dropping it and picking it up again. Otters love to play with round pebbles or balls and enjoy sliding down a chute, and I have often seen foxes playing with feathers or dry leaves bowling along in the wind.

All our animals are tame and for them human contact is something they enjoy, for though some are more confiding than others, we can go in and talk to any of them without fear of alarming them. The form of contact varies. For some voice and sight are sufficient, particularly with adult grazing animals. For others, some physical contact is pleasurable. Pooh loves to have her back rubbed, the foxes like to be rolled over on their backs and have their tummies scratched. Badgers prefer to nose about in one's hair while Bubo, believe it or not, likes me to blow down her neck.

Some animals cannot be kept together in pairs the whole year round if successful breeding is to be achieved. Otters are a good example and in America, where they are bred in several collections, it has been found best to keep the sexes separate except during the mating season. Otters kept together in pairs seem to develop a brother-sister relationship which inhibits sexual behaviour. Bears are notoriously bad fathers and if we ever found a mate for Pooh, she would probably tolerate his presence only during the breeding season, for in the wild, bears are solitary creatures. It is quite possible that these solitary animals derive more pleasure from human association than those which live in pairs or family groups.

Wild animals as pets present a host of new problems (if by pets one means household companions). Far too many pet animals die young whether lions, otters, seals or monkeys. In some instances ignorance or inefficiency in practical animal husbandry on the part of their owners is no doubt the primary cause; but in others the animal has still died young despite apparently first-class care and an ideal environment. One cannot help wondering how much mental strain and too much human intrusion have contributed to early mortality. Animals which enjoy some privacy and peace in their own quarters certainly seem to live longer, and it seems likely that too much intrusion and interference bring a mental strain on the animal so that it develops an anxiety neurosis, perhaps akin to ulcers in over-worked high-pressure business executives. Shepherds often reach a remarkable degree of mutual understanding with their dogs, yet these men rarely make household pets of them. The circus lion-trainer reaches a working partnership with his charges, and the falconer with his hawk, yet in no case does the animal become a pet. The routine is unvaried and it knows exactly what is wanted of it when it comes to work and when not working it is left in peace in the security of its own quarters.

We pride ourselves on being far superior to any animal in intelligence and capacity for learning. Yet how often do we expect an animal to do all the learning and to adapt itself to our form of life. We have no right to endow animals with human values and should endeavour to establish a mutual understanding on grounds of common experience by trying to appreciate the animal's viewpoint. In this way a relationship can develop in which cruelty does not exist and which is pleasurable to both animal and man.

It may be asked, why do we want to establish this contact with animals? In my own case it is simply that I find observing their behaviour and trying to unravel the obscure workings of their brains intensely interesting and rewarding.

" Man may learn from the animals, for they are his parents."
Paracelsus.

THE ORNAMENTAL PHEASANT TRUST

The Ornamental Pheasant Trust is a recognised charity whose chief objectives are:

(a) To maintain and exhibit a representative collection of pheasants and other game birds under suitable conditions for scientific study and research.

(b) To protect and save from extinction all species of pheasants and other game birds by breeding numbers in captivity and especially to encourage their preservation in the wild by such means as are available including, where practicable, the re-introduction of any species to its native land.

(c) To sponsor scientific study of these birds in every part of the world both in captivity and in the wild.

(d) To enable the public to see as many kinds of pheasants as possible thereby fostering their interest in these birds and in problems concerning their conservation.

In many parts of the world pheasants and other members of the Phasianidae, partridges, francolin, quail, etc., are declining in numbers. The progress of civilisation is steadily reducing the kind of habitat they need for their existence, and in many places pheasants are ruthlessly hunted by the natives for food and for their beautiful plumage. If some of these species are to survive, positive steps must soon be taken to propagate their numbers in captivity and to carry out further research into their lives and habits.

To carry on with its work the Trust needs more money and this in turn means more members. Will you join and so help to preserve these rare and beautiful birds? Ordinary membership costs £1 per year payable on 1st January, sustaining membership £5 per year and Life Membership a single payment of £30.

Members receive an illustrated Annual Report, first option on any young birds surplus to the requirements of the collection and free admission both to the Trust's breeding and rearing pens and to the famous Norfolk Wildlife Park.

NORFOLK WILDLIFE PARK

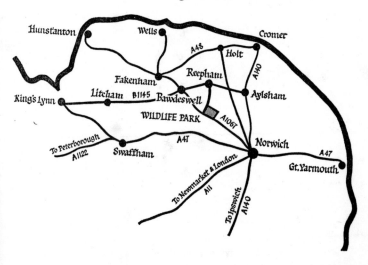

255